13 THINGS
THEY WON'T
TELL YOU

13 THINGS THEY WON'T TELL YOU

375+ Experts Confess the
INSIDER SECRETS
They Keep to Themselves

Marty Munson and the
Editors of Reader's Digest

The Reader's Digest Association, Inc.
New York, NY / Montreal

A READER'S DIGEST BOOK

FOR READER'S DIGEST
Senior Editor: Katherine Furman
Manager, English Book Editorial, Reader's Digest Canada: Pamela Johnson
Project Designer: Jennifer Tokarski
Managing Editor: Lorraine Burton
Senior Art Director: George McKeon
Associate Publisher, Trade Publishing: Rosanne McManus
President and Publisher, Trade Publishing: Harold Clarke
Executive Editor, Reader's Digest North America: Courtenay Smith
Creative Director, Reader's Digest North America: Robert Newman
Editor-in-Chief and Chief Content Officer, Reader's Digest North America: Liz Vaccariello
President, Reader's Digest North America: Dan Lagani
President, Reader's Digest Association, Inc.: Robert E. Guth

Contributing Editor: Marty Munson
Illustrations ©shutterstock.com
Indexer: Jay Kreider

Library of Congress Cataloging in Publication Data

13 things they won't tell you : 120+ experts confess the secrets they keep to themselves / Liz Vaccariello and the editors of Reader's digest.
   p. cm.
   Summary: "Behind-the-scenes advice from hundreds of service professionals that will shock you--and save you time and money.OVER 1,300 EYE-OPENING MONEY-SAVING TIPS! Our experts reveal how to avoid being scammed, what services you don't need to pay for, behind-the-scenes deals (but you have to know how to ask), and how to get the best value for your money"-- Provided by publisher.
   ISBN 978-1-60652-499-2 (pbk.) -- ISBN 978-1-60652-503-6 (adobe) -- ISBN 978-1-60652-502-9 (epub)
   1. Consumer education. I. Vaccariello, Liz. II. Reader's Digest Association. III. Title: Thirteen things they won't tell you.
   TX335.A13 2012
   640.73--dc23
                          2012008838

We are committed to both the quality of our products and the service we provide to our customers. We value your comments, so please feel free to contact us.

   The Reader's Digest Association, Inc.
   Adult Trade Publishing
   44 South Broadway
   White Plains, NY 10601

For more Reader's Digest products and information, visit our website:
   www.rd.com (in the United States)
   www.readersdigest.ca (in Canada)

Printed in Canada

1 3 5 7 9 10 8 6 4 2

WARNING
All do-it-yourself activities involve a degree of risk. Skills, materials, tools, and site conditions vary widely. Although the editors have made every effort to ensure accuracy, the reader remains responsible for the selection and use of tools, materials, and methods. Always obey local codes and laws, follow manufacturer's operating instructions, and observe safety precautions.

NOTE TO OUR READERS
Reader's Digest publishes the advice of expert authorities in many fields. But the use of a book is not a substitute for legal, accounting, or other professional services. Consult a competent professional for answers to your specific questions.

CONTENTS

INTRODUCTION

Wouldn't you love to know what goes on in the mind of burglars and identity thieves so you can outsmart them? Or contractors, movers, and car mechanics so you don't get fleeced?

Now you don't have to wonder, because we here at *Reader's Digest* found out the truth for you in our most popular service column, "13 Things!" The article is such a hit that we wanted to give our readers more, and that's what you have in your hands: the comprehensive, info-packed book that grew from the column that asks hundreds of people—from former inmates to the sales and servicepeople you encounter every day—to cough up the juicy secrets about what really goes on when you're not looking. We made hundreds of phone calls to find out what these experts want people to know, what they *don't* want people to know, and what people would be shocked to know (we had to promise some of them anonymity to fork over the most jaw-dropping tidbits).

Once you understand what really happens behind the scenes, not only will you save huge amounts of money, you will also get better service—and even better health care. For instance, being wise to the games at the car dealership will make you a player, not a victim. And knowing what we found out about how everyone from debt collectors to dentists operate can keep you from gnashing your teeth—or losing them.

We paired these top-secret confessions from the experts with practical sidebars that will help you take action: Find out when you need to call in a professional and when you can easily take care of something yourself on the cheap. Learn how to get on the good side of everyone from your waiter to your pediatrician. Take a deep breath and see how you can maximize your work life, all the way from getting a job to asking for a raise to avoiding a stress meltdown.

From wedding planners to marriage counselors, baristas to weight-loss experts, real estate agents to travel agents, bankers to TV salesmen, dentists to nannies and many, many more, our experts offer you the new dos and don'ts for smart people, and our expert advice shows you how to use these secrets to your advantage.

Among the eye-opening, money-saving, health-friendly tips, we got insiders to reveal:

* Why plumbers see dollar signs when they see "flushable" baby wipes.
* The $100 item you should never let a TV salesman sell you.
* What time of day gas station owners hike up their prices.
* The top things that horrify your nanny.
* What really happens to your pizza between the call and the delivery.
* How to get your insurance to pay for LASIK surgery.
* And over 1,000 other essentials!

You'll benefit from this insider information by becoming not just wiser, but more compassionate, too. By taking a glimpse behind the scenes of dozens of professions, you'll see what it's like in the break room, on the other side of the cash register, in the work van, and behind the service desk. Once you know why you're waiting for so long in the ER, you'll be incredibly relieved. And when you get a feel for what it's like to wait on hungry, cranky grownups acting like kids or worse, your tipping habits might change forever.

Thanks to everyone who told us what their industries don't want you to know, this book can change your mind, your bank account, and even your life. Read on to get savvy!

Liz Vaccariello

Liz Vaccariello
Editor-in-Chief, *Reader's Digest*

Part One

WHAT YOU DON'T KNOW ABOUT
YOUR HOME

Is your home a well-oiled machine or a money pit? When you know the tricks shady contractors try to pull, what turns a quick plumbing fix into a pricey project, and how movers will try to overcharge you, you'll get the house you want minus the overspending and stress.

Beyond the remodelers, the plumbers, the exterminators, and the power companies, we didn't rest until we got you the complete story. Real estate brokers, house cleaners, and sketchy locksmiths showed us their cards. But the info that's worth its weight in gold? Convicted burglars told us what makes them pick your place over the neighbor's.

To keep your home safe and saleable, and keep your stress level at an all-time low, check out—and heed—the top secrets we got hundreds of insiders to reveal.

WHAT BURGLARS WON'T TELL YOU

We got convicted thieves to reveal their sneakiest secrets. Here are the top 13 things to know to avoid being a victim.

1. Of course I look familiar. I was here just last week cleaning your carpets, painting your shutters, or delivering your new refrigerator.

2. And hey, thanks for letting me use the bathroom when I was working in your yard last week. While I was in there, I unlatched the back window to make my return a little easier.

3. Sometimes I carry a clipboard. There are times when I dress like a lawn guy and carry a rake. I do my best to never, ever look like a crook.

4. The two things I hate most: Loud dogs and nosy neighbors.

5. I'll break a window to get in, even if it makes a little noise. If your neighbor hears one loud sound, he'll stop what he's doing and wait to hear it again. If he doesn't hear it again, he'll just go back to what he was doing. It's human nature.

6. Your alarm only works if it's on. I'm not complaining, but why would you pay all that money for a fancy alarm system and leave your house without setting it?

7. A good security company alarms the window over the sink. And the windows on the second floor, which often access the master bedroom—and your jewelry. It's not a bad idea to put motion detectors up there, too.

8. Don't let me see your security system. If decorative glass is part of your front entrance, don't let your alarm company install the control pad where I can see if it's set. That makes it too easy.

> 🔒 **TOP SECRET!** If you don't answer when I knock, I try the door. Occasionally, I hit the jackpot and walk right in.

9. I love looking in your windows. I'm looking for signs that you're home and for flat screen TVs or gaming systems I'd like. I'll drive or walk through your neighborhood at night, before you close the blinds, just to pick my targets.

10. Lock your windows. To you, leaving that window open just a crack during the day is a way to let in a little fresh air. To me, it's an invitation.

11. I always knock first. If you answer, I'll ask for directions somewhere or offer to clean your gutters. (Don't take me up on it.)

12. Do you really think I won't look in your sock drawer? I always check dresser drawers, the bedside table, and the medicine cabinet.

13. You're right: I won't have enough time to break into that safe. . . . The one where you keep your valuables. But if it's not bolted down, I'll take it with me.

SOURCES: Convicted burglars in North Carolina, Oregon, California, and Kentucky; security consultant Chris McGoey, who runs crimedoctor.com; and Richard T. Wright, a criminology professor at the University of Missouri–St. Louis, who interviewed 105 burglars for his book *Burglars on the Job*.

Great Advice

4 WAYS TO KEEP YOUR HOME SAFE WHILE YOU'RE ON VACATION

1. **Burglars really do look for newspapers piled up on the driveway.** They might even leave a pizza flyer in your front door to see how long it takes you to remove it. Have a neighbor collect this stuff while you're gone, and no one will know you aren't home.

2. **Avoid announcing your vacation on your Facebook page.** It's easier than you think to look up your address.

3. **If it snows while you're out of town,** get a neighbor to create car tracks into the driveway and foot tracks into the house. Virgin drifts in the driveway are a dead giveaway that you've taken a trip to warmer climes.

4. **A loud TV or radio can be a better deterrent than the best alarm system.** If you're reluctant to leave your TV on while you're out of town, you can buy a $35 device that works on a timer and simulates the flickering glow of a real television. (Find it at faketv.com.)

7 TIPS FOR TOTAL HOTEL SAFETY

Burglars told us you're a target in your home-away-from-home, too. These tips for keeping protected while you're traveling will make sure you can relax to the max.

1. **Ask for a room on the third floor or higher.** Most thefts occur on the first two floors. Stay below the seventh floor, however; few fire engine ladders can reach above it.

2. **Choose a hotel over a motel.** Burglaries are easier when your room's door is quickly accessible from the parking lot.

3. **Make sure the front-desk person doesn't say your room number aloud** when you're registering. They should write it down and hand it to you. If he does say it aloud, ask for another room and ask that he write down the number.

4. **Ask who is at your door and verify before opening.** If you didn't order room service, or don't know why the "employee" is there, call the front desk and verify that they sent someone.

5. **Use the main entrance of the hotel** when returning in the evening.

6. **Use all locking devices for your door,** and lock all windows and sliding glass doors.

7. **Don't leave the "Please Make Up Room" sign outside your door unless you want to tell the whole world you're not there.** Instead, put the "Do Not Disturb" sign on the door. If you want your room made up while you're out, call housekeeping and let them know.

WHAT YOUR CONTRACTOR WON'T TELL YOU

Here are some of the best ways to avoid home remodeling hassles and headaches.

1. Triple-check financing before you start. You don't want to run out of money to pay me because your lender decides to lower or eliminate your home equity line of credit. (And it can, at any time.)

2. Avoid surprise fines by asking your municipal building department about permits that homeowners might need to get for construction-related services like Dumpsters. Also make sure you're familiar with noise and nuisance ordinances so you're not hit with a costly complaint from neighbors annoyed by the 6 a.m. symphony hammered out by the crew.

3. The National Association of Home Builders has a Green Building Program. Search its website for a green builder in your area: Go to nahbgreen.org and click on Certified Green Professional.

4. Look at work I've done in the past 12 months, on a budget similar to yours. (Older projects likely had bigger budgets and more expensive materials.)

5. Check me out: Any liens? Pending lawsuits? Do I have a valid state license? Do my subcontractors?

6. Test-drive me on a smaller project before you commit.

7. Do I have insurance? Check directly with my insurance company. Those papers I waved in front of you may have expired years ago.

8. Don't overimprove, especially since home values are falling. If a contractor is trying to bolster his pitch with potential resale value, cross-check his claims with a real estate agent or appraiser.

9. Spell everything out. Otherwise, I may not prime the walls before I paint or I may not build that closet shelf and put up that rod. Expect nothing that's not in writing.

🔒 **TOP SECRET! Ask if you're getting a dedicated crew. If not, your project may drag on while I juggle multiple jobs. Tie the contract to deadlines for each phase.**

10. Reduce the risk of upcharges. Some contractors may charge extra for upgrades required by municipal inspectors to cover extra costs—all the more reason to review your plans in advance with your municipal building staff. You can change the plans, and the project budget, to reflect the cost of complying with the code from the start.

11. Find out who will actually be doing the work on your project by requesting a list of the subcontractors. If there's an apprentice, who will be supervising him to be sure the work is done correctly?

12. Get the details of the project schedule and how the contractor has prioritized your job compared to all his work. Ask for a job schedule broken down by phase—demolition, rough construction, plumbing, electrical, and finish work.

13. Ditto for the brand and precise quality of the materials, appliances, and fixtures you are ordering. Don't let us sub in materials of "equal or better quality" that aren't.

SOURCES: Harvard Joint Center for Housing Studies; Roger Peugeot, president of Roger the Plumber, Inc., Overland Park, Kansas; Collin Johnson, director of inspection services for the City of Glendale, Wisconsin; Bruce Case, president of Case Design/ Remodeling, Inc., based in Bethesda, Maryland.

Great Advice

HOW TO AVOID HIRING A SHADY CONTRACTOR

1. **Be cautious:** Don't do business with someone who comes to your door without an appointment. Be especially wary if the contractor drives a vehicle with no company name and phone number or with out-of-state license plates.

2. **Do your research:** Before working with a contractor, research the company. Check out its rating and complaint history with the Better Business Bureau (www.bbb.org).

3. **Ask around:** Ask neighbors, friends, relatives, or local consumer advocates for recommendations of reliable contractors.

4. **Explore your options:** Get at least three written bids for the work you want done from three different contractors before choosing one.

5. **Check the contractor's background:** When you're ready to hire a contractor, ask for proof that the company is properly licensed and bonded (to protect you against theft and damage), that it carries liability insurance, and that it provides workers' compensation insurance.

6. **Get references:** Ask the contractor for references from the company's last three jobs—and check those references!

7. **Get a contract:** Demand a written contract that lists the specific work to be done, costs, materials to be used, start and completion dates, and warranty information on products and installation. Read the fine print carefully before signing it.

8. **Be smart about payments:** Do not pay more than 33 percent of the total job cost as a deposit. Hold off on your final payment until the job is finished and you are satisfied with the completed work.

WHAT YOUR EXTERMINATOR WON'T TELL YOU

You don't always need to call in the experts for ants. Try these common ways to nix them first.

1. Create a "moat" around the object the ants are going for. Simply surround it with adhesive tape placed sticky side up.

2. Draw a line with chalk around home entry points. The ants will be repelled by the calcium carbonate in the chalk, which is actually made up of ground-up and compressed shells of marine animals. Scatter powdered chalk around garden plants to repel ants and slugs.

3. Some other household things ants hate are talcum powder, cream of tartar, borax, powered sulfur, and oil of cloves. You can put these items around your foundation and other points of entry to keep ants out.

> **TOP SECRET!** Stop ants from carrying off your picnic. Place each picnic table leg in a plastic container, and fill them with water. The ants won't be able to crawl past.

4. A baster is the right tool for hard-to-reach spots. If you've sprinkled a powdered ant deterrent, like boric acid, along any cracks or crevices where you've spotted the intruders, use a baster to blow small amounts of the powder into hard-to-reach corners and any deep voids you come across.

Note: Keep in mind that boric acid can be toxic if ingested by young children or pets.

5. A flowerpot can help squelch fire ants. Place the flowerpot upside down over the anthill. Pour boiling water through the drain hole and you'll be burning down their house.

6. You don't need insecticides or ant traps to ant-proof your kitchen. Just give it the lemon treatment. First squirt some lemon juice on door thresholds and windowsills and into any holes or cracks where the ants are getting in. Then scatter small slices of lemon peel around the outdoor entrance.

7. Deter ants that are beating a path to your home by sprinkling salt across the doorframe or directly on their paths. Ants will be discouraged from crossing this barrier.

8. In a blender, make a smooth puree of a few orange peels in 1 cup of warm water. Slowly pour the solution over and into anthills in your garden, on your patio, and along the foundation of your home to send the little pests packing.

9. Cayenne pepper sprinkled in spots where the ants are looking for sugar, such as along the backs of your countertops or on your baseboards, will tell them that no sugar is ahead.

10. Keep cooking essentials, including sugar and paprika, safe from ant intruders by slipping a bay leaf inside your storage containers. If you're concerned about the sugar picking up a bay leaf flavor, tape the leaf to the inside of the canister lid.

11. An anti-ant aromatherapy trick is to tape sachets of sage, bay, stick cinnamon, or whole cloves inside cabinets. This will smell pleasant while discouraging ants.

12. Ants hate the smell of vinegar. So pour equal parts water and white vinegar into a spray bottle. Then spray it on anthills and around areas where you see the insects. Also keep the spray bottle handy for outdoor trips or to keep ants away from picnics or children's play areas.

13. If you have lots of anthills around your property, try pouring full-strength vinegar over them to hasten the bugs' departure.

Great Advice
NATURAL REPELLENTS FOR OTHER COMMON PESTS

The Pest: Slugs
The Remedy: These slow-moving insects are very attracted to beer. Fill an empty tuna or cat-food can with beer, and bury it in your garden soil up to its rim. Overnight, slugs will move into the beer and drown. Throw out the entire can in the morning and replace it with a fresh batch.

The Pest: Snails
The Remedy: Put a board or two on the garden soil, and snails will take shelter in the damp shade beneath them. Pick up the boards and scrape the creatures into the trash. Always water your garden in the morning. If the soil is dry at night, critters like slugs and snails will be less active.

The Pest: Earwigs
The Remedy: In the evening, roll up sheets of wet newspaper and lay them around the garden. At sunrise, earwigs will crawl inside the wet pages to take shelter. Collect the papers before they dry out, bugs and all. Don't throw the newspapers into your trash cans, or the earwigs will soon escape and make their way back to the garden. Either burn the papers and bugs, shake the earwigs into a toilet or sink and flush them down the drain, or tie up the papers and bugs tightly inside a plastic bag—with absolutely no openings— and put them in the garbage can.

The Pest: Aphids
The Remedy: Make your own citrus-rind spray by grating the rind of one lemon or orange and combining it with 1 pint (500 ml) boiling water. Let it steep overnight, then strain through a coffee filter to remove the bits of rind. Add the mixture to a spray bottle, and spray the aphids on the leaves of the plants. Make sure to spray underneath the leaves, too. Reapply every four to seven days as long as the problem persists.

WHAT YOUR HOUSECLEANER WON'T TELL YOU

Learn how a good relationship makes for a clean house—and other neat secrets—from the people who see (and sometimes put away) your dirty laundry.

1. Please say thank you, even if it's just on a Post-it. Or if you really like me, leave something like a $5 gift card to McDonald's. If I feel like someone appreciates me, I really go the extra mile.

2. Make sure you have all the cleaning products I will need. Sometimes I show up, and my clients have nothing for me to use. You know best what kind of cleaners you want used in your home; some people want only organic cleaners, some are picky about brands, and others have allergies.

> **TOP SECRET!** I know more than you think. I see the piles of bills marked "past due" and know you're having money problems. I find drugs and condom wrappers in kids' bedrooms. And I can tell who's unfaithful because the cheaters always start hiding dirty laundry.

3. Don't forget that I need equipment! One of my bosses kept forgetting to get me a mop so I had to wash her floors on my hands and knees with a cloth. Not only is that inconsiderate, it's harder for me to get the results you want.

4. Please do not ask me to sew on buttons . . . clean the wheels of your bike, scrub out your mailbox, or pull out the refrigerator in order to clean behind it.

5. Letting us work "by the job" sometimes means you get less for your money. It can be more cost effective to pay an hourly rate, especially if it's a maintenance cleaning.

6. It's helpful if you soak dirty pans so that I can clean them more easily when I get there.

7. I need reasonable notice if you are going to move or stop hiring me. Too many clients don't think to tell me until the week they're moving. A month's notice would be nice. You give your landlord a month's notice. Please do me the same courtesy.

8. Tiny kindnesses mean a lot. One time a client left me a gift from a trip abroad, which delighted me. Those small appreciations keep me working hard.

9. It's a huge relief when clients allow me to take my child with me to work. Sometimes I just can't find a sitter, but I still need the money.

10. Please write a list of the things you would like me to do, in addition to giving me verbal instructions, to ensure I don't forget anything.

11. Be wary if I give you my price over the phone. Reputable cleaners come to your home and give you a free estimate.

12. If your house is a disorganized mess, it makes it harder for me to clean, and if you pay me by the hour, you'll pay more. Please pick up toys, piles of papers, and clutter from surfaces so that I can actually get to them.

13. Think our insurance will cover you? Hmm, maybe not. Insurance companies expect us to be trained professionals, so if we use the wrong product on your expensive furnishings, the insurance company might deny the claim.

SOURCES: Tangela Ekhoff, a housecleaner in Tulsa, Oklahoma; Lynette Haugen, owner of True Blue Maids of Pasadena, California; Theresa Peterson, owner of Quality Cleaning "Maid to Order" in Fremont, California; Torrey Shannon, former maid service owner in Westcliffe, Colorado; and house cleaners in Louisiana, New York, Vermont, Washington, and London.

Become an Instant Expert
Squeaky-Clean Tips Your Housekeeper May Not Even Know

* **The best way to dust blinds?** Close them, then wipe up and down with an old dryer sheet. It'll create an antistatic barrier that helps prevent dust from building up again.
* **The Mr. Clean Magic Eraser is your friend.** It will cut your cleaning time in half for bathtubs, sinks, countertops, and dirty walls.
* **To clean glass and mirrors, use coffee filters,** not paper towels. They leave no streaks or lint—and they're cheap.
* **Vinegar and water is a great deodorizer for a musty bathroom.** Spray your shower down as you're getting out. It really absorbs the odors, and the smell of vinegar goes away in an hour.
* **A wet pumice stone will clean a dirty oven** faster than any spray-on product. Trust us.
* **Vacuuming bathroom mats is a nightmare.** Toss them in the wash every week or two instead.
* **To damp-mop wood floors, use plain water** or a water-based floor cleaner like Bona. Don't use vinegar. The acid in it will pit your polyurethane finish, can void your warranty, and may reduce shine over time.
* **Our biggest secret weapon?** A powdered product called Bar Keepers Friend. We use it on everything. Its active ingredient is rhubarb powder, which really cuts through grit and grime. It cleans glass-top stoves, counters, toilets, porcelain, and more. Your sink will never be shinier.
* **To clean your microwave oven,** microwave a cup of water with some baking soda in it until it's boiling. This eliminates odors and makes it super easy to wipe away all that stuck-on stuff.
* **Clean cobwebs with a yardstick covered by a tube sock.** This also works for cleaning under stoves and refrigerators.
* **Shine your bathroom tiles with lemon oil.** It also helps prevent mold and mildew.
* **To eliminate that ring in your toilet,** drop in a bubbling denture-cleaning tablet and leave it for at least 30 minutes or overnight. The stain will come off with just a few swishes of the brush.

WHAT YOUR LOCKSMITH WON'T TELL YOU

These secrets will keep you from getting gouged—or worse—when you lock yourself or other people out.

1. Many locksmiths in the phone book or online are scam artists. They'll quote you a great price, but when they get there, they'll say you have a special lock they can't pick, so they have to drill it open. Then they charge you $125 for a replacement lock you can buy at Home Depot for $25. You can find someone reputable at findalocksmith.com.

2. It's easy to defeat the cheapo locks from big-box stores. Most are mass-produced by reputable manufacturers but to very low standards. Look for at least a grade 2.

3. The best lock is a dead bolt that's properly installed. It should have at least a one-inch "throw," and on the "strike side," there should be a security plate with screws at least three inches long that go all the way into the door's wood frame.

4. If you have a window on or near your door, a thumb-turn dead bolt won't do much good. Burglers knock out the glass, stick a hand in, and turn. Get a double cylinder lock that needs a key on the inside.

5. Keys stamped "Do not duplicate" are duplicated all the time. Ask me about high-security locks with keys that can't be replicated at the hardware store.

6. When you buy a new house, always have your locks rekeyed. Otherwise there's probably a master key out there that can easily open your home.

7. Don't believe a car dealer who says only he can duplicate keys. In most cases, a locksmith who specializes in automotive work can make you a key—usually cheaper.

8. Divorce lock-outs are a challenge. The soon-to-be-ex wife will call and say she's locked out, so I get her in and change the locks. Then the husband calls with the same request. I refer him to a competitor.

TOP SECRET! If you're locked out, please call just one of us. More than once, I arrived at a lock-out to find two competitors' trucks already there. At that point, we all agreed to leave and abandon the inconsiderate victim.

9. Have a housekeeper who needs a key? Ask me to key your door so that your master key works on both the dead bolt and the doorknob, but hers works just on the knob. On the day she comes, lock only the knob.

10. A lot of us do undercover work for the cops. We make keys for them and get them into places at 3 a.m. so they can set up surveillance equipment or put the bugs in place. It's part of the thrill of doing what we do.

11. I've seen my share of dead bodies. It's always a bad sign when the landlord calls to get into an apartment, and nobody's seen the tenant for ten days.

12. Try the door even if you don't have your keys. I've gone to houses and found the door unlocked. (I'm still going to charge you for the service call.)

13. Don't feel bad if you have to call me twice in a short span of time. I once had a guy lock himself out of his house three times in one day.

SOURCES: Tom Rubenoff, a hardware salesman and former locksmith in Brookline, Massachusetts; Charles Eastwood, who operates Locksmith Charley in Phoenix, Arizona; Bob DeWeese, a locksmith in Baltimore, Maryland; and Rick Bayuk, owner of Karpilow Safe & Lock in Bridgeport, Connecticut.

Great Advice

5 WAYS TO MAKE YOUR FRONT DOOR MORE SECURE

1. **Add a heavy-duty dead bolt.** A dead bolt is a low-cost, high-value addition to your security system. Varieties include double-cylinder dead bolts, which are keyed on both sides, and single-cylinder dead bolts, keyed on one side. Whichever type you choose, make sure it has a grade-2 security rating.

2. **Add a strike box.** A strike box is something you can add to your lock that toughens up your entry and deters intruders by replacing existing strike plates with a structure that includes a metal pocket, oversized plates, and a solid connection into the wall stud behind the doorjamb with three-inch screws. To accommodate this addition, you'll need to enlarge both the hole in the jamb and the cover plate recess.

3. **Add a reinforcement plate.** Three-sided metal reinforcement plates add an extra layer of security by encasing a door around its handset or dead bolt. To select the correct size for your door, measure its thickness, the handset or dead bolt hole diameter, and the distance between its edge and the center of the handset or dead bolt (known as the setback).

4. **Rekey the lock.** If you're not the first to live in your present abode, rekeying the entry locks is yet another way to enhance security. Rekeying kits matching most lock brands can be found at hardware stores and home improvement centers, and work on both entrance and dead-bolt locks. They also allow up to six locks to be rekeyed for the same key.

5. **Install a wide-angle peephole.** You'll be able to do a larger scale screening of unexpected visitors with a wide-angle peephole viewer. This easy-to-install safety accessory is designed to fit any door up to two inches thick.

WHAT YOUR PLUMBER WON'T TELL YOU

Here are the smartest ways to avoid costly plumbing mistakes.

1. Monday is our busiest day. That's the day wives call us to correct the "work" their husbands did over the weekend.

2. Know where the main turnoff source is. I can't tell you how many calls I get from people screaming and crying that their house is flooding and they don't know what to do.

3. Pay me by the job, not by the hour.

4. Don't get wrapped up in how much I'm charging for the materials. Sure, my material cost is different than the guy who runs his business out of his garage. But it's not the copper you're paying for—it's the experience. At the end of the day, my material cost is between 25 and 30 percent of the cost of the job.

5. A company that has a good reputation for quality service might charge a little more up front, but you'll save in the long run by avoiding callbacks and extra charges. Look for a company that warrants its service for up to a year for major installations or repairs.

6. Be wary of price quotes that are strikingly lower or higher than competitors. Get a minimum of three bids. Estimates for an average-size job should be within a few hundred dollars. Be suspicious of anything that is substantially lower or double the price of the rest, and watch out for hidden fees, like charges for travel expenses. A good plumber will not nickel and dime you like this, and many of us will offer free estimates.

7. Yes, it's against the rules to remove flow inhibitors from your showerheads, but some of us will do it if you ask.

8. Sure, we'll be happy to check those supply valves under your sink free of charge after we finish the work you're paying us for. Just ask. Same goes for checking your water pressure.

🔒 **TOP SECRET!** There's often an Allen wrench that comes with the garbage disposal. I keep it under the sink. When the thing jams, follow the directions in the manual and I won't need to come out.

9. I'm not a babysitter, a mover, or an auto mechanic. Don't ask.

10. You're calling to say your garage-door opener doesn't work ever since I fixed your faucet? Get a clue—and an electrician.

11. I see this all the time: Women want a new toilet seat and ask their husbands to make the switch. If the seat is old and has metal bolts, you probably need to cut it off with a hacksaw, not unscrew it. A wrench may slip, damaging the bowl and bloodying your knuckles.

12. Don't hang clothes on those exposed pipes in your basement. I've seen them break and flood a basement.

13. I was working in one bathroom while my client was using the whirlpool in another one. And blow-drying her hair at the same time. Her husband had told her it was fine. I told her he was trying to get rid of her.

SOURCES: Bill Stevens, owner of Berkey's Plumbing, Heating & Air Conditioning in Texas; plumbers in California, Connecticut, New Jersey, New York, Texas, and Wisconsin.

Great Advice

HOW TO FIND A PLUMBER WHO WON'T DRAIN YOUR WALLET

. . . .

"Don't go to the Yellow Pages to find a plumber," says Berkey's Bill Stevens. "It's like guessing lottery numbers. Anyone can make an appealing ad, but that doesn't mean they are legitimate. In this industry, it's easy for a plumber who develops a poor reputation to advertise under a different name. They come and go."

Don't assume that every Mr. Fix-it advertising his services in the local Pennysaver or on craigslist is a licensed plumber. There is no national standard for issuing licenses. Some plumbers are licensed by the state, others by the counties they work in. Check with your local city hall or chamber of commerce. They should be able to direct you to the appropriate source for a list of licensed plumbers in your area.

Look for a plumber who is well established in your community. Check the Better Business Bureau and read customer reviews at sites such as ServiceMagic.com, AngiesList.com, or Citysearch.com.

Local contractors or plumbing fixture stores can also refer you to a quality plumber, according to Grady Daniel, who owns a plumbing company in Austin, Texas. "Most of these firms won't work with bad plumbers." Or simply ask your neighbors for a referral. A trusted plumber who consistently delivers quality service does not remain a secret for very long.

SIMPLE TIPS AND FIXES THAT WILL KEEP YOUR WALLET FLUSH

A burst washing machine hose is a top homeowner-insurance claim. I'd replace those flimsy rubber hoses with stainless steel ones.

No bricks in the toilet tank. They can keep your toilet from flushing correctly. No liquid drain cleaners either. They eat away at the pipes. Try a plunger or, better yet, a $30 auger.

If you're going away for any length of time, like on vacation, turn off your water, and if on any of those days the temperature drops below freezing have someone check in on your house. I've been called to homes where the family returned from vacation and there was water flooding out from the front door.

Buy a drain strainer or hair snare if you've got a Rapunzel at home (or even a rapidly balding man). Or tell her to use a paper towel to clear the drain. (Soap can gum up the pipes, too, so use as little of that as you can.)

Small drips can waste over eight gallons of water a day, and a continuously running toilet can waste more than 200 gallons of water daily. If you ignore them, you'll pay for it when your water bill arrives.

Those "flushable" baby wipes are one of the main culprits for clogging pipes. They don't break down the way toilet paper does.

Always jiggling the toilet handle? You need to replace the flap valve. The part costs $4, and it's an easy fix. I charge $100 just to walk in the door.

WHAT YOUR HARDWARE STORE WON'T TELL YOU

It's easy to spend money at the hardware store. But we got home-repair experts to cough up their secrets about what you don't need to buy—so you can spend more on what you want.

1. One way to condition tools and keep rust from invading is to rub them down with hair conditioner when you clean them.

2. You don't have to have a fancy drawer system. Keep nuts and washers on metal shower curtain rings hung from a hook in your workshop. The ring's pear shape and latching action ensure secure storage. Put nuts and washers of similar size on their own rings so that you can find the right size quickly.

3. An ice cube tray is a great assistant. You're disassembling your latest swap-meet acquisition that has lots of small parts and worry that you'll never be able to get them back together again in the correct sequence. Use an old plastic ice cube tray to help keep the small parts in the right order until you get around to reassembling it. If you really want to be organized, mark the sequence by putting a number on a piece of masking tape in each compartment. The bottom half of an egg carton will also work.

4. Next time you have something that needs painting, place an aluminum pie pan under the paint can as a ready-made drip catcher. You'll save a lot of time cleaning up, and you can just toss the pan in the trash when you're done. Even better, rinse it off and recycle it for future paint jobs.

5. **To keep small items like screws, nuts, and nails handy without taking up workbench space,** drill a hole near the top of empty coffee cans so you can hang them on nails in your workshop wall. Label the cans with masking tape so you will know what's inside.

6. **If you like to see everything you have at a glance,** keep all your nails, screws, nuts, and bolts organized by screwing jar lids to the underside of a wooden or melamine shelf. (Make sure the screw won't poke through the top of the shelf.) Then put each type of hardware in its own jar, and screw each jar onto its lid. You'll keep everything off the counters, and by using clear jars, you can find what you need at a glance. Works great for storing seeds in the potting shed, too.

TOP SECRET! Clean up and organize glue and caulk tube piles by cutting a strip of adhesive or duct tape several inches long and folding it over the bottom of each tube, leaving a flap at the end. Punch a hole in the flap with a paper hole puncher and hang the tube on a nail or hook. You'll free up counter space, and you'll be able to find the right tube fast.

7. **Since they're highly resistant to corrosion,** aluminum pie pans are especially well suited for storing hardware accessories in your workshop. Cut a pan in half and attach it (with staples or duct tape around the edges) open side up to a pegboard. Now get organized!

8. **Hold small tools with an old leather or canvas belt.** Tack it along the edge of a shelf, leaving small loops between nails. Slip tools into the loops.

9. **Hinged handles like those found on metal garbage cans are great ways to hold large tools.** Mount them so the handle hangs away from the wall. You can slip a hammer or wrench into the handle for safe storage.

10. **Don't confine perforated hardboard to workshop and garage walls.** It's also great for inside cabinet doors and on the sides of your workbench. Lightweight 1/8-inch perf board is fine for hand tools, but you'll want to use 1/4-inch perf board for heavier items. To keep perf-board hooks from coming loose, put a dab of hot glue on the end that hooks into the board. If you need to rearrange items and move the hook, a light tug will usually free it without much difficulty.

11. Round up rolls of tape by slipping them onto a toilet paper holder mounted on a wall or workbench.

12. Tires are great places for "snakes." An old bicycle tire is just the right size to store metal snakes used to clean plumbing lines or "fish wires" used to run electrical cables inside walls. Just lay the snake or fish wire inside the tire, where it will expand to the shape of the tire and become encased within it. Then you can hang the tire conveniently on a hook in your workshop, garage, basement, or shed.

13. Repairing small items, such as broken china, with glue would be easy if you had three hands—one for each piece along with one to apply the glue. Since you only have two, try this: Stick the biggest part of the item in a small container of sand to hold it steady. Position the large piece so that when you set the broken piece in place, the piece will balance. Apply glue to both edges and stick on the broken piece. Leave the mended piece there, and the sand will hold it steady until the glue dries.

Who Knew?
AMAZING USES FOR WD-40

Protect a Bird Feeder

To keep squirrels from taking over a bird feeder, spray a generous amount of WD-40 on top of the feeder. The pesky squirrels will slide right off.

Separate Stuck Glassware

What can you do when you reach for a drinking glass and get two locked together, one stuck tightly inside the other? You don't want to risk breaking one or both by trying to pull them apart. Stuck glasses will separate with ease if you squirt some WD-40 on them, wait a few seconds for it to work its way between the glasses, and then gently pull the glasses apart. Remember to wash the glasses thoroughly before you use them.

Get Off That Stuck Ring

When pulling and tugging can't get that ring off your finger, reach for the WD-40. A short burst of WD-40 will get the ring to slide right off. Remember to wash your hands after spraying them with WD-40.

Remove Chewing Gum from Hair

It's one of a parent's worst nightmares: chewing gum tangled in a child's hair. You don't have to panic or run for the scissors. Simply spray the gummed-up hair with WD-40, and the gum will comb out with ease. Make sure you are in a well-ventilated area when you spray and take care to avoid contact with the child's eyes.

Remove Tough Scuff Marks

Those tough black scuff marks on your kitchen floor won't be so tough anymore if you spray them with WD-40. In fact, you can use WD-40 to help remove tar and scuff marks on all your hard-surfaced floors. It won't harm the surface, and you won't have to scrub nearly as much. Remember to open the windows if you are cleaning a lot of marks.

Wipe Away Tea Stains

To remove tea stains from countertops, spray a little WD-40 on a sponge or damp cloth and wipe the stain away.

Clean Toilet Bowls

You don't need a bald genie or a specialized product to clean your toilet bowl. Use WD-40 instead: Spray it into the bowl for a couple of seconds and swish with a nylon toilet brush. The solvents in the WD-40 will help dissolve the gunk and lime stains.

Winter-Proof Boots and Shoes

Waterproof your winter boots and shoes by giving them a coat of WD-40. It'll act as a barrier so water can't penetrate the material. Also use WD-40 to remove ugly salt stains from boots and shoes during the winter months. Just spray WD-40 onto the stains and wipe with a clean rag. Your boots and shoes will look almost as good as new.

Prevent Snow Buildup on Windows

Does the weather forecast predict a big winter snowstorm? You can't stop the snow from falling, but you can prevent it from building up on your house's windows. Just spray WD-40 over the outside of your windows before the snow starts and the snow won't stick.

Keep Wasps from Building Nests

Don't let yellow jackets and other wasps ruin your spring and summer fun. Their favorite place to build nests is under eaves. So next spring, mist some WD-40 under all the eaves of your house. It will block the wasps from building their nests there.

Remove Doggie-Doo

Uh-oh, now you've stepped in it! Few things in life are more unpleasant than cleaning doggie-doo from the bottom of a sneaker, but the task will be a lot easier if you have a can of WD-40 handy. Spray some on the affected sole and use an old toothbrush to clean the crevices. Rinse with cold water and the sneakers will be ready to hit the pavement again. Now, don't forget to watch where you step!

WHAT YOUR GAS AND ELECTRIC COMPANY WON'T TELL YOU

These secrets will help you get a lower energy bill every single month.

1. Heat food in your toaster oven—it uses up to 50 percent less energy than a full-size oven. Your stovetop is more efficient than your conventional oven as well, so if you can start something there then transfer it to the oven to cut the cooking time, do so. And when you need to reheat leftovers, use your microwave.

2. Cut the amount of time you use your stove or cooktop by covering pots when you boil things. This brings the pot to a boil faster. If you're boiling potatoes, dice them to roughly ½-inch in size so they cook faster, start them in the cold water, and bring to boil. Once the water has come to a rolling boil, turn off the heat. Leave the pot on the burner, cover, and let sit for 15 to 20 minutes, until fork tender. Do the same for pasta, except add the pasta after the water is boiling and boil it for two minutes before turning off the heat. Let it sit, covered, for the amount of time remaining according to the directions on the box.

3. Your refrigerator and freezer run most efficiently when it's full. A near-empty fridge will run more frequently, sucking up more energy and costing you more money. The same is true for your freezer. You don't have to buy more food. Just fill more ice-cube trays for your freezer and pitchers with water, iced tea, or whatever you like to drink for your fridge. If you're a white wine drinker, keep a few unopened bottles in the fridge. Still empty? You can always load up the spaces with those blue ice packs.

4. Store refrigerated food and beverages in closed containers. If left uncovered, they release moisture and overburden the appliance's compressor.

5. Your programmable thermostat only saves money if you program it right. Many people mistakenly believe that these devices will automatically set themselves to operate in the most energy-efficient way. But they don't. You have to program them so that they stop your ducted air-conditioning coming on when it isn't really needed—at night or when you're at work or on holiday. Learn how to set your thermostat to suit your particular needs—lowering it by just 1° can reduce your bill by up to 15 percent.

6. Place lamps and TVs far away from thermostats so the heat given off doesn't cause air-conditioning systems to run longer than they need to.

7. Keep the heat out by opting for white window shades during warmer weather. Keep them closed during the day to reflect the sun's heat away from your house.

8. Weatherproofing saves. You could weatherproof your home yourself, of course, but even if you delegate the job, you can still come out ahead financially in the long run. Merely sealing leaks in windows and doors and insulating ducts could save you at least $100 a year and reduce CO_2 emissions by at least 1,000 pounds per year—and possibly much more. Adding insulation to your home could double the savings.

9. Water temperature matters. You can easily save money, and hundreds of pounds of CO_2 per year, by lowering the temperature of your water heater to 120° and washing clothes in cold or warm water instead of hot. You can save even more by replacing a water heater that's more than 10 or 15 years old.

10. Run your dishwasher, but only when it's full. Otherwise you are wasting water, energy, and money. And if it's full, it uses less than a third of the water you'd use by doing the job by hand. Next, if you have a six-hour delay button on your model, use it. Start it at 6 p.m. (you can always go back in and add more dishes after dinner). This way it will run at midnight, during off-peak energy hours.

11. Choose an Energy Star–compliant computer, which uses 70 percent less electricity than a non-designated model. Choose other appliances with the Energy Star designation, as well.

12. Don't believe the screensaver myth. All a screensaver does is prolong the life of your monitor by displaying a moving image while you are not using your computer, as any fixed image left on would eventually "burn" itself into the screen, ruining it. Screensavers do nothing whatsoever to save electricity—in fact, they burn up quite a lot. If you want to save energy without turning your computer off, check if it has a special energy-saving mode: Go to your operating system's control panel or preferences and explore the power-management options.

13. Stand-by mode doesn't cost less than turning it on and off. Leaving a machine constantly in stand-by mode consumes a surprisingly large amount of electricity. If you want to save energy—and money—you should always turn your computer off at night or when you will be away from it for a long period of time. Remember also to switch off other computer hardware, such as scanners, printers, external hard drives, and speakers at the mains. If they are powered via a plugged-in transformer, that will remain on even when the power button on the appliance has been switched off.

> **TOP SECRET!** Fans do not actually cool the air in a room. They cool the people in it by creating a wind-chill effect on their skin. So there is no point leaving a fan on when you're no longer in a room. Instead, treat it like a light and turn it off when you leave the room. Otherwise, you will just be wasting electricity and running up a large bill.

Who Knew?

ANSWERS TO YOUR TOP 3 ENERGY QUESTIONS

. . . .

Q. Should I turn off the lights every time I leave the room?

A. Turn off incandescents if you're leaving the room for more than five seconds; compact fluorescent lights, if you'll be gone at least 15 minutes.

Q. I know cold-water washes are greener, but will they get my clothes clean?

A. The good news is, washing your clothes in warm or even cold water will get rid of almost any grime, except for the worst dirt or oily stains.

Q. In public restrooms, paper towel or electric hand dryer?

A. Go for the hot air. Far less energy is needed to heat and blow air at your hands than to make paper towels and haul them around. One study found that nine trees are cut down to supply an average fast-food restaurant with paper towels for a year; the tossed towels then create 1,000 pounds of landfill waste.

WHAT YOUR REAL ESTATE AGENT WON'T TELL YOU

What you don't know can cost you. Here's how to be smart when buying and selling.

1. My number one selling tip: Clear off countertops in the bathrooms and kitchen. Americans love that wide-open counter space.

2. Your open house helps me more than it helps you. The majority of visitors aren't buyers—they're nosy neighbors—and that gives me the opportunity to hand out my card.

3. Plug-in air fresheners are a turnoff to a lot of people. If you want your house to smell good, bake cookies.

4. Yes, staging your home by getting rid of clutter and bringing in furniture or accessories can help it sell. But music, champagne glasses next to the bed, and fake pies on the countertop? That's going overboard, and it will turn off some buyers.

5. If you get a call saying that some buyers want to see your house in 15 minutes, let them in even if it's a bit messy. Those last-minute types typically make impulsive decisions, and they might just decide to buy a house that day.

6. In this kind of market, don't be offended by a lowball offer. You have a better chance of getting that person to pay than finding someone new.

7. If I'm hugely successful, you may not get the benefit of my experience. A well-known agent may pass you off to a junior agent after you sign the contract. Ask me exactly who you will be dealing with.

> **TOP SECRET!** Houses without furniture don't look larger. Empty rooms may actually appear smaller because the buyers can't get a sense of how much furniture will fit.

8. The commission is always negotiable upfront, before you sign a contract. You can even make it part of the transaction. If you and your buyer are $4,000 apart, for example, ask the agents if they are willing to reduce their commissions by $2,000.

9. Make sure you read my listing or buyer's contract carefully before signing it. There may be an extra "administrative fee" ranging from $250 to $1,500 on top of my standard commission, intended to cover my brokerage's administrative costs. Similar to my commission, this fee is negotiable.

10. Don't skip the final walk-through. Make sure that repairs were done properly, the owner's personal items have been removed, and the items you agreed should stay are still there. I've seen stoves, washers, and dryers walk right out the door.

11. Beware of sellers' agents who overestimate your house's selling price. They're hoping you'll choose them over other agents who will price it more realistically. We call that "buying your listing," and it guarantees your house will sit on the market for a very long time.

12. If I'm new in the business, my references are likely to be relatives or friends. Always ask how they found me.

13. Even if I've had my license a few years, I may be a soccer coach moonlighting as a real estate agent, and yours may be the first home I've tried to sell in years. Ask how many transactions I completed last year, and Google my name to see if it comes up on real estate forums and websites.

SOURCES: Licensed real estate agents Nicole Tucker in Dallas and Eric Bramlett in Austin, Texas; broker Karyn Anjali Glubis in Tampa, Florida; Rob Foley, a former real estate lawyer who now owns Vermont's Flat Fee Real Estate; and a realtor in Los Angeles, California.

Great Advice

10 WAYS TO INCREASE YOUR HOME'S VALUE WITH EXTERIOR PAINT

....

1. **Color can ratchet up the price.** An effective use of color on the exterior of your home can add thousands of dollars to its value, says James Martin, who has been hired by landlords and real estate developers to increase the market value of their properties or improve occupancy rates in their buildings with eye-catching color schemes.

2. **Perception of color is relative.** If you put a mid-value color, such as tan, next to pure white, it will look beige. But if you put it next to dark green, it will look off-white. Keep this in mind when choosing colors. And when you are choosing a color from a fan deck at the paint store, you should mask off the colors next to it with a white sheet of paper.

3. **Begin with the value.** Design your color scheme first according to value. That is, decide whether you want a dark, medium, or light main color.

4. **Highlight detail carefully.** Create a balanced effect between the top and bottom of your home. For instance, if there is a lot of detail on the top of your home, you will need to create detail and interest on the bottom.

5. **Don't be top-heavy.** Put darker colors toward the bottom of the house to avoid creating an "uncomfortable, top-heavy feel," says Martin.

6. **Choose colors in the right light.** Pick colors outside in natural light on a cloudy day or in open shade. Bright light creates glare and can distort your perception of the color.

7. **Be material-minded.** Make sure the paint colors you choose complement the colors of the other materials of your home, such as the roof, brick, stone, or stucco.

8. **Brighten things up.** Paint window sashes and overhead surfaces, such as porch ceilings and soffits, a lighter color to reflect light and lift the spirit of your home.

9. **Go warm, not cool.** Use warm colors as opposed to cool. For instance, use a warm yellow-white as opposed to a cool blue-white.

10. **Play up the size.** Use light colors to make a small house look bigger, and dark colors to make a large house that is squeezed onto a small lot look smaller.

4 SMART WAYS TO KEEP YOUR HOME'S VALUE ON THE UP AND UP

1. **Find problems early.** Every two or three years, have your house examined by a certified home inspector (see ashi.org or nahi.org), says Steve Berges, a builder and author of 101 *Cost-Effective Ways to Increase the Value of Your Home*. This person inspects the roof and basement for leaks and structural damage; checks the foundation for termites and moisture; and tests heating, air-conditioning, plumbing, and electrical systems. An inspection costs about $400 but could save you thousands later.

2. **Upgrade regularly.** Replace your roof about every 15 years (depending on type), paint the exterior every five years, and review the gutter system every six months. "Tighten the screws connecting the gutters to the fascia board against the house and examine the boards for cracks and rot," Berges recommends.

3. **Watch for water.** Moisture usually enters a home through cracks in the roof and foundation. "During a heavy rain, go in your attic with a flashlight to check for leaks," Berges says.

4. **Change the scenery.** Cut back shrubs that touch the house. They trap moisture and let bugs inside. Consider hiring a certified arborist for tree pruning. Doing it yourself could weaken trees, increasing the risk that limbs will fall on your roof during a storm.

WHAT YOUR MOVER WON'T TELL YOU

Here's what you need to know before you make your big move—including who's legit and how long it really takes.

1. Make sure your mover is legit. If you're moving interstate, search for companies that are registered with the Federal Motor Carrier Safety Administration (FMSCA) at protectyourmove.gov. For an in-state mover, visit the American Moving & Storage Association's (AMSA) consumer website at moving.org to find screened and approved companies.

2. Beware of rogue movers. Movers should answer the telephone with the company's name, rather than a generic term like "moving company." Once you've chosen a company, stop by its office to make sure it exists and is in good condition. On moving day, make sure a company-owned and marked fleet truck—not a rental truck—arrives.

3. Movers covered by federal law must view your belongings in person before giving you an estimate if they have an office within 50 miles of your home.

4. Beware those that try to give you a phone estimate; they can later say you have more stuff than you told them about.

5. Get in-person estimates from at least three companies, and don't hire one that quotes a price much higher or lower than competitors.

6. We can charge extra fees. Consider a binding agreement, which means you'll pay what the movers estimated regardless of what your shipment ends up weighing. Caveat: The movers can still charge extra for moving into a home on a steep hill, with many steps, or in a crowded city. Ask about fees ahead of time.

7. We can charge up to 110 percent of the original estimate. But under federal law, movers cannot charge you more than that (not including fees and extras), even under a non-binding agreement. They also cannot require full payment before final delivery.

8. Movers are responsible for items that are damaged or lost if you purchase insurance with full liability. Be sure to list china, antiques, and anything with a value of more than $100 per pound on shipping documents.

9. Take jewelry, important papers, and other valuable small items with you rather than packing them.

10. Pack only one room at a time. Don't start the next room until you're finished. It'll keep you organized and allow you to tackle the move in smaller steps.

> **TOP SECRET!** Everybody underestimates how long moving takes. Estimate how long it will take you to pack everything and then double (at least) that number. You'll need plenty of time to discard, sort, and pack your things.

11. Don't try to move without a permanent marker. Label, label, label. Write down the contents and the destination room on every box. This may seem obvious, but it can fall by the wayside during a busy move.

12. If you move between October and May, it's considered off-peak, and you'll likely receive better service. If you must move during peak season, try to move mid-month and mid-week.

13. Believe us when we say we can move your car cheaper than you can. Moving your car across the country can cost you at least $1,000, but that's less than the roughly $1,500 in mileage and gas at current prices (plus food and lodging along the way) it'll cost you to drive.

SOURCES: Associated Press; Federal Motor Carrier Safety Administration; American Moving & Storage Association.

Great Advice

DON'T TOSS IT! HERE'S HOW YOU CAN RECYCLE HAZARDOUS STUFF

In your rush to whittle down your belongings, make sure you do the right thing with the environmentally unfriendly finds you're likely to encounter. Here are the recommended methods for recycling from the EPA, Earth911.com, and call2recycle.org.

The Hazard: CFL Bulbs

What to do: Because compact fluorescent light bulbs (CFLs) contain toxic mercury, which can be released into the environment when they break, CFLs shouldn't be disposed of with household trash or recycled with glass. Visit Earth911.com to find out whether your bulbs can be collected by or dropped off at a local waste removal agency. Several hardware and home store chains also have CFL recycling programs, including Home Depot, Lowe's, Ace Hardware, and Ikea.

The Hazard: Dry-Cell Batteries

What to do: Dry-cell batteries are what's used to power most of our cord-free toys and home appliances. Button, AAA, AA, C, D, and 9-volt are all varieties of dry-cell batteries, which fall into two categories:

Single use: Single use batteries come in several varieties, including alkaline, carbon-zinc, lithium, nickel-cadmium (NiCad), nickel metal hydride (NiMH), and button cell (lithium manganese). All contain elements or heavy metals that can become environmental hazards when they end up in dumps and waste treatment facilities. Not all states require recycling of single use batteries, but there are local battery recycling agencies in most cities and towns. Do a quick Internet search to find one near you.

Rechargeable: Rechargeable batteries last longer than their single-use predecessors, but they still contain environmental toxins. Visit call2recycle.org to find a drop-off location in your neighborhood.

The Hazard: Cell Phones

What to do: In most cases, recycling a cell phone means donating it to a worthy cause. Next time you upgrade, free up some storage space and bring that drawer full of older models to your local wireless retailer (AT&T, Verizon, T-Mobile, LG, Sony, Best Buy) or big box office supply store (Staples, Office Depot). Many charities and local government offices also accept cell phone donations.

The Hazard: Household Cleaners and Containers

What to do: Unless they're labeled nontoxic, many household cleaners contain potentially hazardous chemicals. If the label doesn't contain disposal instructions, determine whether the cleaner is water-soluble (mixes with water). If so, pour it down the drain under running water. Sponges, wipes, and mopheads can be thrown in the trash. For products that contain harsher chemicals, such as oven cleaners and drain openers, contact the manufacturer for disposal instructions if none are provided. In many areas, household cleaner containers can be recycled curbside, but it's a good idea to check your local recycling guidelines.

WHAT YARD SALE FANATICS WON'T TELL YOU

Here's the inside scoop on what really draws buyers and how to get the best price for your stuff.

1. Get your neighbors involved. A group sale will draw more lookers than a one-family sale.

2. There's more than one pricing strategy. Decide whether you're selling things to make money or to get rid of them. Price items accordingly.

3. Ask for 25 to 33 percent of the item's original cost.

4. Be less flexible about price at the beginning of the sale and more flexible at the end.

5. We can't come to your sale if we don't know it's there. Go to yardsalequeen.com for ideas about lettering, sign place-ment, and free ways to advertise your sale.

6. A great way to create a sign is with a brown paper bag. Write on it using big, fat, thick lettering—definitely no wispy ballpoint pen—then fill it with rocks, and tape it shut.

7. Non-holiday weekends after local paydays are the best time to schedule a sale.

8. Put the nice stuff closer to the road. Place tools and gadgets out front, too, to draw men who might otherwise try to overrule their wives about stopping at your sale.

9. Do your own math. Say no to helpful calculations from customers, thanks just the same.

10. Your house isn't a dressing room. Don't let strangers into your house to try on clothes or use the restroom.

TOP SECRET! People switch tags. Seriously. As if you're not already giving a discount. Just keep your eye on who's looking at your stuff.

11. Wear a fanny pack; don't keep money in a shoebox. Keep all the money in it, along with a cell phone just in case.

12. Check the bills people give you. It's not that uncommon for people to tell you they gave you a $20 when they gave you a $10.

13. Watch out for sneaks. People will take things out of boxes, put them under their clothes, and leave the empty boxes behind.

SOURCES: J. D. Roth, writer for *Time*'s Moneyland blog; and the experts at yardsalequeen.com and blog.movebuilder.com.

Great Advice

6 THINGS YOU SHOULD NEVER BUY USED

1. Bike or Motorcycle Helmets

Helmets are meant to protect you from one accident. Sometimes damage isn't visible, so you need to buy a new helmet to make sure you're getting all the protection you need.

2. Child Car Seats

A car seat that has been in an accident may not protect your child in another. Damaged car seats are common; about one in ten have been in an accident, found one survey conducted in England. Brand-new car seats can cost as little as $50, and safety technology improves each year. Don't risk your child's life.

3. Tires

If they've been in an accident, tires are likely to be unstable and unreliable.

4. Mattresses

With bedbugs infesting homes in record numbers, chances are the critters could lurk in any used mattress. You might also end up sleeping with other people's mold, mites, bacteria, and bodily fluids (yuck!).

5. Cribs

Scores of crib recalls, as well as changing safety standards, make it hard to verify the safety of a used crib.

6. Laptops

Laptops are more likely to be dropped, knocked around, and spilled on simply because they're out in the world, while a desktop computer sits (mostly) safe at home.

WHAT PROFESSIONAL ORGANIZERS WON'T TELL YOU

It's not that hard to get and stay organized. You just have to know how to go about it— here are some tips.

1. Clients tell me the same thing: When they go to clean their closets, they tend to pull everything out and then they run out of time and they push it all back in, which makes it worse than it was to begin with. So my suggestion is to divide and conquer. On a Saturday morning do your shoes, then at other times do your slacks. People have told me that breaking it up into small projects has changed their life.

2. I always recommend grouping "like with like." It enables people to find items quickly. All tank tops together, all capri pants together in one area. Some people like to group items by sleeve length—and there are a few in the spring and summer seasons.

3. I've even seen people use color-coded hangers, but I don't recommend it—too time consuming!

4. Purses on shelves tend to get messy. For those who have wall space in their closets, a great solution would be to purchase belt racks and hang them vertically instead of horizontally. That way, the bottoms of the purses don't bunch up in the same place. This also works great for ties!

5. **Look around your home for things that are going unused, that might be empty**—like file drawers—and store things away in there. I have had a lot of clients who collect old suitcases and use them for storage—those don't take up much room.

6. **Use clear shoeboxes for hair accessories and light-weight scarves.** You can even use a clear bin for small tank tops, shorts, etc. Take a Polaroid or cut out a magazine photo and tape it so you know what's in the box. Those are fun and it will make getting to things so easy.

7. **I grew up in an apartment, and we had to get creative with our winter clothing storage.** One solution is to purchase plastic bags that you can suck the air out of. The clothes then take up much less space and can be placed under a bed, a couch, or on a high shelf.

TOP SECRET! When you get out your spring clothes, put the hangers in backward on the rod but then when you wear a piece of clothing, hang it up facing the front. At the end of the season you'll know what you've never worn.

8. **Also, some local dry cleaners will store winter clothes** for people (as long as they're dry cleaning them for you, too).

9. **Get together a group of friends and host a clothing swap.** Have them bring clothes they are not using and certainly don't want to discard—someone's going to want it! Have a little cocktail party, and everyone gets new clothes without spending money . . . it's a win-win situation for everyone.

10. **Return anything you bought more than four months ago and never used.** Many stores won't let you return for cash clothing you loved in the shop but never got around to wearing. However, they are likely to offer you store credit if you insist. So instead of letting unwanted clothes pile up in your closets, a better idea is to return them for store credit.

11. **Sometimes, you can sell store credit** for cash on eBay. There's a very vibrant market for store credit receipts and gift cards, which trade for very close to face value. I've seen $200 gift receipts from stores like Macy's, Tiffany, and Bloomingdale's

fetch $180, so you get most of your value back without having to find a buyer for your specific item or dealing with packing and shipping it.

12. Keep winter clothes dry when you're storing them in the basement by putting pieces of chalk into a small cloth bag that you can pack with the clothes you're storing. The chalk will absorb all the moisture, keeping your clothes protected.

13. Literally clean your closet. Before you put the upcoming season's clothes back into the closet, take the opportunity of having empty shelves to replace your shelf paper, vacuum the closet floor, and make the closet fresh and clean.

SOURCES: Ann Bingley Gallops, professional organizer from The Organized Life; Beth Levin, professional organizer of Closet Queen; Stacey Agin Murray, professional organizer of Organized Artistry; Dan Nissanoff, author of *FutureShop*; Mary Pankiewicz, professional organizer and author of *You Can Be Clutter-Free & Organized*.

Become an Instant Expert
Incredibly Clever—and Cheap!—
Ways to Clean and Store Clutter

* **Tennis Rackets, Baseball Bats** Keep a decorated empty wine or liquor carton—with partitions and the top cut off—in your child's room and use it for easy storage of tennis rackets, baseball bats, fishing poles, and such.
* **Coins** Instead of emptying the coins from your pockets into a jar for later sorting, cut off a four-section piece of an egg carton and leave it on your dresser. Sort your quarters, dimes, nickels, and pennies as you pull them out of your pockets.
* **Junk Drawer Items** If your junk drawer is an unsightly mess, insert a plastic ice cube tray for easy, low-cost organization. One "cube" can hold paper clips, the next, rubber bands, another, stamps. It's another small way to bring order to your life.
* **Utility Closet Clutter** A hanging shoe bag is a great organizer in the utility closet. Use its pockets to store sponges, scrub brushes, and other cleaning utensils—and even some bottles of cleaning products.

Big Advice

HOW TO AVOID LOSING MONEY ON REPAIRS YOU DON'T NEED

Each spring and summer, professional home improvement scammers roam the United States in search of victims. They often target people who live in areas recently damaged by weather events—such as the tornado-ravaged Midwest—and older adults, offering "deals" on home repairs. So how can you avoid being fooled by one? Use these tips.

1. Leaky Roof Wrangling

Water is coming through your roof. Or is it? A con artist will say water is seeping through the shingles and you need to tear off all the old layers and build a new roof, a job that typically costs $5,000 or more.

The Reality: Most of the time, roof leaks occur because the sealing around vent pipes has failed, the metal flashing on the chimney has deteriorated, or the connections between roof sections have eroded. Replacing the sealing or flashing, simply and cheaply, will often solve the problem.

Normally, an asphalt shingle roof lasts 15 to 20 years. You need to replace the roof if you see curling or missing shingles or a large amount of granular material from the shingles collecting in gutters. Don't get talked into having the bad roof torn off, at a potential 50 percent increase in costs, unless your building code demands it. Many towns will allow a second or even third asphalt roof to be installed if the home's framing can support the extra weight. And beware a roofer who says you need an entirely new deck, the wood base beneath the shingles. A completely new deck is needed only one in 1,000 times.

2. Basement Boondoggle

If your basement is chronically wet, unscrupulous contractors might tell you they need to dig out your entire foundation and waterproof it, for anywhere from $5,000 to $15,000. More often, though, the solution is simple and costs very little.

The Reality: Many basement leaks are caused by overflow from clogged gutters, misrouted downspouts, unsloped land around the house, or even improperly aimed lawn sprinklers.

"Think of your masonry foundation as a rigid sponge," explains waterproofing expert Richard Barako. If the water volume is above normal, water will wick through the cinder blocks. So before calling in professional help, try to reduce the moisture along the foundation by cleaning gutters, rerouting downspouts, repositioning sprinklers, or packing fresh soil six inches high against the foundation and sloping it back to level within about three feet.

Damp walls may be caused by high humidity. To test, attach a piece of aluminum foil to the foundation wall; if moisture shows up on the patch in a day or two, it's just condensation. Start shopping for a dehumidifier.

If water is still seeping in, repair any cracks with hydraulic cement, available at home stores, and apply a quality waterproof paint such as Latex Base Drylok Masonry Waterproofer. As a last resort, consider hiring a professional engineer, whose impartial advice would be worth the expense. Home inspectors are less expensive, but be sure they're certified by the American Society of Home Inspectors.

3. Termite Treatments

Myths about termites abound. In a recent survey by the University of Kentucky, 60 percent of people thought termites could take a house down in six months or less. Nothing could be further from the truth, yet con artists use this fear to pressure homeowners into quickly signing on the dotted line for unnecessary or shoddy work that could cost up to $3,000.

The Reality: By arming yourself with a few facts, you'll be able to ask informed questions and avoid a scam. The most common termite in the United States is the subterranean, of which there are two main kinds: workers and swarmers (or winged) termites. The workers hollow out the wood, while swarmers mate and create new colonies. Termites live underground and burrow through soil until they find wood, or woodlike products, and water. To get into your house, they'll often build moist, earthen tunnels across foundations to your home's lower frames, a clear sign of infestation.

Wood that's been damaged by termites is hollowed out along the grain, with bits of dried mud or soil lining the feeding galleries. Be wary of exterminators showing you termites on woodpiles or fences unconnected to your house: This may be a scam. You have a problem only if there's evidence of termites inside the house or close to the foundation.

Bugs flying in the home during the spring are another sign of infestation. These may be flying ants, however. Termites have a full waist, straight antennae, and wings of equal length; ants have elbowed antennae, pinched waists, and forewings longer than hindwings.

There are more than 17,000 pest control companies in the United States, but bigger doesn't always mean better. You want a firm with good recommendations, lots of experience, and a fair price. Michael Potter, a professor of entomology at the University of Kentucky, recommends questioning the company carefully about its history and asking that it send an experienced technician. If an exterminator claims you have termites, he should show you the evidence.

Some companies charge thousands for a typical job that could be done for less than $1,000, so take notes on the exact kind of treatment and compare apples to apples when getting estimates.

4. Chimney Sweep Swindle

In a classic bait-and-switch scam, a chimney sweep calls from a "boiler room" or comes to your door telling you he's just fixed a neighbor's chimney and is offering an inspection for the low price of $39.95. Once inside the chimney, he may claim to find problems, saying you need a new liner, for instance. Suddenly that $39.95 price tag rises thousands of dollars.

The Reality: There's no question that fireplace chimneys can be hazardous. An oily, blackish substance called creosote accumulates inside the chimney and may catch fire if it's more than a quarter-inch thick. Occasionally, but not as often as chimney sweeps would have you believe, a blocked chimney can route carbon monoxide into your house.

Experts recommend an annual inspection to check for creosote buildup and the structural soundness of the chimney. This usually costs $100 to $250 (not that ridiculous $39.95), and if cleaning is required, an additional $100 to $150. Hire only certified chimney sweeps who've been taught and tested by the Chimney Safety Institute of America. Also, watch the technician as he makes his inspection. Lately, sweeps are using video cameras fed down the flue, so ask to see the video and have the technician explain it as you watch. If he balks, he's scamming you.

Chimneys for oil and gas burners are far less a concern. "An oil-heat system that's serviced every year before winter hardly ever causes problems," says Kevin Rooney, CEO of the Oil Heat Institute of Long Island. But before you look for a professional chimney sweep, call your local fire department; some conduct inspections for free.

5. Mold Mayhem

Mold is making a comeback—not in your home, necessarily, but with con artists, especially since Hurricane Katrina. Playing up fears about disease from mold, particularly over the Internet, they try to convince you to run tests costing anywhere from $300 to $600 to identify your mold. Then they recommend a remediation company for removing the mold—a firm they're in cahoots with.

The Reality: Healthy people usually have nothing to worry about. "If you're immunosuppressed or have allergies or asthma, it can be problematic," says David B. Callahan, MD, medical epidemiologist at the Centers for Disease Control and Prevention (CDC). "Other than that, mold isn't dangerous."

The CDC doesn't even recommend testing mold, because if it's a problem to the occupants, it should be removed no matter what kind it is. And you don't need a remediation company for small areas. Just clean nonporous surfaces with soap and water, followed by a solution of one cup of bleach mixed with one gallon of water. To control future growth, eliminate excess moisture by keeping humidity levels between 40 and 60 percent. Promptly fix leaky roofs, windows, and pipes, and ventilate shower, laundry, and cooking areas.

Part Two

WHAT YOU DON'T KNOW ABOUT
YOUR FOOD

Do waiters ever do things to your food when you're not looking? And how do you know if you're really getting decaf? Veteran staff from restaurants high and low held open the kitchen door so we could see what's really in the "vegetarian stock," the truth behind why kids love the pizza at their favorite places, and how to tell if a restaurant is really clean.

Waitpeople aren't the only ones who spilled industry secrets. Bartenders exposed what whistling and waving money at them really gets you (a nice, long wait). Baristas point out that "I'll take a..." does not mean "please." And the pizza guy? Heck yes he speeds (at least once a day), and he's accidentally dropped your pizza more than once, but he's also helped you move your sofa. Welcome to the secret world of food and how consumers can be smarter about what goes in their mouths, and savvier about what comes out of them, to guarantee a great experience every time.

WHAT YOUR WAITER WON'T TELL YOU

Here are the top 13 things restaurants don't want you to know about what goes on when you're out of view.

1. Don't order fish on Sunday or Monday. Fish is usually delivered twice a week, so you'll get the freshest fish when you order any day between Tuesday and Friday. To be sure, you can always ask the restaurant when they get theirs.

2. I've seen some horrible things done to people's food: steaks dropped on the floor, butter dipped in the dishwater.

3. I never ask for lemon in a drink. Everybody touches them. Nobody washes them. We just peel the stickers off, cut them up, and throw them in your iced tea.

4. We put sugar in our kids' meals so kids will like them more. Seriously. We even put extra sugar in the dough for the kids' pizzas.

5. At a lot of restaurants, the special is whatever they need to sell before it goes bad. Especially watch out for the soup of the day. If it contains fish or if it's some kind of "gumbo," it's probably the stuff they're trying to get rid of.

6. Your "fresh" salad might not be. At one restaurant where I worked, the salads were made up to three days before they're served. They were sitting on a tray with a thousand other salads in the refrigerator. The waiters went back, grabbed a plate and some dressing, and handed it to the customer.

7. Sometimes, we stick a fork in it. At one bakery restaurant, they used to make this really yummy peach cobbler in a big tray. A lot of times, servers don't have time to eat. So we all kept a fork in our aprons, and as we cruised through the kitchen, we'd stick our fork in the cobbler and take a bite. We'd use the same fork each time.

> **TOP SECRET!** I have seen servers mess with your credit card. If a server doesn't like you, he might try to embarrass you by bringing your credit card back and saying, "Do you have another card? This one didn't go through."

8. There really is no caffeine in there. In most restaurants, after 8 p.m. or so, all the coffee is decaf because no one wants to clean two different coffeepots. I'll bring out a tray with 12 coffees on it and give some to the customers who ordered regular, others to the ones who ordered decaf. But they're all decaf. Oh, and if you order specific milk, very few restaurants carry whole milk, 2 percent milk, skim milk, *and* half-and-half; it's just not practical.

9. Water has a cost. My biggest pet peeve? When I walk up to a table of six or seven people and one person decides everyone needs water. I'm making a trip to deliver seven waters, and four or five of them never get touched.

10. Use your waiter's name. When I say, "Hi, my name is JR, and I'll be taking care of you," it's great when you say, "Hi, JR. How are you doing tonight?" Then, the next time you go in, ask for that waiter. He may not remember you, but if you've requested him, he's going to give you really special service.

11. If you're worried about cleanliness, check out the bathroom. If the bathroom is gross, you can be sure the kitchen is much worse.

12. If you walk out with the slip you wrote the tip on and leave behind the blank one, the server gets nothing. It happens all the time, especially with people who've had a few bottles of wine.

13. Always examine the check. Sometimes large parties are unaware that a gratuity has been added to the bill, so they tip on top of it. Waiters "facilitate" this error. It's dishonest, it's wrong—and I did it all the time.

SOURCES: Interviews with more than two dozen servers across the country at restaurants including well-known pizza chains, casual restaurants, Mexican restaurants; Charlie Kondek, former waiter at a Denny's in Central Michigan; Kathy Kniss, who waited tables for ten years in Los Angeles; Judi Santana, a server for ten years; Charity Ohlund; Jake Blanton; Chris, a New York City waiter and the founder of bitterwaitress.com; Steve Dublanica, veteran New York waiter and author of *Waiter Rant: Thanks for the Tip— Confessions of a Cynical Waiter*; and JR, waiter at a fine-dining restaurant and author of the blog servernotslave.wordpress.com

Great Advice
THE NEW RULES ON TIPPING

Twenty percent (or close to it) is the standard amount to leave on a restaurant check. But other tipping-related matters aren't so clear-cut. Steve Dublanica, former server and author of the blog *Waiter Rant* and *Keep the Change: A Clueless Tipper's Quest to Become the Guru of the Gratuity*, weighs in on some hot-button tipping issues.

1. **Should you tip on the tax?** I like it when you do, but you don't have to.

2. **What is the correct amount to tip on drinks?** At the bar, you should leave 15 to 20 percent of the total cost of that drink, which may seem kind of ridiculous. But think of it this way: At the table, you're paying 15 to 20 percent. Why does the bartender not get that money, but the waiter—who doesn't make those drinks—does?

3. **When, if ever, is it acceptable to leave a bad tip?** I don't suggest stiffing servers on the tip, because you are punishing all the other people connected to that food chain. I tell people to talk to the manager and say, "I had very poor service, but I'm leaving a tip anyway."

4. **Should a server be able to automatically include gratuity if it's not a large group?** I don't support waiters deciding who they're going to attach a tip to. That's not their job—that's management's job—and they need to have a very well thought-out policy about it.

WHAT YOUR BARISTA WON'T TELL YOU

Get what you want—including a fast-moving line and good service—with these 13 things to know before you caffeinate.

1. If you're not at Starbucks, don't order like you are. If you want a Venti Caramel Frappuccino, you're in the wrong place. Order from our menu.

2. There is an art to pulling a perfect shot of espresso. The ideal shot takes 18 to 22 seconds to pull. I have to make sure that the espresso grounds are packed to just the right firmness, that the right amount of water filters through, and that the temperature is controlled. If a shot isn't perfect, I won't serve it.

3. Just because they're vegan doesn't mean our cakes are good for you. They are LOADED with white sugar.

4. Yes, I went to school for this. Starbucks sends employees to barista school for two weeks, where they study the history of coffee, the entire coffee menu, and how to turn milk into velvety foam.

5. Latte art isn't merely decorative. If a heart or a pinwheel design holds in the milk, it means that the consistency of the foam is good and the shot was pulled well. If you're at a place that does foam artwork, and you don't get a good picture, that means your drink is not well made.

6. **Please believe me.** If you asked for decaf, I gave you decaf. You don't need to ask me repeatedly. I am not out to get you.

7. **Sometimes the owners of independent coffee/espresso carts buy cheap coffee and sell it as a respected brand.** Not that any of our customers noticed.

8. **Tip.** I know your coffee is already overpriced, but a dollar bill in a tip jar earns you infinite goodwill.

9. **You are the reason for the wait.** When there's a line to the door, I hate it when customers spend the whole time talking on the phone and only think about what they want when they get to the register. They are the reason the line takes forever.

TOP SECRET! Buy whole beans. Experts and coffee connoisseurs agree that the only way to prepare a decent cup of joe is to buy beans whole and grind them immediately before brewing. Oxygen causes coffee to lose flavor rapidly, and preground coffee has far more surface area for oxygen to come in contact with.

10. **A real macchiato has just a stain of milk foam and no sugar.** Because Starbucks uses the names of authentic espresso beverages for sugary, milky confections that bear no resemblance to the real thing, they confuse people. I'll make someone an authentic drink and they'll say, where's the milk and syrup?

11. **Be nice.** No matter how tired you are, it's nice to say "please" when you're ordering your first coffee of the day. "I'll take a . . ." or "Give me a . . ." is NOT "please" in anyone's language.

12. **A bigger cup doesn't mean more coffee.** Starbucks' Venti (20 oz.) and Grande (16 oz.) each contain two shots of espresso. The Venti just has more milk. So if it's caffeine you're after, size doesn't matter.

13. **Buy the right amount of coffee.** As with most things we consume, when it comes to coffee, fresh is best. So if you're going to buy something from our shop, buy the bag, and only buy what you'll use within a week or two—within a month at max.

SOURCES: Baristas from Starbucks and independent cafés and coffee carts in Seattle, New York, Pennsylvania, and London, England.

Who Knew?
COFFEE, THE MIRACLE DRUG

When was the last time you heard a doctor use the word *miracle?* Well, wake up and smell the coffee: "It's amazing," says liver specialist Sanjiv Chopra, MD, professor of medicine at Harvard Medical School. "Coffee is truly a lifesaving miracle drug."

Though he says it's still a "scientific mystery" how a simple cup of coffee works its wonders in the body, large epidemiological studies repeatedly verify its astonishing benefits. Some recent research highlights we got from the National Coffee Association of the USA, Food.com, and the website *Home and Garden Ideas* say:

More than three cups a day lowers women's risk of developing the most common skin cancer by 20 percent.

More than six cups a day cuts men's risk of dying from prostate cancer by 60 percent.

Drinking at least one cup of coffee a day lowers women's risk of stroke by up to 25 percent.

Consuming at least two cups daily reduces women's chances of becoming depressed by up to 20 percent.

"Drink it black, or at most put a little skim milk in it" to minimize calories, recommends Dr. Chopra, who is also the author of *Live Better, Live Longer: The New Studies That Reveal What's Really Good—and Bad—for Your Health.* The benefits from decaf may not be as prodigious, so stick with regular if you can tolerate the buzz. Dr. Chopra drinks at least four cups a day himself, though most people should limit themselves to two. And no, he jokes, "I'm not sponsored by Starbucks."

WHAT YOUR GROCER WON'T TELL YOU

Find out where and how to get the best bargains at your supermarket—and what they really think about people who graze while filling their carts.

1. If you hate crowds and lines, shop at dinnertime (5 to 9 p.m.) or even later. Only 4 percent of shoppers hit the aisles between 9 p.m. and 8 a.m. Least-crowded day of the week? Wednesday.

2. That star fruit has been here a lot longer than the broccoli. Familiar produce turns over more quickly than exotic things.

3. Dig and reach for the freshest produce. Older merchandise gets pushed to the front of the bin and spread across the top to encourage customers to take it first.

4. The more products you see, the more you are likely to buy. That's why the aisles are so long and the milk is usually in the far corner. Skip the center aisles. That's where you'll find the junk food, like sodas and snack foods.

5. Like employees with a good attitude? Shop at chains that are employee-owned and suggest customer-satisfaction surveys. When employees have a stake in the profits, it shows in their attitude.

6. The "grazers" order food at the deli, eat it as they're shopping, and get rid of the wrappers before they check out. We also call that stealing.

7. We're marketing to your kids, too. That's why we put the rainbow-colored cereals and other kiddie catnip at their eye level.

8. Be wary of "specials." When people see signs with numbers "8 for $10!" "Limit: 5 per customer"—they buy 30 to 100 percent more than they otherwise might have.

9. The baby formula is locked up because thieves resell it on the black market. Ditto for the cough and cold medications, smoking-cessation products, razor blades, and batteries.

10. Bring back your recyclable cans and bottles, but please rinse them out first. Leaving soda inside is unsanitary, and we find it disgusting.

11. Attention, shoppers: Don't start your shopping just as we're closing. We just want to leave. It's been a long day.

12. Signs of a store in trouble: Stocking fewer perishable items, storing nonperishables in refrigerated cases to make them look full, and "dummying up" shelves with empty boxes. If we were offering the best prices and highest quality, wouldn't there be more people shopping here?

13. Check sizes. Manufacturers are constantly trying to repackage things to make them sound like a better deal. A new peanut butter container may look the same, but look closely and you'll see it actually has less peanut butter inside. Most customers don't watch this kind of stuff.

SOURCES: David Livingston, a supermarket industry consultant; Marion Nestle, author of *What to Eat*; Maurice Nizzardo, former supermarket executive in Connecticut; David J. Livingston, an industry consultant; Brian Wansink, author of *Mindless Eating*; and others.

Great Advice

PREPACKAGED GOODS THAT AREN'T WORTH THE CONVENIENCE

1. "Gourmet" Frozen Vegetables

Sure, you can buy an 8-ounce packet of peas in an herbed butter sauce, but why do so when you can make your own? Just cook the peas, add a pat of butter, and sprinkle on some herbs that you already have on hand. This homemade version is almost as easy and will taste a lot fresher. The same thing goes for carrots with dill sauce and other gourmet veggies.

2. Powdered Iced Tea Mixes

It's much cheaper to make your own iced tea from actual (inexpensive) tea bags and keep a jug in the fridge. Plus, many mixes are loaded with high fructose corn syrup and other sugars, along with artificial flavors.

3. Salad Kits

Washed and bagged greens can cost three times as much as buying the same amount of a head of lettuce. Even more expensive are "salad kits," where you get some greens, a small bag of dressing, and a small bag of croutons. Skip these altogether.

4. Trail Mix

We checked unit prices of those small bags of trail mix hanging in the candy aisle not that long ago and were shocked to find that they cost about $10 a pound! Make your own for much, much less—and you can include only the things you like!

5. "Snack" or "Lunch" Packs

These "all-inclusive" food trays might seem reasonably priced (from $2.50 to $4.00), but you're actually paying for the highly designed label, wrapper, and specially molded tray. They contain only a few crackers and small pieces of cheese and lunchmeat. The actual edible ingredients are worth just pennies and are filled with salt.

6. Preformed Meat Patties

Frozen burgers—beef or otherwise—are more expensive than buying the ground meat in bulk and making patties yourself. We timed it—it takes less than 10 seconds to form a flat circle and throw it on the grill! Also, there's some evidence that preformed meat patties might have a higher chance of containing E. coli than regular ground meat. In fact, most of the recent beef recalls have involved premade frozen beef patties. Fresh is definitely better!

WHAT **YOUR BUTCHER** WON'T TELL YOU

Here are delicious ways to eat better for less money when beef, pork, and chicken are on the menu.

1. Don't be fooled by supermarket brand names like Butcher's Brand, Rancher's Reserve, and Blue Ribbon. The label to look for is USDA Quality Grade. Prime is the best (and most expensive), followed by choice, select, and then standard.

2. Your beef may get ground in Iowa, stuffed in a long tube of plastic, and trucked to our store, where we regrind and package it.

3. Despite all the hype, most of us think "Certified Angus Beef" is a marketing gimmick that doesn't necessarily indicate the meat is any better than other beef with the same USDA grade. Though it does look spiffy on that black tray.

4. Make sure you check the price per pound or per serving. The per-pound price of the regular-size package is often cheaper than the family pack.

5. You don't have to be so wedded to the cut of beef your recipe calls for. We can suggest cheaper options.

6. My favorite cut? The hanging tender. Also known as a hanger steak or a bistro steak, it's got great flavor at a good price.

7. Take the meat tray at the bottom of the stack or the farthest in back. Just like milk, it tends to be fresher. And check the pack date. Ideally you want packages dated that day or the day before.

8. Save $1.50 to $2 a pound on boneless pork chops. Buy a whole boneless pork loin roast and slice it into chops an inch thick.

9. Want to save a few bucks per pound on beef? Try buying a whole top sirloin and asking me to cut it into steaks. Or get a whole chuck and ask me to make you some chuck roasts, beef stew cubes, and ground meat out of it. The bigger the cut, the more money you'll save.

10. Yes, that 92/8 ground beef is lean, but if you make burgers with it, you might be disappointed. Your favorite burger joint probably uses beef that's much fattier.

TOP SECRET! If you throw your meat straight into the freezer in the packaging it came in, freezer burn is a virtual certainty. Instead, take the meat off the tray, rewrap it with plastic food wrap, then put it in a freezer bag and squeeze out as much air as possible.

11. Even if those chicken breasts say "100 percent natural," they may still be injected with sodium-laden broth, salt water, or seaweed extract. Always check the label.

12. Some of the best tasting cuts are the ugliest ones, like the flap meat on the belly part of beef.

13. Ask me to help. Even if it's already on a tray wrapped in cellophane, I can cut the fat off a roast, trim a flank steak into stir-fry strips, or grind up a chuck roast. Then I'll neatly wrap it back up for you. All for no extra charge.

SOURCES: Butchers in New York City; Charlotte, North Carolina; San Francisco; Kingston, New York; and Timberville, Virginia; Lee O'Hara, author of *Beef Secrets Straight from the Butcher*; and the National Cattlemen's Beef Association.

Great Advice
WHAT YOU REALLY NEED TO KNOW ABOUT YOUR KNIVES

. . . .

Cutting board materials matter. Using a proper cutting board and hand washing your knives are absolutes; you're either doing it or you're not. Wood, bamboo, and plastic are better for your knives than composite boards; harder boards like glass, metal, stone, and ceramic will quickly destroy knives.

A sharp knife actually causes fewer cuts. The reason you cut yourself less with a sharp knife is because it takes less force to cut through anything. Sharp knives aren't scary—blunt ones that need loads of force and are liable to go anywhere are. Use the right tool for the job and use it the right way.

Proper cutting technique is easy to learn. Tuck your fingers under and use the knuckles as a guide for the knife. Watch your thumb too!

Choose a knife that works for you. The ultimate knife for your best friend may not be the right knife for you. If possible, cut with a knife before you buy it to see how it feels in your hands.

Don't use a knife for anything other than cutting food. As a general rule, if you wouldn't bite into it with your teeth, don't touch it with your chef's knife.

Don't use a steak knife for food preparation. Use a chef's knife or paring knife, even if these are the only two knives you own. In many households, the serrated steak knives are often the only sharp knives capable of cutting at all. (That's not a good thing.)

A serrated knife is not a saw. Most items can be cut in a nice slice with a single long draw of a serrated knife.

Keep your cutting area clear. Don't place any item on your cutting board that you don't want to be cut.

Don't toss knives into a sink. Sharp knives + bowls full of soapy water + unsuspecting hands = nasty surprise. Wash your knives after using, dry, and put away in a knife block, knife drawer insert, or secure magnetic rack.

A falling knife has no handle. Don't grab for it. Just let it go and watch your feet. Also, don't cook barefoot.

Skip the huge gift sets. You are better off buying a couple of really good knives than a huge block set of mediocre knives.

Safety first. Brace your cutting board with a kitchen towel for more stability.

The blade is for cutting, not corralling. Many people use the blade edge of a knife to corral the food to the edge of the board. Avoid that. Instead, turn it over and use the spine of the knife, which will keep the working edge sharp.

SOURCES: Adam Marr of Marr Knives; Christopher Miller, owner of Industri Café; Mark Richmond, owner, Chefknivestogo.com; Sebastians; Tom Bolton; Kenny Chan; and Mike Zollner of Zollners.blogspot.com.

WHAT YOUR FARMERS' MARKET WON'T TELL YOU

Find out when to look for a bargain and when a specialty item is worth the price with these top secrets straight from the farmers themselves.

1. Many of us depend on this for our survival. Almost all farmers who participate in farmers' markets run very small operations, and the profit margin is slim.

2. We don't do deals. I don't encourage "dealing" with a farmer. The prices are fair, and this is a symbiotic relationship.

3. If you want a discount, the best way to get one is through consistent patronage.

4. Your money supports your community. If you spend $100 at a farmer's market, $62 goes back into the local economy—and $99 out of $100 stays in the state. If you spend $100 at a grocery store, only $25 stays here. So, where do you want your money to go?

5. Please stop saying how expensive I am. My products would sell for much more in any specialty store and are NOT available in a supermarket.

6. I love my job because my business is not about retailing and then good-bye. It's about cultivating relationships with people who are willing to spend a little bit more for something better.

7. Standing out in the summer sun is nice, but this job isn't easy. It is tough being outdoors all day in July. I'm not just working a register; I'm loading and unloading heavy boxes every day.

8. Rain is good for crops during the growing season but bad for business. When it rains, that keeps customers inside and can easily damage my products.

9. I care about where the products are coming from. If a vendor has a retail store, I WILL NOT purchase from the vendor because I do not feel they belong in a farmers' market. Unfortunately some markets are letting in franchise/chain businesses, and that hinders the small vendor.

TOP SECRET! Many produce vendors are really only retailers. Ask yours if they buy from wholesalers. If they do, shop at your supermarket instead for a better price on the exact same produce.

10. We cannot get you everything all the time. We work very hard to provide you with the freshest, best tasting food we can at a reasonable price. There are seasons when certain produce isn't available (even in California). No peaches in January!

11. Some farmers say their produce is organic, but in order to say that, they must be certified by an organic agency and undergo an inspection. Most organic farmers are proud to display organic certification, and you can always ask to see it.

12. We are sick of these buzzwords, too: Natural, specialty, estate, artisan, local, and organic.

13. If a vendor sells citrus products or tropical products in an area of the country where those clearly don't grow, they are not farmers. They are having their produce shipped in.

SOURCES: Nancy Gammons of Four Sisters Farm and Watsonville Farmers' Market; Ersilia Moreno, owner of Olive Oil of the World; Adriana Silva, owner of Tomatero Organic Farm; cowtownfarmersmarket.com; Mark Santoro, owner of Gaia's Breath Farm.

MAKE A MEMORABLE CRUDITÉS PLATTER

Ask about these delicious veggies on your next trip to the farmer's market, and you'll be sure to create a party platter that no one will forget.

1. **Fennel**
   The crisp anise flavor of fennel is perfect with creamy dips. Fennel also pairs exceptionally well with roasted red peppers.

2. **Jicama**
   Crunchy jicama is a sweeter alternative to celery.

3. **Endive**
   Bitter endive leaves are perfect for scooping up hummus, dip, and even salsa. The vegetable goes especially well with blue cheese.

4. **Tiny Purple Carrots**
   Purple carrots will add color and the wow factor to your crudités platter. Blanch until al dente and chill. Try the red and yellow varieties for extra color.

5. **Asparagus**
   Grilled asparagus adds an upscale finger food to your platter.

6. **Fingerling Potatoes**
   Get the longer ones and blanch. Chill.

7. **Green Beans**
   Blanched green beans are easy to dip. You can use fresh green beans, but frozen work just as well.

8. **Radishes**
   Peppery radishes can be a delicious counterpoint to dips.

WHAT YOUR PIZZA DELIVERY GUY WON'T TELL YOU

Have you ever wondered what is happening behind the scenes at your favorite pizza place—and on the way to your house?

1. It's a pizza, not a lifetime commitment. My other line is ringing, so choose the toppings before you call.

2. Patience, please! It takes about 20 minutes to go from raw dough to fully baked pizza. And then I have to drive to your house.

3. Why won't we deliver to some neighborhoods? In some neighborhoods, a kid getting out of a car with a pizza in his hands is like screaming, "Rob me! I have cash!"

4. At our shop, we use our own cars to deliver pizza. Last week one of our guys smashed his car into a pole on an icy road. Now he's using a rental car.

5. I'm just a kid. Many delivery drivers are teenage boys, and most parents don't like their teenage boys driving around at night in downpours or blizzards. Yet these same people have no qualms about having other teenage kids deliver their pizza in these conditions.

6. I probably break a speeding law once a day.

7. I'm a human being. When you see me drenched and shivering in the rain, it's not nice to close the door in my face while you search for some quarters in the sofa cushions.

8. I will try to be as nice to you as possible. But if you complain that I'm late, or if you get nasty about a problem with your order, I won't be so nice.

9. There are always special customers. Like the little old lady who wants to pay her bill with a $5 check. I'll take it because none of us want to be mean to a grandmother. But if she hasn't ordered from us before, I won't take it.

> **🔒 TOP SECRET!** Accidents happen. If I drop your pizza on the way, sometimes I'll shake the box to get the cheese to slide back on right.

10. Tips should be 10 to 15 percent of your order. If you order a lot of pizza—say, hundreds of dollars' worth, for a party or something—but give me a $1 tip, well, I'm going to have a problem with that.

11. The more gated the community, the more guarded the wallet. The best tips actually come from middle- and lower-class people who know what we go through.

12. The majority of our employees work 12 to 14 hours a day. At the end of the day, we just want to go home. So please don't call for a delivery at closing time and then complain that we can't accommodate you.

13. Some people want more than just pizza. A guy once ordered pizza from me just so he'd have some help moving his sofa up a flight of stairs. I agreed to help him. He gave me a few extra bucks. I took it.

WHAT YOUR BARTENDER WON'T TELL YOU

Here's how to get served first at a crowded bar—every time—plus more tips for making the most of your next night out.

1. Know what you want, and have your money ready. Yell, whistle, or wave money, and I'm going to make you wait. Make eye contact and smile, and I'll come over as soon as I can. Don't create a traffic jam.

2. Start a tab. If I swipe your card five times this evening, that's five times as much paperwork I have to do at 4 a.m.

3. You want a drink made strong? Then order a double—for double the price.

4. You get what you pay for. Bars that don't have regulars (in hotels, airports) have started using wireless gadgets that measure how much is poured and automatically ring up each shot. They're meant to prevent overpouring and to cut losses, but I don't like them—neither do customers.

5. I've heard it all. One guy told me I had the worst smile he'd ever seen. I found out that he thinks a girl won't remember him unless he puts her down. I guess it worked; I'm telling you this story three weeks later.

6. I have the police on speed dial. And I never hesitate to call.

7. Don't order a round of drinks after last call. Last call applies to everyone—even you.

8. If I cut you off, don't argue. If anything, you should apologize if you've made a scene.

9. Get a room. The more you make out with your date, the closer you are to being cut off.

10. I can tell if your date is going well or not. And I notice if you bring in a new date every week.

TOP SECRET! We'll call you a cab. Some of us get a cut from the cab company when we call a taxi for a tipsy patron. Not that I've ever done that, of course.

11. Think tending bar isn't a real career? You're wrong. The craft of bartending is appreciated in the food industry, and some of us are even called "mixologists" now.

12. I love sharing what I know. If it's not busy, ask me about the history of drink or the latest cocktail I've invented. You'll learn something new.

13. I like a sophisticated palate. You'll win points with me if you request gin in your martini.

SOURCES: David Craver, president, National Bartenders Association; and anonymous bartenders in Boston, Kentucky, Florida, California, and Illinois.

Who Knew?

NIFTIEST THINGS TO DO WITH BEER (OTHER THAN DRINK IT)

....

Use as setting lotion. Put some life back into flat hair with some flat beer. Before you get into the shower, mix 3 tablespoons beer in ½ cup warm water. After you shampoo your hair, rub in the solution, let it set for a couple of minutes, then rinse it off. You may be so pleased by what you see that you'll want to keep a six-pack in the bathroom.

Soften up tough meat. Who needs powdered meat tenderizer when you have some in a can? You guessed it: Beer makes a great tenderizer for tough, inexpensive cuts of meat. Pour a can over the meat, and let it soak in for about an hour before cooking. Even better, marinate it overnight in the fridge, or put the beer in your slow cooker with the meat.

Clean wood furniture. Have you got some beer that's old or has gone flat? Use it to clean wooden furniture. Just wipe it on with a soft cloth and then off with another dry cloth.

Polish gold jewelry. Get the shine back in your solid gold rings and other jewelry by pouring a bit of beer (*not* dark ale and *not* on gemstones!) onto a soft cloth and rubbing it gently over the piece. Use a clean second cloth or towel to dry.

Remove coffee or tea stains from rugs. Rub the beer lightly into the material, and the stain should disappear. You may have to repeat the process a couple of times to remove all traces of the stain.

WHAT ETIQUETTE EXPERTS WANT YOU TO KNOW

These expert table manner tips are the best ways you can make your mom proud— and avoid being the one everyone IMs about in the morning.

1. Whoever arrives at a door first holds it for the next person. It doesn't matter the gender of either.

2. All things not having to do with food (and decoration) should remain off the table: keys, clutch bags, cigarette packs, sunglasses, cell phones.

3. A napkin is there to protect your clothes; use it to dab the corners of your mouth but never to polish your teeth.

4. If you're seated at a table with eight or fewer guests, wait for everyone to be served and for the host or hostess to begin eating before you dig in. At a long banquet table, it's OK to start when several people are seated and served.

5. Never cut bread or bread rolls. Break the bread with your fingers and butter a small piece at a time. Breakfast toast is the only exception.

6. Don't insult your host by adding salt before you have tasted your food.

7. Let your food cool of its own accord—don't blow on it.

8. Use your hand to shield your lemon as you squeeze it into your iced tea so you don't inadvertently squirt your dining companion in the eye.

9. Grabbing a bowl of salad or a saltshaker as it's being passed to someone who asked for it is the equivalent of cutting in line: greedy and rude.

TOP SECRET! Here's how to remember which bread plate and wine glass are yours: Make an OK sign with each hand by touching the tips of each thumb to the tips of your forefingers. Your left hand will form a lowercase b (for bread), and your right will form a d (for drinks). Or remember the acronym BMW: bread, meal, water/wine.

10. On the subject of passing: Dishes go counterclockwise, but if someone to your left asks for something, you can hand it directly to him.

11. When you excuse yourself to go to the restroom, just say, "Please excuse me."

12. It's OK to ask for your leftovers to be wrapped when out with friends or family— even at a fancy restaurant. But don't do it at a business lunch or dinner.

13. When you've finished eating, place your knife and fork or spoon and fork together, vertically on your plate. Leave your plate where it is—never push it away from you.

SOURCES: Anonymous etiquette experts and Nicholas Clayton of the Guild of Professional English Butlers.

Great Advice
THROW A FLAWLESS DINNER PARTY

There are two ground rules for a smooth-running dinner party: Plan ahead and don't overexert yourself. Here's how:

Invite no more people than your table can accommodate. Six is a good number (including yourself) that facilitates around-the-table conversation. Eight is a sensible maximum number.

Ask in advance if your guests are vegetarian or have other special dietary requirements. (A polite guest will volunteer this information, rather than come and refuse your food.)

Plan your menu so it's full of contrasts: veggie starter, fish main; rich main, light dessert; no more than one spicy course, etc. Avoid repetition: Don't serve a creamy chicken casserole followed by a vanilla pudding, say, or a potpie followed by apple pie.

Choose tried-and-true recipes that you know you can duplicate on the night. Don't treat your guests as guinea pigs for your culinary experimentation.

Serve one course that you can prepare entirely in advance—say, a chilled soup. You don't want to neglect your guests while you slave away at the stove. Avoid dishes, such as individual steaks, that require last-minute attention.

Make sure there are enough drinks—don't rely on guests to bring bottles. As a rule, keep white wine chilled, allow red wine to breathe, and be sure to have soft drinks and water on hand.

Above all, be attentive to your guests. Making them feel at home and at ease is at least as important as the food you put on the table.

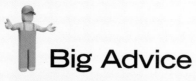

Big Advice

HOW TO BE A GREAT RESTAURANT CUSTOMER— WHO GETS GREAT SERVICE

People in the service industry are really hustling to give you a great dining experience—and get great tips. This advice straight from the waitstaff will help you get the best service by keeping on the good side of your waiter or waitress.

It's much easier to be recognized as a regular on Mondays, Tuesdays, or Wednesdays. Once you're recognized as a regular, good things start to happen. You'll find your wineglass gets filled without being put on your bill, or the chef might bring you a sample.

If you find a waiter you like, always ask to be seated in his or her section. Tell all your friends so they'll start asking for that server, as well. You've just made that waiter look indispensable to the owner. The server will be grateful and take good care of you.

Don't snap your fingers to get our attention. Remember, we have shears that cut through bone in the kitchen.

Splitting entrées is OK, but don't ask for water, lemon, and sugar so you can make your own lemonade. What's next, grapes so you can press your own wine?

We want you to enjoy yourself while you're eating. But when it's over, you should go. Do you stay in the movie theater after the credits? No.

If you're having a problem, speak to the owner if you can. Managers may have very little power. They're less likely to comp a meal, and most aren't authorized to give away free alcohol. They'll also take it out on the server if you have problems.

If you don't like something, don't muddle your way through it like a martyr and then complain afterward. If you don't like it, don't eat it. Send it back and get something else.

People think that just because your food took a long time, it's the server's fault. Nine times out of ten, it's the kitchen. Or it's the fact that you ordered a well-done burger.

Trust your waitress. Say something like "Hey, it's our first time in. We want you to create an experience for us. Here's our budget." Your server will go crazy for you.

Don't order meals that aren't on the menu. You're forcing the chef to cook something he doesn't make on a regular basis. If he makes the same entrée 10,000 times a month, the odds are good that the dish will be a home run every time.

You'll get better food if you avoid holidays and Saturday nights. The sheer volume of customers guarantees that most kitchens will be pushed beyond their ability to produce a high-quality dish.

In many restaurants, the tips are pooled, so if you have a bad experience with the server, you're stiffing the bartender who made your drinks, the water boy who poured your water, sometimes the hostess, the food runners, and maybe the other waiters.

Kindness pays. Sometimes, if you've been especially nice to me, I'll tell the bartender, "Give me a frozen margarita, and don't put it in." That totally gyps the company, but it helps me because you'll give it back to me in tips, and the management won't know the difference.

Part Three

WHAT YOU DON'T KNOW ABOUT
YOUR HEALTH

Think you know the rules of health? Sure, staying off the sugar, piling on the produce, and getting some exercise are all smart moves. But what really gets your attention at the ER? When is the worst time to have surgery? And why don't docs choose department heads as their own physicians?

We worked hard to get the answers to these questions and more. With interviews with scores of medical professionals—from nurses to pediatricians, podiatrists, general practitioners, eye doctors, pharmacists, and more—we uncovered the facts professionals usually only reveal to one another.

In addition to these hassle-saving—and potentially life-saving—facts, we're boldly revealing some things that usually go unsaid, like what grosses out even your doctor or what can land you next-to naked in a hospital gown (Hint: It might have less to do with how sick you are and more to do with how much you're annoying them). Find out why your yoga instructor is OK with your bodily functions but has issues with your shorts. We even found out the number one thing *never* to say to a nurse. We did the work, now you get the benefits!

WHAT YOUR NURSE WON'T TELL YOU

Here are some words to the wise from the one who's often handling the needle.

1. We're not going to tell you your doctor is incompetent, but if I say, "You have the right to a second opinion," that can be code for "I don't like your doctor" or "I don't trust your doctor."

2. When a patient is terminally ill, sometimes the doctor won't order enough pain medication. If the patient is suffering, we'll sometimes give more than what the doctor said and ask him later to change the order.

3. I've had people with brains literally coming out of their head. No matter how worried I am, I'll say calmly, "Hmmm, let me give the doctor a call and have him come look at that."

4. If you're happily texting and laughing with your friends until the second you spot me walking into your room, I'm not going to believe that your pain is a 10 out of 10.

5. When you tell me how much you drink or smoke or how often you do drugs, I automatically double or triple it.

> **🔒 TOP SECRET!** No matter how many times you use your call light, even if it's every ten minutes, I will come into your room with a smile. However, if you don't really need help, I will go back to the nurses' station and complain, and this may affect how the nurses on the next shift take care of you.

6. Your life is in our hands—literally. We question physicians' orders more often than you might think. Some of the mistakes I've headed off: a doctor who ordered the incorrect diet for a diabetic and one who tried to perform a treatment on the wrong patient.

7. If you ask me if your biopsy results have come back yet, I may say no even if they have, because the doctor is really the best person to tell you. He can answer all your questions.

8. When you ask me, "Have you ever done this before?" I'll always say yes. Even if I haven't.

9. Every nurse has had a doctor blame her in front of a patient for something that is not her fault. They're basically telling the patient, "You can't trust your nurse."

10. I once took care of a child who had been in a coma for more than a week. The odds that he would wake up were declining, but I had read that the sense of smell was the last thing to go. So I told his mom, "Put your perfume on a diaper and hold it up by his nose to see if it will trigger something." The child woke up three hours later. It was probably a coincidence, but it was one of my best moments as a nurse.

11. Some jobs are physically demanding. Some are mentally demanding. Some are emotionally demanding. Nursing is all three. If you have a problem with a nurse, ask to speak to the charge nurse (the one who oversees the shift).

12. For some reason, when I ask "Are you having pain?" a lot of patients say no, even if they are. But I've found that if I say, "Are you uncomfortable?" people are much more likely to say yes. Please tell us if you're in pain. We have all sorts of medications we can use to help you.

13. If a patient is incontinent, I'm just supposed to use a washcloth to clean them. But if you're really nice, I'll get heated wipes.

SOURCES on page 97.

Great Advice

HOW YOU CAN HELP PREVENT MEDICAL MISTAKES

According to the medical journal *The Lancet*, medical errors might be a leading cause of death, but that doesn't mean you can't help change the numbers. Use these strategies to help keep mistakes from happening:

Trust your instincts. If you have questions about a lab result, diagnosis, or treatment, speak up. And be persistent. After you have a lab test or diagnostic image, call your doctor to make sure he received the results. Don't worry about hurting your doctor's feelings. This is about you.

Choose wisely. The doctor you pick is only the first member of a team of specialists involved in your care. She'll likely assemble the rest of the team, so finding the right doctor is doubly important. So, too, is the hospital you choose. There are no guarantees, but usually, the better the hospital, the better the team.

Read the label. Many lab mix-ups start in your doctor's office. When giving a blood or other specimen, ask the nurse, politely, to show you the identification sticker to make sure it's accurate.

Carry a medical passport. A summary of your vital health information is a must. It should list diseases, medications and doses, food and drug allergies, and phone numbers of your physician and nearest relative. Take it with you to every doctor you see—even the radiologist.

Get a second opinion. It's crucial to your health. If a diagnosis requires surgery, chemotherapy, or medications with side effects, find another specialist (call the hospital's referral service for help), and send him all your pathology and radiology lab work for review, both the images and reports.

WHAT YOUR NURSE WISHES YOU KNEW

We got so many great tips from nurses that we couldn't fit them all on just one list. Now that you know what your nurse won't tell you, find out what you can do to make his or her job a lot easier so you can get the best care possible.

1. The number one thing you should never say to me: "You're too smart to be a nurse." I went to nursing school because I wanted to be a nurse, not because I wanted to be a doctor and didn't make it.

2. This is a hospital, not a hotel. I'm sorry the food isn't the best, and no, your boyfriend can't sleep in the bed with you. I know you asked for mashed potatoes, but that sound you hear is my other patient's ventilator going off.

3. If you have a really great nurse, a note to her nurse manager that says "So-and-so was exceptional for this reason" will go a long way. Those things come out in her evaluation—it's huge.

4. If you're going to get blood drawn, drink two or three glasses of water beforehand. If you're dehydrated, it's a lot harder for us to find a vein, which means more poking with the needle.

5. Never let your pain get out of control. Using a scale of zero to ten, with ten being the worst pain you can imagine, start asking for medication when your pain gets to a four. If you let it get really bad, it's more difficult to get it under control.

6. Never talk to a nurse while she's getting your medications ready. The more conversation there is, the more potential there is for error.

7. Positive attitude is everything. I have seen many people think themselves well.

8. Feel free to tell us about your personal life, but know that we're here for 12 hours with nothing to talk about. So the stuff you tell us will probably get repeated.

9. At the end of an appointment, ask yourself: *Do I know what's happening next?* If you had blood drawn, find out who's calling who with the results, and when. People assume that if they haven't heard from anyone, nothing is wrong. But I've heard horror stories. One positive biopsy result sat under a pile of papers for three weeks.

🔒 **TOP SECRET!** Don't hold your breath when you know we're about to do something painful, like remove a tube or take the staples out of an incision. Doing that will just make it worse. Take a few deep breaths instead.

10. Husbands, listen to your wives if they tell you to go to the hospital. Today a man kept fainting but wouldn't go to the hospital until his wife forced him. He needed not one, not two, but three units of blood—he was bleeding internally. He could have had a cardiac arrest. Another man complained to his wife that he didn't feel "right." His wife finally called me to come over to their house. His pulse was 40. He got a pacemaker that evening.

11. Please don't get mad at me because your scan was supposed to be at noon and you didn't have it until three o'clock. Unfortunately, I have no control over that.

12. The doctors don't save you; we do. We're the ones keeping an eye on your electrolytes, your fluids, whether you're running a fever. We're often the ones who decide whether you need a feeding tube or a central line for your IV. And we're the ones who yell and screech when something goes wrong.

13. When you're with someone who is dying, try to get in bed and snuggle with them. Often they feel very alone and just want to be touched. Many times my patients will tell me, "I'm living with cancer but dying from lack of affection." You can never say "I love you" too much.

SOURCES FOR BOTH NURSE SECTIONS: Mary Pat Aust, RN, clinical practice specialist at American Association of Critical-Care Nurses in Aliso Viejo, California; Kristin Baird, RN, a health-care consultant in Fort Atkinson, Wisconsin; Nancy Beck, RN, a nurse at a Missouri hospital; Linda Bell, RN, clinical practice specialist at the American Association of Critical-Care Nurses in Aliso Viejo, California; Nancy Brown, RN, a longtime nurse in Seattle, Washington; Theresa Brown, RN, an oncology nurse and the author of *Critical Care: A New Nurse Faces Death, Life, and Everything in Between*; Barbara Dehn, RN, a nurse-practitioner in Silicon Valley, California, who blogs at nursebarb.com; Karon White Gibson, RN, producer-host of *Outspoken with Karon*, a Chicago cable TV show; Theresa Tomeo, RN, a nurse at the Beth Abraham Center for Nursing and Rehabilitation in Queens, New York; Kathy Stephens Williams, RN, staff development educator for critical care at St. Anthony's Medical Center in St. Louis, Missouri; Gina, a nurse who blogs at codeblog.com; a longtime nurse who blogs at head-nurse.blogspot.com; and anonymous nurses and nurse supervisors in California, Florida, New York City, New Jersey, Pennsylvania, and Texas.

 Become an Instant Expert

This Won't Hurt a Bit . . .

A nurse rarely tells you when a needle will be painful. That's because research shows that when you're told something may hurt, you imagine the discomfort. If you overreact, your body may actually create symptoms. (It's called the "nocebo" effect.)

WHAT YOUR DOCTOR DOESN'T TELL YOU

Don't want a grumpy, tired doctor? Stay on his good side by knowing what he's thinking.

1. We generally know more than a website does. I have patients with whom I spend enormous amounts of time, explaining things and coming up with a treatment strategy. Then I get e-mails a few days later, saying they were looking at this website that says something completely different and wacky, and they want to do that. To which I want to say (but I don't), "So why don't you get the website to take over your care?"

2. When a patient isn't listening or cooperating, I was told in school to put a patient in a gown. It casts him in a position of subservience.

3. Thank you for bringing in a sample of your (stool, urine, etc.) from home. I'll put it in my personal collection of things that really gross me out.

4. It bugs me when you leave your cell phone on. I'm running on a very tight schedule, and I want to spend as much time with patients as I possibly can. Use your time to get the information and the process you need. Please don't answer the phone.

5. I wish you would take more responsibility for your own health and stop relying on me to bail you out of your own problems.

6. **Doctors often make patients wait** while they listen to sales pitches from drug reps.

7. **Those so-called free medication samples** of the newest and most expensive drugs may not be the best or safest.

8. **Bring a spouse, but not an entourage.** I know why you're bringing your husband and three kids, all of whom are also sick, with you today. No, they are not getting free care.

> **TOP SECRET!** We don't make the money you think we do. Just how much of the $100 your doctor charges for taking 30 minutes to investigate your stomach pain goes into his pocket? After paying the bills, he gets less than half.

9. **Avoid Friday surgery.** The day after surgery is when most problems happen. If the next day is Saturday, you're flying by yourself without a safety net, because the units are understaffed and ERs are overwhelmed because doctors' offices are closed.

10. **If you want experience, go long.** In many hospitals, the length of the white coat is related to the length of training. Medical students wear the shortest coats.

11. **Often the biggest names, the department chairmen, are not the best clinicians,** because they spend most of their time being administrators. They no longer primarily focus on taking care of patients.

12. **If a sick patient comes to me with a really sad story** and asks for a discount, I take care of him or her for no charge. And though we don't cry in front of you, we sometimes do cry about your situation at home.

13. **In many ways, doctors are held to an unrealistic standard.** We are never, ever allowed to make a mistake.

SOURCES: Daniel Amen, MD, psychiatrist, Newport Beach, California; cardiologist, Bangor, Maine; James Dillard, MD; ear, nose, throat, and facial plastic surgeon, Dallas/Fort Worth, Texas; ER physician, Colorado Springs, Colorado; family physician, Washington, D.C.; Vance Harris, MD, family physician, Redding, California; heart surgeon, New York, New York; internist, Philadelphia, Pennsylvania; Evan S. Levine, MD; obstetrician-gynecologist, New York City; oncologist, Santa Cruz, California; pediatrician, Baltimore, Maryland; pediatrician, Chicago, Illinois; pediatrician, Hartsdale, New York; physical medicine and rehabilitation doctor, Royal Oak, Michigan; Tamara Merritt, DO, family physician, Brewster, Washington; surgeon, Dallas/Fort Worth, Texas.

Great Advice

8 TIPS FOR DOCTOR VISITS THAT WORK

1. **Study up before your visit.** Research your condition, as well as any other medical conditions or concerns you may have, by gathering information from reputable websites. But don't hand your doctor a huge sheaf of printouts and expect her to respond to them during your visit. And don't try to diagnose your symptoms or self-prescribe your remedies. It's still up to your doctor to do that.

2. **Make a list of questions and prioritize them.** In one review of 33 office-visit studies, researchers found that people who brought checklists got more time with their doctors. Once you're in the exam room, don't be afraid to give your doctor the list—or ask for it back so you can refer to it.

3. **Rehearse.** When older people practiced their questions just before a doctor's appointment, according to one study, they were nearly twice as likely to speak up during the visit than people who didn't rehearse.

4. **Bring a family member or friend along.** Another person who knows about your health and your concerns can help you listen carefully, ask the right questions, and even help you make important decisions during an appointment.

5. **Carry a tape recorder.** Replaying an audiotape of your visit could assist you in better understanding instructions and information that you may have missed or not fully understood at the time.

6. **Bring in your meds.** Get a bag, toss in all your prescription drugs as well as herbal supplements, vitamins, and over-the-counter remedies, and bring it to your appointment. This will help your doctor understand if you're experiencing any problems with drug interactions or if you're taking any drugs you really don't need.

7. **Ask what tests you need and when and where to get them.**

8. **Evaluate your doctor.** Is she too bossy? Is he too deferential? Does your doctor interrupt you? Does he take your views as seriously as you'd like? Try discussing your concerns first, and make a good-faith effort to build a relationship of trust and respect with your physician. But if it's not working out, don't feel obligated to stay. Studies show that patients who don't trust their doctors simply don't get well as quickly, probably because they're less motivated to follow advice and treatment.

Great Advice

WANT BETTER DOCTORING? GIVE THEM THIS

If you want to get the best care possible, you have to be the best patient you can be. That means being thorough and honest. Here's what your doctor needs to know:

Your past health history, including major illnesses, allergies, and drug reactions.

Your family's health history that summarizes the major illnesses of your first-degree relatives (parents, aunts and uncles, grandparents). Pay special attention to medical conditions—such as diabetes—that seem to run in the family.

Your lifestyle history, such as how much you exercise, what and how you eat, whether you have a pet you enjoy, how stressed you are, whether you smoke tobacco or drink alcohol, any over-the-counter or prescription drugs (from another doc) that you take regularly. Include any risky sports you enjoy: Do you bungee-jump, skydive, or ski down the expert slopes?

WHAT YOUR ER STAFF DOESN'T TELL YOU

Take special note of these life-saving ER facts they usually don't show on TV doctor dramas.

1. We're not in it for the money. We're the only doctors who will take care of you first and ask questions about payment later, so we end up giving one third of our care for free—and lose about $100,000 of income a year. Yet we still do it. This is the best specialty in the world.

2. Say thank you. In the ER, nurses provide most of the hands-on care. So be nice.

3. Waiting is good. It means you're not going to die. The person you need to feel sorry for is the one who gets rushed into the ER and treated first.

4. We mean it. If we tell you to stay in bed, do it. Some medications make you uncoordinated, and we hate it when people fall down.

5. We don't believe you. One of our favorite lines is "You can't fix stupidity." If you complain of nausea and then eat a bag of chips, that's what we're thinking.

6. We can only do so much. Not all ERs are equally equipped to deal with children. Check with your pediatrician in advance of an emergency to see which local ER he or she recommends.

7. If you haven't had your child immunized, admit it. That's important information for us to have.

8. Get the details. If you don't understand what you're supposed to do when you leave the ER, ask—and ask again if necessary. We don't want you to have to come back.

9. Call, don't drive. It's incredible how many people having a heart attack drive themselves to the emergency room instead of calling 911. That's just dumb. What are you going to do if you're driving and your heart stops?

10. We don't usually speed. If the patient is stable, and 97 percent are, there's no reason to drive 60 miles an hour on city streets. Have you ever tried to put an IV into someone's arm in the back of a speeding ambulance?

11. Never tell an ER nurse, "All I have is this cut on my finger. Why can't someone just look at it?" That just shows you have no idea how the ER actually works.

TOP SECRET! Use a landline. Calling 911 from a landline can save your life because we can pinpoint your location instantly. If you call from a cell phone, we waste a lot of time asking where you are or searching for you.

12. Help us out. We don't have time to read the background on every patient. So if you're having stomach pain, and you've had your appendix or gallbladder removed, tell us so we don't go on a wild-goose chase. Be honest about whatever happened. Don't be a hypochondriac, know what medications you are on, and don't answer yes to every question. It will only screw up your care.

13. Speak up, please. An ER in a rural area might not have a doctor who is certified in emergency medicine, and the likelihood of having specialists on staff is very low. If you wind up in one, ask to transfer to a hospital that has more resources.

Become an Instant Expert

*How to Save Your Own Life if You Think
You're Having a Heart Attack*

If you're experiencing crushing chest pain with or without pain in your left arm, are short of breath, or have a sense of impending doom, you may be having a heart attack. Women are more likely to have atypical symptoms like severe fatigue, nausea, heartburn, and profuse sweating. If you are having the symptoms of a heart attack, even if you're a twenty-something, vegetarian triathlete, you need to:

* **Call 911 and chew one 325 mg uncoated aspirin** to get it into your bloodstream fast. This will thin your blood, often stopping a heart attack in its tracks.
* **While waiting, lie down so your heart doesn't have to work as hard,** says Sandra Schneider, MD, a spokeswoman for the American College of Emergency Physicians.
* **If you think you might pass out, try forcing yourself to cough deeply.** It changes the pressure in your chest and can have the same effect as the thump given in CPR, says Dr. Schneider. "Sometimes it can jolt the heart into a normal rhythm."
* **If someone else goes into cardiac arrest,** note that the American Heart Association now recommends CPR without the mouth-to-mouth. Call 911, then push hard and fast on the person's chest until help comes.

SOURCES: Jeri Babb, RN, Des Moines, Iowa; Marianne Gausche-Hill, MD, emergency physician, Torrance, California; Dana Hawkins, RN, Tulsa, Oklahoma; Leora Horwitz, MD, assistant professor, Yale University School of Medicine, New Haven, Connecticut; Arthur Hsieh, paramedic; Ramon Johnson, MD, emergency physician, Mission Viejo, California; Denise King, RN, Riverside, California; Linda Lawrence, MD, emergency physician, San Antonio, Texas; Don Lundy, paramedic, Charleston County, South Carolina; Donna Mason, RN, ER consultant, Nashville, Tennessee; Connie Meyer, RN, paramedic, Olathe, Kansas; Allen Roberts, MD, emergency physician, Fort Worth, Texas; Dennis Rowe, paramedic, Knoxville, Tennessee; Joan Shook, MD, emergency physician, Houston, Texas; Robert Solomon, MD, emergency physician, Waynesburg, Pennsylvania; Joan Somes, RN, St. Paul, Minnesota; emergency medical technician, Middlebury, Vermont.

WHAT YOUR PEDIATRICIAN WON'T TELL YOU

Find out how to make the most out of each trip to the pediatrician with these behind-the-stethoscope secrets.

1. Want to avoid the wait? Schedule your appointment for the middle of the week, and ask for the first time slot of the morning or right after lunch.

2. When you tell me you gave a decongestant to your toddler, I cringe. Studies show that cold medicines never work well for children under age six, and the risk of overdose and side effects far outweigh any benefit.

3. Want to make vaccines less painful for your child? Ask if you can breast-feed while we give your infant his shots. Or if you have an older child, see if we can use cold spray or a numbing cream to decrease the pain.

4. Do you really believe that we'd be recommending vaccines if we had any concerns about their safety? Almost all pediatricians immunize their own children.

5. If I prescribe a newer, more expensive medication, it may be because a drug rep just left my office. They constantly bring us presents and flatter us, and their only goal is getting us to prescribe the latest medication, which is usually no better than the older ones. In fact, the older ones have longer safety track records and really should be the ones we prescribe first.

6. Don't ask if I'll take a "quick look" at the sibling who doesn't have an appointment. If your mom went with you to the gynecologist, would you ever say, "Doc, would you mind putting her on the table and giving her a quick look?" Every patient deserves a full evaluation.

7. As soon as you say, "He doesn't like it when you look in his ears," you remind your child of the last time and set us up for another failure. Be matter-of-fact: "It's time for the doctor to look in your ears." Kids have also figured out that "This won't hurt" is code for "This is going to hurt," and they get all worked up. It's really best not to even use the word *hurt*. It just creates anxiety.

8. Sometimes we have less than ten minutes per patient, so make the most of your time and ask about the most pressing problems first. If you have a lot of questions, request an extra-long appointment.

9. Even though I tell you to let your baby cry himself back to sleep once he's older, don't ask me if I always followed that advice with my own kids. I didn't.

🔒 **TOP SECRET!** If you have an urgent concern and the front desk tells you there are no appointments available, ask for a nurse and explain your situation. Often she can work you in even if the schedule indicates there's no time.

10. Don't tell your kid the doctor will give him a shot if he doesn't behave. I won't.

11. Yes, you can talk to your pediatrician on the phone. Be persistent, be polite, and explain to the staff that you have a pressing, personal issue that you think would be best handled over the phone. We'll call back as soon as we can. This especially applies to older children, who often don't even need a visit. It may only take a call to find out that your child's fever, cold, sore throat, ear infection, and even pinkeye will most likely get better on its own.

12. Listen to your intuition. You know your child better than anyone, and that's why when you tell me something "isn't right," my ears perk up.

13. Don't delay treating your child because you want me to see the symptoms. People do this a lot: "I didn't give him Tylenol, because I wanted you to feel the fever." "I didn't use the nebulizer, because I wanted you to hear the wheezing." Trust me, I will believe you that the child had a fever or was wheezing. Delaying the treatment only makes your child suffer.

SOURCES: Pediatricians David L. Hill, MD, in Wilmington, North Carolina; Robert Lindeman, MD, in Framingham, Massachusetts; Allison Fabian, DO, in Grand Rapids, Michigan; Amanda Moran, MD, in Charlotte, North Carolina; Roy Benaroch, MD, author of *A Guide to Getting the Best Health Care for Your Child*; and a pediatrician in Virginia who preferred not to be named.

Great Advice

11 TIPS FOR A HEALTHIER AND MORE ACTIVE FAMILY

1. **Go on a treasure hunt.** Take your kids to a local park and set an expedition course on a map, circling various "checkpoints." Take turns navigating to each point on the map and leading the team to each destination.

2. **Hold a sports party.** Rather than the typical pin-the-tail-on-the-donkey birthday party, hold your child's birthday party in an active location, such as a roller-skating or ice-skating rink, laser tag center, wall-climbing gym, or indoor playground center. Or you can have your own "no particular reason" party. Kids won't think of what they're doing as exercise—but it is.

3. **Wash the car together.** The scrubbing is good exercise, but everyone getting wet and soapy is just plain fun for kids.

4. **Plant a garden together.** Digging holes, planting seeds, and pulling weeds build upper body strength. As an added bonus, research shows that children are more likely to eat the vegetables they help grow, which means your gardening forays will help your child follow a more nutritious diet.

5. **Take a hike at least twice a month.** Grab a backpack, plenty of water (everyone should drink eight ounces every half-hour), and a light lunch and head to a local trail for a hiking expedition. Wear hiking boots for rocky terrain or sneakers for smoother trails, and pack sunscreen and insect repellent. To make this more fun for kids, make it about something else, such as looking for a particular animal or bird, climbing to see a lake or pond, or seeing how many rocks you can scamper over without touching the ground. Kids like hiking much better when they don't realize it's about hiking!

6. **Dance during commercial breaks.** Make it a family rule that whenever you watch television, you have to stand up and dance around during the commercials. This goes for everyone! Whoever gets caught sitting on the couch during a commercial break must perform his or her least-liked household chore for one week.

7. **Sign up for a race.** Check your local paper for a list of 5K and 10K walk/run events in your area. Many of these events also raise money for charity, which can inspire your children to train for the event.

8. **Walk around the world.** Place a map of the country, state, or world somewhere prominently in your home. Work with your children to arrive at a walking destination. Then, based on your daily family walks, plot your progress on the map using thumbtacks. There are about 2,000 steps in a mile, so you can plot your progress by using a pedometer. To add some incentive, promise to actually take a vacation to your walking destination once you complete the number of steps to get there.

9. **Act like a child.** Remember duck-duck-goose, hopscotch, and red-light-green-light-one-two-three? You probably thought of these games as just that, games. But they also require movement and count as exercise. Teach them to your kids and play along. As you laugh, you'll burn extra calories. Don't forget Simon Says!

10. **Place small children on the floor at least once a day**—and let them crawl, move, and toddle. Children are inherently active when given the opportunity to move. Yet we often confine children and prevent the very exercise they need.

11. **Design your backyard for activity.** What you put in your backyard helps determine how fit your children become. If they see it, they will play. If they don't, they will watch TV. Older children enjoy climbing on ropes or ladders and playing in forts. Make sure you have a swing set, sprinkler attachment for your hose, sandbox, wagon for hauling toys and dolls, and outdoor sporting equipment for basketball, badminton, soccer, and other games.

WHAT YOUR DENTIST WON'T TELL YOU

You can't sneak as much past your dentist as you think you can. Here are 13 things they know about you—and what you need to do to see them less.

1. No pain doesn't mean "no problem." Some truly educated people think that if nothing in their mouth hurts, they're fine. High cholesterol doesn't hurt, either, but it's a big problem.

2. Bleeding is not OK. If your hands bled when you washed them, you'd run to the doctor. But in the public's mind, bleeding gums are okay. Unless you're really whaling away with your brush, if your gums bleed even a little, that's periodontal disease, period.

3. Your dentist does need to see you. The advice to see your dentist twice a year applies only if you have healthy gums. Most people don't.

4. The problem might not be what you think it is. People come to me with a mouthful of tooth decay and say, "I got my grandfather's soft teeth." I don't even know what soft teeth are.

5. The more time you spend, the less we have to. Proper oral hygiene requires ten minutes of brushing and flossing every day. The average adult spends two or three minutes total, and kids do even worse.

6. Chewing gum can be good. If you want to reduce the bad bacteria in your mouth, you should be all over xylitol, a sugar substitute found in chewing gum. It changes the chemistry of your mouth. Six or seven pieces of xylitol gum every day will help keep cavities away.

7. Mouthwash is a very short-term strategy. A mouthwash with alcohol dries out your mouth—you'll smell nice and minty for a half hour, but then the bad breath comes back worse than ever.

TOP SECRET! Minty mouthwash or breath mints don't fight bad breath! Most mouthwashes contain alcohol, which dries up saliva and makes your breath worse afterward. Mint candy is just a cover-up; it actually feeds the odor-causing bacteria more sugar! For a natural mouthwash, mix 1 tablespoon of baking soda with 1 cup of a 2 to 3 percent solution of hydrogen peroxide. The foam it kicks up has a powerful oxidizing effect that kills odoriferous bacteria.

8. The electric toothbrush is one of the best things to ever happen to dentistry. The newer ones replicate professional cleaning—they won't reach much below the gum line, but they're far superior to regular toothbrushes. The cheap ones are okay for kids, but you'll have to pay more than $75 for a really good brush with a warranty and replacement heads.

9. We think X-rays do more good than harm. A lot of patients are worried that dental X-rays can cause cancer, but if you're outside for an hour, you're exposed to more radiation than you'd get from a full set of dental X-rays. What I worry about is that if I don't take an X-ray, I might miss something serious.

10. There's no way to make implants cheaper. If you're missing teeth, chances are that your insurance company won't cover implants—only one out of 22 insurance companies I deal with covers them, even though they're better than dentures in every way.

11. Sometimes, we can fix your headache. Misaligned teeth can cause migraine headaches. If we can align the teeth and fix the bite, the pain often goes away.

12. Teeth get whiter when they dry out. Some dentists promise that their office procedures will make your teeth four shades whiter. But if you leave your mouth open for an hour, you could easily be two shades whiter just from dehydration.

13. We need you to know what your insurance covers. People think we have a crystal ball that tells us everyone's insurance information. We don't. And we need to find out what's covered before we can do anything.

SOURCES: Michael Alkon, DMD, general dentist, Holmdel, New Jersey; Damian Dachowski, DMD, general dentist, Horsham, Pennsylvania; Danine Fresch Gray, DDS, general dentist, Arlington, Virginia; Jay Grossman, DDS, cosmetic dentist, Brentwood, California; Gary Herskovits, DDS, family dentist, Brooklyn, New York; Paul Hettinger, DMD, general dentist, Orlando, Florida; Jennifer Jablow, DDS, cosmetic dentist, New York, New York; Jim Janakievski, DDS, periodontist, Tacoma, Washington; Chris Kammer, DDS, cosmetic dentist, Middleton, Wisconsin; Mark Mutschler, DDS, pediatric dentist, Oregon City, Oregon; Mai-Ly Ramirez, DDS, general dentist, San Francisco, California; Ron Schefdore, DMD, general dentist, Chicago, Illinois; Bryan Tervo, DDS, expert at JustAnswer.com; Joel Slaven, DDS, general dentist, Valencia, California; Ned Windmiller, DDS, general dentist, Stillwater, Minnesota; Careen Young, DDS, prosthodontist, Beverly Hills, California.

Great Advice
INSTANT BAD BREATH FIGHTERS

Dry mouth is a haven for the bacteria that cause bad breath. So find a tap, and swish the water around in your mouth. Water will temporarily dislodge bacteria and make your breath a bit more palatable.

At the end of your power lunch or romantic dinner, munch the sprig of parsley that's left on your plate. Parsley is rich in chlorophyll, a known breath deodorizer with germ-fighting qualities.

If you can get your hands on an orange, peel and eat it. The citric acid it contains will stimulate your salivary glands and encourage the flow of breath-freshening saliva.

Cloves are rich in eugenol, a potent antibacterial. Simply pop one into your mouth and dent it with your teeth. The pungent aromatic oil may burn slightly, so keep that spicy nub moving. Continue to bite until the essence permeates your mouth, then spit it out. Don't use clove oil or powdered cloves—they're too strong and can cause burns.

Chew on fennel, dill, cardamom, or anise seeds. Anise, which tastes like black licorice, can kill the bacteria that grow on the tongue. The others can help mask the odor of halitosis.

Suck on a stick of cinnamon. Like cloves, cinnamon is effective as an antiseptic.

Vigorously scrape your tongue over your teeth. Your tongue can become coated with bacteria that ferment proteins, producing gases that smell bad. Scraping your tongue can dislodge these bacteria so you can rinse them away.

WHAT YOUR EYE DOCTOR WON'T TELL YOU

Here are 13 things about what helps and hurts your eyes (carrots included).

1. Never use tissues or toilet paper to clean your eyeglasses. Paper is made of wood, and it will scratch your lenses. I like to use my tie because it's silk and really smooth.

2. Polarized sunglasses are great at reducing glare, but they can make it difficult to see the LCD on your cell phone or navigation system. It's harder to see an ATM screen when you've got polarized sunglasses on, too.

3. Life doesn't go on as normal after I dilate your eyes. It'll be two or three hours before you can do anything that requires concentrated visual attention.

4. You wear your sunglasses only when it's sunny? That's like saying "I only smoke sometimes." Most people know that UV radiation can damage skin, but they don't realize it's also bad for eyes. Wear sunglasses big enough to block the light from above and below—they should have thick sides or wrap around.

5. Eyedrops (any kind) sting less if you keep them in the refrigerator.

6. Some doctors pressure patients to have cataract surgery right away, but if it creates financial problems for you, there's usually no harm in waiting. Cataracts rarely hurt you—they just make it hard to see, like looking out of a dirty window.

7. Reading in dim light won't hurt your eyes, but you might get a headache.

8. Take extended-wear contacts out before bed. Your chance of infection is 10 to 15 times greater if you sleep in them.

> 🔒 **TOP SECRET!** Carrots aren't the best food for your eyes, despite what generations of parents have told their kids. That honor goes to spinach, kale, and other dark, leafy veggies.

9. Don't grab just any old bottle of eyedrops out of your medicine cabinet when a new problem comes up. If you have an infection, steroid drops might make the redness look better, but the infection could get worse. I've had to remove people's eyes because of that!

10. Pinkeye isn't always benign. A number of patients end up with light sensitivity and even vision loss. But many physicians treat it with antibiotics that won't help if the cause is a virus. We do a rapid test for adenovirus—if that's what you have, we treat it very differently than if your pinkeye is bacterial.

11. No, it's not OK to wait for symptoms to appear. Some blinding eye diseases have few warning signs. A yearly exam is the only way to catch things early.

12. If you're over 60, considering LASIK, and at risk of developing cataracts, wait until you develop one. Then we can fix your vision as part of the cataract surgery and your insurance may pay for it.

13. If you wear contacts, ask for UV coating.

SOURCES: Brian Bonanni, MD, an ophthalmologist at Gotham LASIK, New York City; Stephen Cohen, OD, past president of the Arizona Optometric Association; Eric Donnenfeld, MD, editor of *Cataract and Refractive Surgery Today*; Paul Harris, OD, associate professor at the Southern College of Optometry, Memphis, Tennessee; Janice Jurkus, OD, professor of optometry at Illinois Eye Institute; Robert Noecker, MD, an ophthalmologist at Ophthalmic Consultants of Connecticut; Robert Sambursky, MD, an ophthalmologist in Sarasota, Florida; Andrea Thau, OD, associate clinical professor at the SUNY College of Optometry.

Be an Instant Expert
Easy Ways to Improve Your Vision

1. **Mix a cup of blueberries with a cup of yogurt for breakfast.** In one study, women and men who ate the greatest amount of fruit were the least likely to develop age-related macular degeneration (ARMD), the leading cause of blindness in older people. While you're getting fruit, why not go for blueberries, one of the richest fruit forms of antioxidants?

2. **Cook with red onions, not yellow.** Red onions contain far more quercetin, an antioxidant that may protect against cataracts.

3. **Aim your car vents at your feet**—not your eyes. Dry, air-conditioned air will suck the moisture out of eyes like a sponge. Aim the vents in your car away from your eyes, or wear sunglasses as a shield. Dry eyes can be more than an inconvenience; serious dryness can lead to corneal abrasions and even blindness if left untreated.

4. **Move your computer screen to just below eye level.** "Your eyes will close slightly when you're staring at the computer, minimizing fluid evaporation and the risk of dry eye syndrome," says John Sheppard, MD, who directs the ophthalmology residency program at Eastern Virginia Medical School in Norfolk, Virginia.

5. **Walk at least four times a week.** Some evidence suggests that regular exercise can reduce the intraocular pressure, or IOP, in people with glaucoma. In one study, glaucoma patients who walked briskly four times per week for 40 minutes lowered their IOP enough so they could stop taking medication for their condition. It's also possible—although there's no proof yet—that walking could reduce your overall risk of developing glaucoma.

6. **Eat fish twice a week.** A study from Harvard researchers evaluated the diets of 32,470 women and found those who ate the least amount of fish (thus getting the least amount of omega-3 fatty acids) had the highest risk of dry eye syndrome. If you can't stand fish or are worried about mercury consumption, try fish-oil supplements to get your omega-3s.

7. **Turn down the heat in your house.** Heat dries out the air, which, in turn, dries out your eyes. In the winter, you might also try adding some humidity with a humidifier or even bunching a lot of plants together in the room in which you spend the most time.

WHAT YOUR PODIATRIST WON'T TELL YOU

These 13 secrets can keep your feet from hurting—or stinking—for good.

1. Your feet don't have to smell. You use antiperspirant on your armpits to keep them from getting stinky, don't you? The same stuff works on your feet. Try the spray kind.

2. You can fight stink without buying anything. Make some really strong black tea, then soak your feet in it two or three times a week for 20 minutes. The tannic acid has been shown to temporarily shrink sweat ducts so they don't work as hard. Always alternate your shoes so they have a chance to dry completely, and wear socks. Otherwise, the sweat will promote the growth of bacteria that stay in your shoes.

3. Infections from nail salons keep us in business. If you want a pedicure, book the first appointment of the day, when the equipment is cleaner. Those footbaths can be especially germy. Even if technicians spray the basin between customers, many of the tubs have drains and filters that don't get cleaned. No matter what, don't shave before you go. Bacteria and fungus can enter the microscopic nicks on your ankle and give you an infection.

4. Toe separators, bunion splints, and "yoga toes" may help you feel better, but they aren't going to get rid of hammertoes and bunions. You've got to come to me for that. If you have a structural problem, a $6 device isn't going to reverse anything.

5. Some podiatrists will shorten toes or do injections so you can wear high heels more comfortably. But I don't believe in cosmetic surgery for feet. You shouldn't have surgery if you're not in pain, because you will have pain after surgery—that's a guarantee. It has to be worth it. Otherwise, you're asking for trouble.

6. Get your bunions taken care of now. If you wait until they get really bad, they'll be much harder to fix.

7. I've seen all sorts of things, including people who have shot their feet. You really shouldn't clean your loaded gun after you've had a couple of beers. Another dumb move: mowing the lawn in flip-flops. The first weekend of every spring, doctors see a lot of injuries.

> **TOP SECRET!** I wear flip-flops, too, but if you wear them every day, all day, you will end up in my office eventually. Those shoes are designed for the beach and pool, not for walking all over the place.

8. Over-the-counter "custom-fit" orthotics are a bit of a gimmick. They'll help if you just need some arch support and padding, but they're nothing like the orthotics I make after creating a mold of your feet in my office. Orthotics and arch supports should be firm. If it's jellylike or soft and smushy, then that's not support—that's cushioning—and it's probably not going to help your problem.

9. A lot of you hurt your foot or ankle exercising and head straight to an orthopedic surgeon. But unless he or she is specifically trained in the foot and ankle, coming to me is a better bet.

10. Your cuticles are there for a reason. You can push them back, but don't cut.

11. I have people who tell me that I changed their life, and it turns out all I did was tell them to wear a bigger size shoe. I think, *did that really change your life?* But if they had a lot of pain, it's a big deal.

12. When you go into a shoe store, your salesperson should measure your feet. A lot of you have been wearing the same shoe size for the past 30 years because no one measures you anymore, but feet often get bigger as you age.

13. The best socks today are not 100 percent cotton. Look for materials that promise to wick moisture away.

SOURCES: Jane Andersen, a podiatrist in Chapel Hill, North Carolina; Marlene Reid, a podiatrist in Naperville, Illinois; Carly Robbins, a podiatrist in Columbus, Ohio; Jacqueline Sutera, a podiatrist in New York, New York; Cary Zinkin, a podiatrist in Deerfield Beach, Florida.

Become an Instant Expert
Give yourself a foot massage.

When you massage the thousands of nerve endings in the foot, you can feel relaxation throughout your body. It doesn't just feel good: Regular massage keeps the foot flexible and healthy. Treat your feet with these techniques:

* **To give yourself a deep massage,** grip your foot in your hands with fingers on the sole and thumbs on top. Work the bones by pressing down with the thumbs and heels of the hands, and up and in with your fingers. Then move one hand up the length of the foot while moving the other hand down.
* **Thumb presses are great.** Hold your foot with your thumbs on the sole and fingers on the top. Press in hard, firm circles over the sole. Repeat over the top of the foot. Be thorough, covering the entire area. Use your fingers to press near the ankle and heel.
* **Toe stretches will relieve tension.** Hold the heel firmly with one hand. With the other hand, push the toes forward and backward (omit the little toe if you wish). Hold the stretch for several seconds each way, then repeat.
* **End off your massage with toe tugs.** Gently tug each toe with your index finger and thumb. Then, starting with the big toe, twist each toe from side to side; let the thumb and forefinger slide off the end. Don't crack the toe knuckles.

WHAT YOUR PHARMACIST WON'T TELL YOU

Here's how to spend less at the pharmacy, get what really works for you, and avoid dangerous—and sometimes deadly—pill mix-ups.

1. Don't try to get anything past us. Prescriptions for pain-killers or sleeping aids always get extra scrutiny.

2. Generics are a close match for most brand names. But I'd be careful with blood thinners and thyroid drugs, since small differences can have big effects.

3. I hate your insurance company as much as you do. Even if something's working for you, the insurance company may insist you switch to something else. I'm stuck in the middle trying to explain this to customers.

4. We can give flu shots in most states.

5. All pharmacists are not created equal. A less-qualified pharmacy technician may have actually filled your prescription. Currently, there is no national standard for their training and responsibilities.

6. We're human . . . And we make mistakes (about two million a year). Ask if we use a bar code system to help keep us from pulling the wrong drug off the shelf or giving the wrong strength of the right drug.

7. If you don't like a generic, ask if there are alternatives. I can give you a generic refill that's different from the one you started with.

8. We'll save you money if we can. A good part of a pharmacist's time is spent dealing with patients and their incomes. Part of that is suggesting generic alternatives. Or if a doctor has prescribed a newer drug with no generic alternative available, I'll call the doctor to suggest an older drug that's equally effective.

9. Look into the $4 generics. Chains like Target, Kroger, and Walmart offer them.

🔒 **TOP SECRET!** There's not some big computer database that tracks your drugs and flags interactions for pharmacists everywhere. Use one pharmacy. If you start using a new one, make sure we know what you're taking.

10. It gets busy Monday and Tuesday evenings, since many new prescriptions and refills come in after the weekend.

11. Don't put up with the silent treatment. Pharmacists are required by law in most states to counsel patients and answer their questions. If your pharmacist seems too busy to talk, take your business elsewhere.

12. People take too many drugs. Two out of every three patients who visit a doctor leave with at least one prescription for medication, according to the Institute for Safe Medication Practices. Drugs are an easy solution, but there are other solutions.

13. Talk to me—and check my work. Every year plenty of prescriptions are taken wrong—the FDA has recorded an incident where a man overdosed after his wife mistakenly applied six prescription painkilling patches to his skin. And many people don't ask questions about how to use their medications. When you pick up your prescription, at least ask, "What is this drug? What does it do? Why am I taking it? What are the possible side effects? and How should I take it?" Not only does this help you to use the drug correctly; it's also a good way to double-check that you're getting the right drug.

SOURCES: Cindy Coffey, PharmD; Greg Collins, pharmacy supervisor, CVS/pharmacy, California; Stuart Feldman, owner, Cross River Pharmacy, New York; Dr. Daniel Zlott, oncology pharmacist, National Institutes of Health.

Great Advice

HOW TO TELL WHICH ONLINE PHARMACIES ARE LEGITIMATE

Plenty of online pharmacies are honest businesses—experts think they actually outnumber the sham ones—and they offer big advantages. You can shop the Internet for the best prices; you can buy certain drugs without embarrassment; and you can do it all from the comfort of your armchair.

But how can you be confident an online pharmacy is legitimate? One sure sign is if the site has the VIPPS (Verified Internet Pharmacy Practice Sites) seal of approval. That's a certification from the National Association of Boards of Pharmacy (NABP), and the seal must be displayed prominently on the business's website. You can also check the NABP's website for a list of pharmacies that have earned the VIPPS seal (nabp.net).

You should be suspicious of any online pharmacy that:

* Doesn't require you to mail in a prescription.

* Doesn't speak to your doctor to ensure your prescription is valid.

* Doesn't ask you to do more than fill in an online questionnaire.

* Doesn't have a toll-free number and street address listed on its website.

* Doesn't make pharmacists available to answer questions about the medications. Be on guard, too, if the site sells only "lifestyle" medications, like drugs for impotence, obesity, or pain.

WHAT YOUR SLEEP DOCTOR WON'T TELL YOU

A good night's sleep is vital to your health and happiness. Here are 13 ways to get better sleep—and become aware of what's really robbing you of it.

1. We expect to sleep for eight solid hours, but that's actually not normal compared with global populations and our own evolutionary history. People naturally wake up two or three times a night. It's worrying about it that's the problem.

2. Digital clocks blare time at you. If you look at the time when you awaken during the night, it's likely to increase your anxiety about not being asleep. If you need a clock to wake you in the morning, just turn its face to the wall right before bed. You'll hear it just as well.

3. If you're not sleeping well, you may have acid reflux, even if you don't feel heartburn. Try elevating your head by putting blocks under the top of the bed and sleeping on your left side.

4. If you like a firmer mattress and she likes a softer one, you don't have to compromise. Get two singles, push them together, and use king sheets. You can also buy a strap that attaches the mattresses to each other. I also tell couples that each person should have a sheet and blanket. One of the biggest disrupters of sleep is the pulling and tugging of sheets and blankets. If you pull a big comforter or duvet over the top when you make the bed, you really can't tell. Couples call me after I suggest that and say, "Wow—you changed our marriage."

5. Memory foam is very temperature dependent. The foam can get a little hard in a cold bedroom. And if you're a hot sleeper, it may make you hotter.

6. My research has found that any new smell, even one associated with relaxation, like lavender, can make you more alert and vigilant. You're better off with a scent that makes you feel safe and comfortable. There really is something to cuddling up with your spouse's undershirt.

TOP SECRET! Women aren't used to putting their needs ahead of others', but sleep is so necessary to health and happiness, they must. If the dog's snoring wakes you up, put him in another room. If your partner's snoring wakes you up, help him get treatment. If he refuses to cooperate, put him in another room.

7. Watching TV at night may seem relaxing, but it beams light into your eyes, which is an "alert" signal for the brain. Read a book before bed instead.

8. Give yourself an hour—the one right before bed. You need it to wind down and make the transition from the person-who-can-do-everything to the person-who-can-sleep.

9. To keep your room dark, use blackout draperies or shades—not blinds, because they never completely block out light. Install the shades as close to the glass as possible. If you don't have the depth for an interior mount, extend the fabric several inches past the width of the window.

10. A hot bath will increase your skin temperature, which eventually decreases your core body temperature, and that's helpful for sleep. Do the same thing for yourself that you'd do for a young child—make sure you take a bath a half hour or so before bedtime.

11. There's no solid explanation for it, but studies have found that wearing socks to bed helps you sleep. It may be that warming your feet and legs allows your internal body temperature to drop.

12. A lot of people take bedtime pain relievers that contain caffeine and don't even realize it. Excedrin has 65 milligrams of caffeine per tablet—if you take two, that's as much as a cup of coffee. Check the label: Caffeine is always listed as an active ingredient.

13. I'm not a fan of sleeping with two pillows if you're a back sleeper because it makes your upper back curve and strains the neck and back. If you need to sleep up high for medical reasons, get a wedge and put your pillow on it.

SOURCES: Tara Brass, MD, a psychiatrist in New York, New York; Pamela Dalton, PhD, odor-perception expert and sensory psychologist at Monell Chemical Senses Center, Philadelphia, Pennsylvania; Jan Engle, professor of pharmacy at the College of Pharmacy, University of Illinois at Chicago; Karen Erickson, a chiropractor in New York, New York; Mary Susan Esther, MD, director of the Sleep Center at South Park in Charlotte, North Carolina; Ian Gibbs, cofounder of the Shade Store in New York, New York; Colin Grey, a time-management coach in London, England; Alan Hedge, PhD, professor of ergonomics at Cornell University, Ithaca, New York; Robert Oexman, chiropractor and director of the Sleep to Live Institute in Joplin, Missouri; Patricia Raymond, MD, a gastroenterologist in Virginia Beach, Virginia; Carol Worthman, PhD, an anthropologist at Emory University in Atlanta, Georgia.

Great Advice

HOW TO STOP STRESS FROM WRECKING YOUR SLEEP

When worry drives your life, studies show you're more likely to develop chronic insomnia. Here's how to prevent that—and get a good night's sleep.

Stop those thoughts. Once you hit the sheets, worry time is over—especially about sleeping. There's a therapy trick called "thought-stopping" that works like a charm, says Mary Susan Esther, MD, director of the Sleep Center at South Park in Charlotte, North Carolina. "If you find yourself thinking about tomorrow and saying, 'It's going to be a bad day because I'm never going to sleep,' immediately think: 'STOP. Don't go there. I know I've done this before. If I don't fall asleep, I'll get out of bed, flip through a magazine, but I am NOT going to focus on this stuff!'" Sounds simple, but once you try it, you'll find it works.

Dump the 24/7 routine. Even if we manage to drop into bed in enough time to get our optimal amount of sleep, our minds are full of what-if's, why-did-we's and what's-on-the-agenda-tomorrow's. All this rumination and agitation ignites stress hormones that keep us in a state of perpetual arousal. That's why we should make a serious attempt to simplify our lives, says Cecile Andrews, PhD, author of *Slow Is Beautiful*. Draw up your to-do list, then take a big breath and start crossing things off, she says. It's a bit humbling to realize, but you really don't have to do it all.

Don't work so late. The prevailing thought is that you have to stay late to get the job done. But working right up until bedtime is bound to affect your sleep. Go home at a reasonable hour. The truth is that it's better to go get some sleep, then come back and do more work in the morning. Studies show that after a good night's sleep, your increased ability to concentrate means that you can work faster and more accurately.

Recognize yourself. How do you deal with stress? Pig out on chocolate mousse? Skip meals? Refill your wineglass a couple of times after dinner? All of these classic stress responses actually make falling asleep and staying asleep more difficult. But if you know your stress response will sabotage your sleep, plan ahead of time how you're going to handle something you just know is going to raise your stress level. If you know the big sales conference is coming up next week, for example, get into bed an hour early every night this week, which will give your body a biochemical boost of stress-proofing growth hormone to ride into the week. If you know you're going to see your ex when he drops off your daughter Saturday evening, take time out and meditate for 20 minutes before he's supposed to arrive.

Get physical. Burn off a rush of stress with a 15-minute walk. Studies show that those who regularly exercise sleep better than those who don't.

Forgive the past. Anger toward someone who has wronged you can trigger a cascade of stress hormones that can haunt you through the night. To prevent that effect, think about how you were hurt, your response, and how you feel right now. Then think about whether or not there's anything in the background of the person who hurt you that explains what he or she did. If there is, put yourself in their shoes—and see if you can't forgive them. If you can, you'll sleep like a baby.

WHAT YOUR AEROBICS INSTRUCTOR WON'T TELL YOU

What's really going through your instructor's head when she's watching you in the gym? It's probably not what you think!

1. Follow my lead. I get aggravated when students do a different workout than the one I'm teaching—and they're in the front row! If you come to class but choose to do your own thing, really, what's the point?!

2. Be careful what you complain about. When I'm cranky and short-tempered I'm more likely to make you do something hard and brutal because you whined about something else.

3. Everyone started somewhere. Don't worry if other people are using heavier weights, higher steps, or going farther while stretching. The fact that you are there participating at all is the most important thing. Work within your own limits and abilities. If I suggest a modification for an exercise, it would be helpful if you'd follow the suggested guideline. It's for your own good!

4. Leave your cell at home. Can you not exercise for an hour without checking your text messages?

5. Dress appropriately. Ladies, consider wearing a cami or additional liner under your low cut Lululemon or Lucy yoga tops. I get an eyeful I really don't wish to see when you're in downward dog. And guys, don't forget your liner shorts! I don't want to see anything poking through your gym shorts in class!

6. It takes a lot to be entertaining, funny, and likeable . . . all while trying to motivate people to do things that will cause them pain. I think the '80s thong leotards and side-ponytails gave aerobics instructors a bad rap. We're also not all super bubbly and rail-thin.

> **TOP SECRET!** You hurt yourself the most when you refuse to try. Fitness is one of the only things in life where you can achieve success simply by trying harder than you did yesterday.

7. Preparing is a lot of work! Pre-choreographed classes, like BodyPump and Turbo Kickboxing, take hours of prep. We're sent materials every six weeks, and we have to review and learn all the music and choreography before we teach it to you.

8. Music helps me connect with you and lets me bring some of my personality to the table. I take requests and will download songs for my students. Who wouldn't want an instructor to play their personal power song?!

9. I'm always learning. I prepare classes by reading, watching videos, attending workshops, and taking other instructors' classes. I can't tell you how many times my family's walked into my office only to find me on the floor contorted into some unusual position for the latest ab or outer-thigh exercise that I have just discovered online. They used to ask what I was doing, but now they leave before I force them to give it a try.

10. Stop weighing yourself constantly. Newbies expect miracles without realizing that while the added muscle may not make the scale drop, it will bring the pants size down. But you can't change your physique simply by working out; 80 percent of any change and fat loss is the result of a clean diet.

11. We don't all have perfect relationships with health and fitness. People assume we spend our days eating salad without dressing and train ALL the time. Sometimes I'm tired, cranky, hungry, or want a pizza, but I have to put on the show. Sometimes I want to veg out and eat junk food, and sometimes I actually do!

12. This isn't my only job, and I wish you wouldn't assume we're all meatheads who enjoy working out 24/7.

13. Some exercises make people fart. Get over it. Reverse crunches do especially, most particularly while squeezing and lifting a fit ball. I think it means that you're working hard and giving a huge effort. Some people are so mortified when it happens that they leave class that day and never come back. I wish they wouldn't care as much. I don't!

SOURCES: Jacky Burke of BodyDefinitions.com; Keri Cawthorne of ironmountainmovement.com; Laura Dow, Josh Guerrieri, ACE; certified personal trainer of FitWit.com; Sara Hauber of sarahauber.com; Andrew Kalley of kalleyfitness.com; Lauren Lorenzo MS, ACE-CPT of Fork in the Road Consulting, LLC; Charla McMillian, JD, CSCS of FitBoot.com; Sharyn Zerello Mastropaolo of teambeachbody.com; Virginia Nicholas MA, RN of Moving Breath Pilates; A.J. Pantoni of www.oxfordathleticclub.com; Mike Tubbs, personal trainer, nutritionist, and martial arts instructor of exhalewellness.com; Cate Wade of fulcrumfitness.com.

Become an Instant Expert
How Much Exercise Do I Really Need?

Most healthy people should aim for at least 30 minutes, five times a week, of moderately intense activity (such as brisk walking), plus 10 to 15 minutes or so of strength-training (digging in your garden counts) two or three times a week. This is enough exercise to help you lower your risk for health conditions like high blood pressure, stroke, coronary artery disease, type 2 diabetes, colon cancer, and osteoporosis, and to prevent the natural loss of muscle mass that slows metabolism and contributes to weight gain in your thirties, forties, fifties, and beyond.

* **If you're trying to lose weight, more activity is better.** An hour or even 90 minutes of moderate exercise, or 30 minutes of vigorous activity such as jogging, strenuous aerobics, or fast-paced cycling, is ideal.
* **Of course, anything you do is better than nothing,** and consistency counts. Fitting in 30 minutes most days of the week, even in 10-minute bursts, is better than playing the weekend warrior by overdoing it once or twice a week.
* **If you're the type who just doesn't enjoy going to the gym** or using a treadmill, choose an activity you enjoy that you can do for 10 to 30 minutes or longer and that raises your heart rate. This could be dancing, playing tennis, chopping enough wood to heat your house for the winter, or lining up strenuous yard work or housework that feels like a workout.

WHAT YOUR DIET BOOK DOESN'T TELL YOU

These secrets reveal why your belt is too tight, beyond your chocolate addiction and french-fry love affair.

1. Your weight really is genetic. When scientists first discovered a gene in certain chubby mice, they called it simply the fatso gene. Turns out, people with two copies of the gene were 40 percent more likely to have diabetes and 60 percent more likely to be obese than those without it. Those with only one copy of the gene weighed more, too.

2. Scientists now suspect that there could be as many as 100 fat genes, each adding a pound or two here and there.

3. You might have more fat cells than your skinny neighbor does. Some people have as much as twice the number of fat cells as others. Even if you've lost a few pounds (or gained some), your fat-cell count remains, holding tight to the fat already inside and forever thirsting to be filled up with more. (To add insult to injury, the fat cells of overweight and obese people hold more fat, too.)

4. New fat cells emerge during childhood but seem to stop by adolescence. Those of us destined to have a lot of these cells probably start producing them as young as age two. The cells' rate of growth may be faster, too—even if kids cut way back on calories.

5. But your "destiny" is no excuse. When researchers at Helsinki University Central Hospital studied sets of twins where one was fat and the other thin, they learned that fat cells in heavier twins underwent metabolic changes that make it more difficult to burn fat. Gaining as little as 11 pounds may slow metabolism, so as you gain more fat, it becomes harder to lose it. What helps? Physical activity.

6. Fat might be your boss's fault. Stress fattens you up, and the most direct route is the food-in-mouth syndrome: Stressful circumstances spark cravings for carbohydrate-rich snack foods, which in turn calm stress hormones. (When researchers in one study took away high-carb food from stressed mice, their stress hormones surged.)

7. Stress hormones also ramp up fat storage. For our prehistoric ancestors, stress meant drought or approaching tigers, and a rapid-storage process made sense; we needed the extra energy to survive food shortages or do battle. Today we take our stress sitting down—and the unused calories accumulate in our midsection. To whittle yourself back down to size, in addition to your usual workout routine, make time for stress relief—whether it's a yoga class or quality time with family.

8. Fat might be your mom's fault. A growing body of science suggests that sugary and fatty foods, consumed even before you're born, can mess with your weight. One study on rodents found that overweight females have higher levels of glucose and free fatty acids floating around in the womb than normal-weight ones do. These molecules trigger the release of proteins that can upset the appetite-control and metabolic systems in the developing brain.

9. Your spouse's ice cream habit is messing with your weight. If one spouse is obese, the other is 37 percent more likely to become obese, too, according to a study in the *New England Journal of Medicine*. Fortunately, slimming down may be contagious, too, if one partner becomes motivated by the other's success.

10. Obesity might be viral. Adenoviruses have been linked to fat by researchers at the University of Wisconsin, who injected chickens with the viruses and found that certain strains fattened them up. Human studies, including comparisons of twins, suggest that obese people are indeed more likely to harbor antibodies for a particular virus, known as adenovirus 36.

11. It's hard to win against a cookie. While food is not addictive the way cocaine or alcohol is, there are some uncanny similarities. When subjects at Monell Chemical Senses Center in Philadelphia were shown the names of foods they liked, the parts of the brain that got excited were the same parts activated in drug addicts.

12. Ear infections can taint your taste buds. In one study of more than 6,000 people, researchers found that people over age 35 who had suffered several ear infections had almost double the chance of being obese. Why? These infections can damage a taste nerve running through the middle ear. And when researchers found that former ear-infection patients were a little more likely to love sweets and fatty foods, they theorized that the damaged nerve may cause them to have a higher threshold for sensing sweetness and fattiness.

13. You may have obliterated your "stop eating" signal. Gorging on candy bars, chips, and other not-too-healthy carbs brings damaging free radicals out in droves (those are also the molecules blamed for making you look old). It's possible that they damage the cells that tell you you're full. Fight that with antioxidant-rich produce.

> **TOP SECRET!** Your bedroom, not the kitchen, might be making you fat. Sleep deprivation upsets our hormone balance, triggering both a decrease in the hormone leptin (which helps you feel full) and an increase of the hormone ghrelin (which triggers hunger). As a result, we think we're hungry even though we aren't—and so we eat. Sleep may be the cheapest and easiest obesity treatment there is.

SOURCES: Zane Andrews, PhD, a neuroendocrinologist at Monash University in Australia; Louis Aronne, MD, past president of the Obesity Society and author of *The Skinny*; Linda Bartoshuk and Derek Snyder of the taste lab at the University of Florida; Claude Bouchard, PhD, executive director of the Pennington Biomedical Research Center at Louisiana State University System; Nikhil Dhurandhar, PhD, associate professor of infections and obesity at Pennington Biomedical Research Center, Baton Rouge, Louisiana; Kirsi Pietiläinen, PhD, an assistant professor of nutrition at Helsinki University Central Hospital; Kirsty Spalding, PhD, of the Karolinska Institute in Stockholm.

Who Knew?
HOW DIFFERENT ARE ALL THOSE DIET BOOKS, REALLY?

. . . .

As established diet books constantly reinvent themselves to sell copies and win converts, a curious phenomenon has emerged: Ornish, Atkins, and everyone in between are sounding remarkably similar. The low-fat gurus now say that certain fats are okay, while the low-carb proponents are beginning to endorse whole grains. With every new guideline and selling point, each diet acknowledges that there are really four basic rules to healthy eating (drumroll, please):

* **Consume carbs** in the form of whole grains and fiber.

* **Avoid trans fats** and saturated fats.

* **Eat lean protein.**

* **Fill up** on fruits and vegetables.

The low-carb South Beach Diet, for example, now espouses the virtues of eating the Mediterranean way—including lots of carbohydrate-rich fruits and vegetables. The latest Atkins book emphasizes the "good carb" message, too. Weight Watchers, a champion of the points system, is now offering a "no counting" option based on healthy choices like those above. Jenny Craig is pushing Volumetrics, a high-volume, low-calorie strategy. Our new book, *The Digest Diet*, reveals the foods that studies show help the body release fat. And everyone gives a thumbs-down to processed and sugary carbohydrates, which cause insulin to spike and can lead to more fat and even diabetes.

The key to all of this, of course, is moderation rather than deprivation—eating in a way you can enjoy for the rest of your life.

WHAT YOUR PERSONAL TRAINER WON'T TELL YOU

What's a waste of energy and what really works? Find out from trainers who've seen it all in the gym.

1. Do not arrive at a training session in the following states: On an empty stomach, coming off a cold/stomach bug, or on four hours' sleep. It wastes your time and mine when your body isn't fueled, hydrated, and ready to work.

2. If you concentrate on the exercise you are doing with me with the same intensity as telling me the latest gossip about your life, you would find it easier.

3. If you're on a budget, recruit a few friends for a small group session. These cost less per person.

4. We know you are eating more than you tell us.

5. It takes more than writing a check or showing up for training sessions to make you fit and healthy. It's what you do before and after you meet with your trainer, including choices with food, alcohol, workouts, and a commitment to a new lifestyle.

6. Ask you trainer what she or he does to keep educated in the field. An educated trainer will get better results and provide variety to keep you engaged and motivated in your workouts.

7. **When you are late it is a waste of your money,** a waste of my time, and disrespectful.

8. **There is a difference between pain and burn.** You need to be honest with your trainer about which you're feeling. If you push so hard that you injure yourself, we both lose.

9. **Whatever the text or e-mail says, it can wait until we're done.** And no, you cannot text and put forth 100 percent effort at the same time.

10. **Gear matters.** Don't expect to get maximum performance and results by working out in the ratty gym shoes and shorts you dug out of that old box of college dorm clothes. Invest in a good pair of sneakers. Your feet and joints will thank you and so will your trainer.

> **TOP SECRET!** Drink a bottle of water on your way to the gym. If you're dehydrated, you can't work as hard, you don't feel as good, and your mental function is compromised. So you won't get as much out of your workout.

11. **We see through your stall tactics.** "I think I need to fill my water bottle." "Let me get a dry towel real quick." "Oh, I need to go to the bathroom again." Nice try. But you're paying for the session, so make every minute count.

12. **Remember that a 30-minute session at max effort is better**—and cheaper—than 60 minutes of dawdling and half-effort.

13. **Turn off the TV when exercising on your own.** Although TV may take your mind off your workout, it also causes you to lose touch with your effort level. You unconsciously slow down or use poor form as you get caught up in what's on screen.

SOURCES: Personal trainers in Vermont, Florida, California, and Louisiana.

Great Advice
SURPRISING TIPS FOR A BETTER WORKOUT

· ·

1. **Avoid the mirrors.** Many fitness centers line exercise rooms with mirrors, yet a study of 58 women found that those who exercised in front of a mirror felt less calm and more fatigued after 30 minutes of working out than those who exercised without staring at their reflections.

2. **Set a short-term workout goal.** Of course, goals motivate you to work harder, and the best exercise programs include measurable goals to achieve weeks or months down the road. Sometimes, though, when your motivation is drooping, a goal focusing on what you can complete over the next 30 minutes is what you need. So pick something achievable: Maintain a sweat for 20 minutes, give your arms a good workout, or cover 2 miles on the treadmill. A target like that gives you focus to get through.

3. **Invent a competition with the person on the next treadmill.** If you're on the treadmill and you're bored, glance at the display on someone else's nearby treadmill. If you're walking at 3.5 miles per hour and he or she is chugging away at 4 miles per hour, see if you can increase your speed and catch up, as if it were a race. The other person won't even know you're racing.

WHAT YOUR WEIGHT LOSS COUNSELOR WON'T TELL YOU

Here are the experts' secrets to resisting food temptation in its many guises.

1. Eat the cake. Just decide how much ahead of time. Passing on your colleague's cake looks as curmudgeonly as refusing to sing "Happy Birthday." The socially acceptable way out is to ask for a thin slice, and then eat a small number of bites you've decided on beforehand. Or just eat the cake and leave the icing.

2. Kiddie cones are not that bad. When your best pal wants to go out for ice cream and you can't shake off 1,360 calories and 89 grams of fat—the going rate for a banana split at Ben & Jerry's Scoop Shops—a 3-ounce kid-sized cone weighs in at about 220 calories at the same shop. Frozen yogurt or sorbet may have even less.

3. Beer isn't off-limits when you choose lite—or right. The most refreshing, easy-to-drink beers are the highly carbonated, lower alcohol "lite" brews. As a rule the darker the beer, the more calories, so if your yen is for craft-beer flavor, stick to the trendy new wheat and white (weiss) beers and avoid higher alcohol ales, even so-called "pale" ones.

4. You can do OK at the drive-thru. The big boys have begun to grasp that customers want some reasonable options: "395-calorie meal for $3.95" read one sign outside a fast food franchise recently. Just stay away from anything with the word "crispy"; steer clear of mayo-heavy sauces (use mustard!); and keep dressings no-fat.

5. Starbucks has low-calorie options. This chain isn't just about additions that turn a cup of coffee into an ultra-sweet high-calorie dessert. While the tempting, calorie-rich offerings are generally at eye level, look down. Starbucks now offers sensible snacks, but they're going to make you find them. As for drinks, begin any order with the word "skinny" and you can cut the calorie count by up to a third.

6. Don't skip the sauce; share. A meal in a top-flight restaurant is all about the sauces and special preparations made by a chef who is closer to an artist than a cook, and you're not going there to skip them. Instead, order less food, and be confident that the intense flavors will satisfy you.

7. Appetizers to share, broth soups, and salads are great options when you're out to eat. If you can't resist a delectable dessert item, share that, too.

> **TOP SECRET!** Toast with a something-and-soda. When you hit the bar to raise a toast to Bob-in-Accounting's promotion, have a lower-calorie cocktail that doubles easily for a soft drink, and then alternate between the two. For example, a gin (or vodka) and tonic has only 180 calories and no one will be the wiser when you make your second round an equally bubbly and transparent zero-calorie diet Sprite, dressed up with a twist.

8. Nibble on the move. If you are shopping and fading from hunger, avoid settling in at the food court. Instead nibble your way through a shopping marathon. Pick up a snack, such as a hot pretzel, a small bag of roasted nuts from a kiosk, or even a chicken taco, and nibble on the move. Portable meals, of course, can still seriously weigh you down; check calorie counts before you go or on your mobile phone.

9. Have the hot dog. If the only foods at the picnic are hot dogs, hamburgers, and drenched-in-mayo "salads," then go ahead and smell the burgers, but eat the hot dog. A dog on a bun with a smear of ketchup will set you back about 250 calories. That's as many as the burger has in fat alone. Load up your plate with the low-calorie burger fixin's, like lettuce, tomato and onions, to round out your meal.

10. Douse your afternoon slump or hunger pangs with water. The energy drop that hits in afternoon is likely a combination of perfectly natural factors: the result of a light lunch, mild dehydration, a momentary lack of iron, or a crash off that coffee you had at the late-morning meeting. Before wandering to the cafeteria or fridge, start your recovery with a tall glass of water, which boosts your blood flow and, as a side benefit, makes you feel full.

11. Ideal snacks for clearing a cobwebby head are hummus or almonds, but if your only option is an office vending machine, look for any hint of protein—those orange crackers with peanut butter, at 200 calories, are better than a sugary cookie. Wash it down with a cup of coffee doused in iron-rich cinnamon.

12. You can eat less and still make Mamma happy. Food is love, and when Mamma tells you "mangia" and you don't, she acts like you're rejecting her, not her pot roast. The answer: Have some of everything pushed at you during the holidays or a weekend visit home, but only a spoonful. That means your plate will be more of a tasting sampler than a full meal. Remember: Just one bite of a dish, preceded by a loud "I can't resist!" will do your parents good and won't kill you.

13. Another strategy: Make yourself useful serving people and cleaning up. It gets you away from your plate, but still makes you a vital part of the meal.

SOURCES: Marion Nestle, nutrition professor at New York University; Elizabeth Somer, author of *Eat Your Way to Happiness.*

Great Advice
WEIGHT LOSS SECRETS FROM AROUND THE WORLD

Start with soup. This Japanese tradition is one of the best weight-loss strategies. That's because eating soup, particularly the broth-based vegetable kind, before your entrée fills you up so you eat less during the meal, explains Barbara Rolls, Guthrie professor of nutrition at Penn State University in University Park, and author of *The Volumetrics Eating Plan*. A two-year French study of 2,188 men and 2,849 women found that those who ate soup five to six times a week were more likely to have BMIs below 23 (considered lean), compared with infrequent- or non-eaters whose BMIs tended to be in the 27 range.

Make lunch your main meal. Although they do this throughout Europe, a good explanation for eating your big meal at midday comes from ayurveda, India's 5,000-year-old approach to wellness. "According to ayurveda, we're actually designed to eat the larger meal at lunch because our digestive 'fire,' called agni, is strongest between 10 a.m. and 2 p.m., so we digest more efficiently," explains Jennifer Workman, a Boulder, Colorado–based ayurveda specialist, registered dietitian, and author of *Stop Your Cravings*. "I've seen people in my practice lose 5 to 10 pounds just by doing this."

Think quality, not quantity. The French snub processed "diet foods" not found in nature, opting instead for high-quality meats, fish, produce, dairy, even desserts. When food is fresh and flavorful, you can be satisfied with smaller portions. This is the opposite of the American approach, which is to fill up on bland diet foods, then gorge on sweets later. "The French set the standard for small portions with their haute cuisine," says David Katz, MD, author of *The Way to Eat*. "If we consider that part of eating is to induce pleasure, if you can get there with quality of choice, you get there in fewer calories."

Big Advice

SHOULD YOU REALLY BE EATING THAT?

The healthy choice isn't always obvious. For optimal weight and health, here's what to pick from these popular pairs.

1. Bacon or sausage?

Answer: Bacon. A slice of bacon, cooked thoroughly, has fewer calories than a typical serving of sausage. Your best bet is a slice of lean back bacon with the rind and fat cut off, rather than fatty, streaky bacon.

2. A packed lunch or a purchased lunch?

Answer: A packed lunch. It'll be healthier; it'll probably have fewer calories; it'll be cheaper; and it'll save you lots of time that you can use for walking, reading, or socializing instead.

3. Lunch or graze?

Answer: Graze. Nibble food throughout the day, rather than having a large, formal lunch. Spreading out your calories stabilizes blood sugar and insulin levels; provides more frequent relief from stress, tension and boredom; and avoids post-meal fatigue, because you don't have a big meal. Plus, you never get really hungry and so are less likely to make the regrettable food choices that you might when you're starving. But if you are going for meals over munching, make lunch your big one.

4. Coffee or tea?

Answer: Tea. Choose black or green tea. These are jammed with heart-healthy antioxidants that provide more than just an energy-boosting punch. As well as contributing to healthier arteries, they may also help to prevent cancer.

5. Natural sugar or white sugar?

Answer: Neither. They're both sugar. Neither has any nutritional benefit or is any better than the other. Here's a case where the brown color does not imply a healthier version.

6. Strawberries or blueberries?

Answer: Blueberries. Of course, both are great for you, so try to eat lots of these two fruits. But when you compare the nutrients in an equal amount of each, blueberries have a slight edge. Blueberries are particularly rich in fiber—four times that of strawberries—and contain much more vitamin E and some unique micronutrients that are good for memory.

7. Fruit juice or fruit?

Answer: Fruit. Get the real thing. Not only are most fruit juices loaded with sugar, they've been stripped of an important element found in fruit—fiber.

8. Broccoli or cauliflower?

Answer: Broccoli. At 2.6 grams of fiber per 100 grams, broccoli has twice the fiber oomph of cauliflower.

9. Apple or orange?

Answer: Apple. The old adage is true after all. A study from the University of Nottingham found that people who ate more than five apples a week had improved lung function, less wheeziness, and fewer asthmalike symptoms. Eat them raw, try them baked, add them diced into a salad, or sauté an apple with onions as a side dish for chicken or fish.

10. Green olives or black olives?

Answer: Green olives. Green olives haven't ripened fully, so they contain roughly half the fat levels that they would have achieved had they ripened and blackened.

11. Sparkling water or club soda?

Answer: Sparkling water. There's a reason soda and sodium sound similar. Club soda is based on the use of sodium bicarbonate to "carbonate" it; thus it should come as no surprise that club soda is salt-rich. With only 3 milligrams of sodium, sparkling water beats club soda's 75 milligrams hands down.

12. Sirloin steak or rib-eye?

Answer: Sirloin. A 300 grams sirloin steak contains 325 calories and 13 grams of fat, 6 of them saturated, compared to the 423 calories and 23 grams of fat (12 of them saturated) found in the same size of rib-eye steak.

13. Soup or salad?

Answer: It depends. Some soups are far healthier than some salads and vice versa. You're better off with a salad of mixed greens and raw vegetables coupled with a light, healthy dressing over a creamy soup. You'll get more fiber and thus more filling for your calories, not to mention the healthy dose of disease-fighting antioxidants found in raw vegetables. But broth-based soups are very healthy and contain way less fat and calories than a salad covered in a creamy dressing.

14. Bottled salad dressing or homemade?

Answer: Homemade. Homemade is healthier almost every time. Not only can you use cholesterol-lowering monounsaturated fats such as olive oil, but also many bottled dressings contain extra salt and additives.

15. Café au lait or caffe latte?

Answer: Café au lait. Café au lait comprises equal parts brewed coffee and steamed milk. A caffe latte is one or two shots of espresso with steamed milk and foam filling the rest of the cup. For a tall drink made with semi-skimmed milk, the au lait has just 91 calories and 3.4 grams of fat, while the tall semi-skimmed latte, because it uses so much more milk, has 148 calories and 5.6 grams of fat. You may find that the au lait has a bolder, more coffee-rich flavor, so you win on all counts.

16. Fresh tomatoes or tomato sauce?

Answer: Tomato sauce. Tomatoes are rich in lycopene, an antioxidant believed to reduce the risk of prostate cancer and possibly several other cancers. But only by cooking it will you release the lycopene from the tomato cell walls so that your body can absorb it. What's more, lycopene is fat-soluble, meaning your body is better able to absorb and use it when you get it with a bit of fat—such as the olive oil found in most tomato sauces.

Part Four

WHAT YOU DON'T KNOW ABOUT
YOUR FAMILY

Who's watching your kids and your spouse when you aren't? Plenty of people, and they'd love to tell you a few things. From marriage counselors and nannies to mall Santas and mothers-in-law, there are a slew of behind-the-scenes insights (and some funny stories, to boot) you'll be glad to know.

What makes a wedding planner pretend to be booked? What do your kids really eat at camp, and should you worry about it? What do all happily married people agree on? (Looking out for each other is one thing, but part two may surprise you.) And Santa? That beard the kids are tugging on may be worth thousands! Learn the secrets to a happy family at all stages of life with these insider truths.

WHAT YOUR WEDDING PLANNER WON'T TELL YOU

What do you get for that often hefty price tag? If only you knew. Wedding planners around the country reveal the good, the bad, and the very ugly secrets about preparing for the big day.

1. I keep secrets. At one wedding I planned, the cake went missing after the bride and groom cut it. The bride soon asked where the cake was. Turns out the servers had taken it upon themselves to eat it! We cut the pieces smaller and the bride never knew. Keeping things quiet is the secret behind making the bride think the wedding was flawless.

2. I hate feeling devalued. When a potential client begins to nickel and dime me, I know they do not understand what it is I will be doing for them.

3. The biggest mistake you can make is choosing the cheapest vendors in the hopes of saving money. You truly get what you pay for.

4. Don't forget the tax and service charge. Many couples overlook the "plus plus" when planning a menu. Everything has a tax and service charge, and it really adds up—trust me!

5. Just because you planned your own destination wedding doesn't mean you can do my job better than I can. Yes, you may have found lower rates on Orbitz, but you don't have access to the contract and package perks that I'm able to offer to my brides.

6. I do manual labor and other dreadful tasks. I cannot even tell you how many times I've been on my hands and knees, sweating. I sometimes have to count the napkins and linens before they go back to the rental company. I'm talking dirty, smelly napkins, with food, lipstick, and whatever else is on them. Talk about gross!

7. Reuse flowers from ceremony to reception if at all possible. Be sure to tell your florist so your flowers aren't arranged to look good from only one side.

8. You can always elope! It's never too late to run away and have a relaxing wedding. You'll have great memories to share with your friends and family once you're home.

9. This is a full-time job, and on the big day we are steaming the bridal gown, pinning boutonnieres, making sure that the timelines are being met, making sure there are no spots on the glasses or silverware, allowing gum to be spit out in our hands before the ceremony, dealing with any situations that arise, and the list goes on!

> 🔒 **TOP SECRET!** If you've been engaged for a week and your wedding planning organizer is thicker than mine (which usually contains paperwork for the five or six weddings I'm currently planning,) then I automatically tell you that I'm booked on your date . . . and your backup date.

10. Make sure the things you spend money on can be reused. Don't have "bride" and "groom" etched on your flutes and toasting glasses. The same rule applies to serving pieces. If you must get something engraved, make it your initials, and then you have an heirloom.

11. Some things will not go perfectly. We'll do our best to fix mistakes without you knowing and bill you later at our discretion. I'll go to great lengths to make sure your wedding is perfect. Your wedding is my job, and I'll do everything I can to make it memorable, including walking miles to a florist in Jamaica to correct the $700 bouquet that arrived spray-painted purple.

12. I'll make sure everything you're offered is in the contract. If the first manager you work with offers you a complimentary toast, get it in writing. If that manager leaves for whatever reason, you won't be forced to argue about these details with his or her replacement.

13. Stay focused on the big picture. It's easy to micromanage all of the details at the expense of the big picture. As long as people marry for the right reasons, the details of wedding

Be an Instant Expert
8 Creative Ways to Cut Wedding Costs

1. **Skip the custom-printed invitations.** Your guests will probably never even notice the scalloped edges and silver ink that cost you an extra $2 per print. They probably also won't know if you've made your invitations yourselves. Although they are the enemy of wedding invitation designers, invitation software packages offer modern fonts and graphics, and they are easy to use.

2. **Book a budding musical talent.** If you have always dreamed of having a live string quartet or even a rock band at your wedding reception, but can't afford their fees, hire music students—just listen to them perform at a concert or gig before you hire them.

3. **Take a class in wedding planning.** Although these courses are designed for people embarking on wedding planning as a career, you'll pick up huge amounts of inside information.

4. **Use local expertise.** Ask around and you'll quickly discover bargain talent in your area, whether you want a wedding dress or outfit stitched, a cake baked, special ties or cravats made for the bridegroom and his party, or flowers arranged for your church and reception.

5. **Consider nonfloral centerpieces.** The flowers in the bride's bouquet and on your mom, dad, bridesmaids, and other relatives are the flowers that will be in your photos, so that's where you want

planning are really secondary. Don't make decisions to please or impress others.

SOURCES: Candice "Candy" Cain, Candy Cain Travel; Karen Clark, SomethingBorrowedSomethingBlue.com; Denise Georgiou-Newell, WPICC, DWC, CSP, TICO, WeDDings Jubilee Planning Services; Wayne Gurnick, AIFD, MomentsByWayne.com; Jill Higgins, Jill Higgins Photography; Lynn Jawitz, Florisanllc.com; Bryant Keller, bryantkeller.com; Gregorio Palomino, CEP, CWP; Tanya W. Porter, Weddings, Etc., LLC; Jules Rupae, Jules Rupae Events; Holly Schoenke, Simply Sweet Weddings.

to invest. Rather than having floral centerpieces, "Put beautiful, tall candles on the tables and surround them with glass pebbles, or float votive candles in water," says Deb McCoy, president of the American Academy of Wedding Professionals.

6. **Buy booze by the head, not by the drink.** Even if most of your wedding guests are nondrinkers, don't let the caterer talk you into paying by the drink. The secret about teetotalers is that many actually do imbibe when the liquor is free, and what's free for them costs you about $7.50 per cocktail. Plus, there will be no surprises when the bill comes.

7. **Cut to the cake.** Cut your cake and toss your bouquet early in the night so your photographer and videographer can leave early. Plus, after the professional photographers leave, your guests will be more likely to start snapping pictures with the inexpensive, disposable cameras on their tables.

8. **Consider your credit card your secret weapon.** Paying for everything related to your wedding and reception with a credit card will protect you should anything go wrong with your vendors. If the first-rate photographer you booked gets hit by a bus the day before the wedding and you put the deposit on a credit card, your money will be refunded. If you had paid with cash, your money would have gone down with the photographer. Your credit card is like a free wedding insurance policy in your wallet, so use it.

WHAT HAPPILY MARRIED PEOPLE WANT TO TELL YOU

Not everything about marriage is pretty. And the couples who make it accept and love that fact. Here's what they want you to know.

1. Only puppies want to be on top of each other—and they get tired of it, too. Sometimes, you need space.

2. Is there anyone who hasn't, at least once, remembered they left the car windows open when the rain, and sex, started at the same time?

3. A date isn't all candlelight and dinner. The true criterion for a date: anything that lets you focus on each other. That could be weeding the garden while you chat amiably, a weeklong trip to Bermuda, or ten minutes over morning coffee.

4. There's a couple who randomly asks each other, "how's your love tank?" They want to see if each other's love tank—how loved they feel—is full, half-full, or getting near empty. If it's low, it's not taken personally; it's just a signal that the other partner needs something.

5. Most people have at least one thing about their partner they really can't stand. Of course you're going to be seriously annoyed at some of a partner's habits. For example: snoring, hygiene, sloppiness, or foot-in-mouth problems. You are lucky if it's just one habit.

6. Over time there is less that you have to say—you know your partner's response! Long silences are OK.

> **TOP SECRET!** Most good friendships are made, not inherited. There is usually at least one friend of your partner you hope will disappear.

7. Almost everyone has had a fantasy lover—either a real one that didn't work out or a movie star or some famous person who you dream about. There is that "What if . . ." thought that comes now and then.

8. Sometimes you just want to chuck it all. Hey, life is sometimes just hellish or boring—or both. Or you feel underappreciated and overworked. Not taking care of yourself happens sometimes, too. Everyone knows it's important to stay fit and attractive, but it's just so much work.

9. Sometimes the mojo isn't working, but you don't want to hurt your partner's feelings. It's normal sometimes to fake more sexual arousal than you're experiencing. Good partners tend to be kind about this sort of thing—angry partners telegraph that, on the whole, they'd rather be watching TV.

10. A calm, mature, trustworthy babysitter is worth her—or his—weight in gold. Even better than one babysitter: Develop a stable of two or three to boost your odds that one will be available when you need a date night.

11. Quiet sex is OK. So is afternoon sex or sex when the kids are out for the evening. But nothing beats unhurried, loud, whenever-you-want-it sex, followed by a cuddle, a nap, a shower, more lovemaking, a wonderful walk. For this luxury of uninterrupted time, you need to get away—or find a trusted friend, relative, or overnight camp so that the kids can get away.

12. There are ways to feel awake after the kids go to bed. One couple used to take turns taking naps during the day so they wouldn't be too exhausted to be together at night.

13. Maybe there are some long-term couples who have never told a lie to each other about anything—yes, conscious omissions count—but I wouldn't make a money bet on that.

SOURCES: Pepper Schwartz, PhD, professor of sociology at the University of Washington in Seattle; Don Howard and Teresa Titus Howard, a married couple in Blue Springs, Missouri; Susan Vogt; and anonymous couples throughout the United States.

 Become an Instant Expert
What to Do Right After You Get Engaged

* **Tell your parents.** Give them the honor of hearing the news first. Have the champagne ready to celebrate.
* **Let your friends know before Facebook does.** Call your best buddies before you log in to Facebook to update your relationship status or tweet your happy news. Be certain everyone who should hear it from you personally has been called.
* **Ladies, get a manicure.** Your finger and its sparkly new adornment will be getting a lot of attention.
* **Speaking of rings,** get yours appraised and insured!
* **Craft a catchall response.** You'll be asked when you're getting married often. Get past the "big day" question by choosing a month, season, or even just a year.

WHAT YOUR MARRIAGE COUNSELOR WON'T TELL YOU

How can you figure out when fighting is a good thing? Find out this and much more with these 13 stable-union secrets that it's never too late to know.

1. I love couples who fight in the waiting room. At least they still care about each other. If one or both of you seems indifferent, my job is a lot harder.

2. The earlier you come in, the quicker you can get the problem solved, the less your therapy will cost.

3. When you say your feelings "just aren't there anymore," I know you're probably cheating.

4. Sometimes I'll tell a couple "no sex until the next session. Don't touch each other, period." What I'm really hoping is that they'll fail and feel a sense of unity from their mutual rebellion.

5. What do I wish I could say? "Grow up!" "Stop whining!" "Get a life!" When I feel this way, I know I need a vacation.

6. Don't try to convince me you're the good one. In most marriages, there isn't a good one.

7. Yes, you should go to bed angry. If you try to resolve everything before you hit the sack, you'll both be sleep-deprived and cranky the next day. Instead, get a good night's sleep and talk once you're rested.

8. Three signs that a couple is not going to succeed: name-calling, finger-pointing, and when one or both partners fails to accept even the tiniest bit of responsibility for the situation.

9. Sometimes two people love each other but have such different styles of living that I recommend they live together in a duplex. It sounds strange, but it works for some people.

10. I've seen couples I thought didn't stand a chance end up staying together. Often it's because they're both willing to try. But sometimes it's just that they are too dysfunctional to leave each other.

TOP SECRET! I'm not going to tell a couple that I have no idea why they're together. But take the hint if I say something like "You both have to make a decision about whether this is going to work long term."

11. Don't expect your spouse to be everything you need: your lover, your best friend, your massage therapist, and your confidant. You need other relationships outside your marriage to fill those roles.

12. The big thing most women don't understand: Men are not mind readers. If you don't tell him how you feel, he's not going to know. The big thing most men don't understand: If you hardly acknowledge your wife all day, she's not going to want to get intimate with you at night.

13. The person who complains about things that happened in the past is usually more of the problem than the spouse they're complaining about. And if I ask you how long you've had problems and your answer is "ten years," you're not going to change things in ten minutes or ten sessions.

SOURCES: Susan Fletcher, PhD, a psychologist in Dallas, Texas; Lawrence J. Levy, PsyD, a licensed psychologist in Boca Raton, Florida; Nancy Mramor, PhD, in Pittsburgh, Pennsylvania; Jeff Palitz, a marriage and family therapist in Chula Vista, California; Meghan L. Reitz, LCPC, NCC, in Schaumburg, Illinois; Karen Sherman, PhD, in New York, New York; Tina B. Tessina, PhD, a psychotherapist in Long Beach, California; and a marriage counselor in Pennsylvania.

Great Advice

HOW TO STRENGTHEN YOUR RELATIONSHIP

As nice as it would be, your relationship won't just thrive on its own while you're taking care of the other business of life. Here's how to take it off autopilot and keep the excitement and partnership.

Schedule time for your marriage first. Don't relegate your relationship to scraps of leftover time. "In mapping out your schedule for the next several weeks, why not start with writing in date times for you and your mate?" suggest Claudia and David Arp, founders of Marriage Alive International and coauthors of marriage books including 10 Great Dates to Energize Your Marriage. "Unless you're willing to make your relationship a higher priority than other relationships and activities, you won't have a growing marriage," notes Claudia Arp.

Create couples rituals. Do something regularly that bonds you, such as 10 minutes to chat before bed, always having morning coffee together, or saving Saturday for date night.

Institute a daily check-in. Marriage experts recommend couples do something that big business has employed for decades to keep workers happy, productive, and in the loop: hold regular team meetings. Luckily yours will be more fun than listening to Bob from accounting go over the last month's sales numbers. In a daily check-in, you might start by appreciating something about each other, offer some new information about your day, and end with a hope that could be small ("I hope we can go see that new movie Friday night") or lavish ("I'd love to retire at age 50 and sail the Mediterranean with you.")

Ask "Is it good for our relationship?" When you bump up against any important decision in your marriage, don't just talk about whether it's good for you and for your spouse. If you don't even want to ask the question, that's a red flag that whatever it is—from working late to "surprising" your spouse with an expensive new living room sofa to making individual plans on your usual date night—isn't going to be good for your marriage.

Cheer each other on. "One of the most important things to me is that my wife, Rebecca, is for me and I'm for her," says Lee Potts, a retired computer programmer from St. Louis, Missouri. "It sounds simplistic, but it's really important. I've been married twice before, and I don't think we had each other's best interests at heart like this. We had our own agendas." Look for the positive in your new spouse; develop a sense of humor; and give honest, specific praise.

Disconnect from the 24/7 office. Push the "off" button! When researchers tracked the technology use and moods of 1,367 women and men for two years, they found that those who sent and received the most calls and messages were also most likely to say that this "work spillover" left them tired and distracted at home. Not to mention stressed: "Your boss doesn't tend to call you with the good news," says lead researcher Noelle Chesley at the University of Wisconsin–Milwaukee. "You do hear that suddenly there's a deadline crisis." Set limits on when you'll check e-mails and when your phone will be on.

Create a code word for love. Find a secret way to express your love that only the two of you understand. It comes in handy if your spouse calls when the boss is standing beside your desk, and creates that "just us" feeling anytime you use it.

In a survey of over 10,000 married couples, 97% of happy couples listed togetherness as a top priority, while only 28% of unhappy pairs listed it. Enjoying free time together and not letting friends and family interfere in the relationship were also valued by the large majority of happy couples.

SOURCES: Pat Love, EdD., marriage and sex therapist; David Olson, PhD at the University of Minnesota, and daughter Amy Olson-Sigg

WHAT YOUR MOTHER-IN-LAW WON'T TELL YOU

Here are some reasons why she's secretly glad you're in her life—even when it doesn't seem like it.

1. It hurts to be downsized. I spent a couple of decades being the leading lady; now I have a smaller role.

2. I know he's your husband now. But he's still my son.

3. You don't have to call me Mom. But it would be nice if you did.

4. Thank you. I don't always say it because I'm afraid you'll think I'm sucking up. But I've never seen my son happier than he is now, married and with children.

5. A little gratitude wouldn't hurt. Every year, I send you a birthday present, but you never even pick up the phone to thank me. This year, I said, "That's it. No more." Yet look at me: I'm about to send another present. I guess that's how I am.

6. I want the best for both of us. We mothers say to our children, "I want you to be happy." And we mean that. What we don't say is, "But I would like to be happy, too."

7. I know a little something. I've bought and sold 13 houses in my life. Why won't you ask for my advice?

8. When I visit you, I'm just coming to see the family. I'm not coming for a white-glove inspection.

9. I'm lucky to have you! Whenever I stay at your house, you always have my room ready, my towels, everything. You do all the right things.

> **TOP SECRET!** I'm in competition with your mother. She takes you on vacations every year and buys things I can't afford. All I can do is love you and babysit for you. I hope that's enough and that it's appreciated.

10. I'm truly appreciative. I'm happy that you allow my son—your husband—to visit me on Mother's Day. It's a long trip and a big expense.

11. I have a dirty little secret. I'm afraid that if I don't get this right, you'll cut me off.

12. I've got his number. When I really want to talk to my son privately, I don't call your house. I call his cell phone.

13. I really want to make you happy. If you hate that green sweater I bought you, please, please tell me.

SOURCES: Susan Abel Lieberman, PhD, author of *The Mother-in-Law's Manual*; Jane Angelich, author of *What's a Mother (in-Law) to Do?*; and anonymous mothers-in-law in four states.

Great Advice

WHAT TO DO IF YOUR MOTHER-IN-LAW TRIPS YOUR SWITCH

Even a great mother-in-law can frustrate you now and then, which is why the coauthors of *Anger Kills*, Virginia Williams, PhD, and Redford Williams, MD, recommend these ways to cope with your ire (and avoid the defibrillator):

1. **Recognize that anger is universal.** We're stuck with it, and making sure it doesn't hurt you means understanding when to express it—and when to let it go. It's having only one way to react—always or never—that can make anger a problem.

2. **Ask yourself if whatever made you angry is important.** Is what you're thinking and feeling appropriate to the objective facts of the situation? Can you modify this situation? Is it worth taking action?

3. **Talk yourself down:** a) yell "Stop!" to yourself (silently) when you start replaying an offense; b) distract yourself (surf travel sites for dream vacations); c) breathe in, clench your fist, breathe out, release fist. Repeat.

More than 60 percent of mothers-in-law see their son's wife as either a daughter, a friend, or the right woman for their son. Just 10 percent see her as the enemy, according to a survey of 1,868 mothers-in-laws and 2,000 daughters-in-laws, conducted jointly by ThirdAge.com and GalTime.com.

WHAT YOUR PARENTS WON'T TELL YOU

Do you still feel like you're seven around your parents even though you're the boss in your own house? Well, here's how to forge a rewarding, adult relationship with your mom and dad.

1. We're adults, too. If your parents still treat you like a kid despite the fact that you have kids of your own, you may have to help them let you "grow up." The key is thinking of them as adults, not parents, and acting like an adult when you're around them. A simple way to do this is to ask yourself a question before each interaction with them: "How would I act in this situation if Mom or Dad was a friend or an acquaintance?" Then behave accordingly.

2. We like to talk about the world with you. Model your conversations with Mom and Dad on those you have with friends. Don't limit conversations strictly to family memories, or gossip about family members, or your personal life. There's a whole wide world out there—why not explore it with Mom and Dad as you would with a friend? Current events, sports, work, local neighborhood issues, or national politics (if you can manage such a conversation and still be on speaking terms the next day) are all fair game.

3. Keep your sense of humor. When you're dealing with your parents, laughter can be a lifesaver—both to help you handle the stress of dealing with sometimes crotchety individuals and to help you bond together. Tell a few jokes you know they'll enjoy, share some comics from the paper, or e-mail with them. If you can laugh together, you're doing OK.

4. Sometimes you have to speak up.

We're not always going to like it. If you love your mom and dad but they drive you batty, your resentment can eat away at your relationship. So don't seethe silently. Communicate, with gentleness and respect. For instance, if your mom keeps calling you at work, tell her that your boss is starting to notice and, while you love talking to her during the day, it's beginning to affect your job performance. Arrange a call you can both count on at a mutually convenient time.

> **TOP SECRET!** Grant us some independence, too. Sometimes it's the grown-up kid who doesn't want to cut the nurturing relationship off. If you are past 25 and still find it necessary to talk to Mom every night, then you may be the problem, not your folks. They deserve freedom, too.

5. Why ask our advice unless you really want it? Some-
times asking for a parent's advice is really a way of asking for Mom's or Dad's approval. If that's the case, remember that you're an adult now, perfectly capable of choosing a living room carpet or a car on your own. If your parents are bent on offering you advice whether asked or not, smile, nod, and take it in (who knows—it may actually be helpful!). Focus on the fact that they have your best interest at heart. Then make your own choice.

6. Don't ask us to help straighten out your latest personal or financial crisis. While you may depend on their emotional support, relying too much upon their resources, rather than your own, can lead to mutual resentment. So get used to solving your problems, big or small, on your own. You'll be amazed how good doing it all by yourself can make you feel—and what a positive effect it can have on your relationship with your parents.

7. Create opportunities for exploring and uncovering memories. If your parents are older, look through old scrapbooks with them, asking them for stories about the people in the photos. We help our parents discover the meaning in their lives by encouraging them to talk about their accomplishments, the high points in their lives, and the joys and sorrows they have experienced.

8. We wouldn't mind creating a video, audio recording, or scrapbook with you. The finished product will not only be a testament to a renewed closeness between you, but also provide a wonderful legacy.

9. Expressing your appreciation is always welcome. Yes, Mom may be a buttinsky, but she always makes your favorite Christmas cookies. Dad is a bit of a stuffed shirt, but just the other day, he came to your rescue when your car died at the mall. The point is, your parents still do things for you that deserve your notice—and gratitude.

10. Rediscover and share mutual interests. When you were a kid, did you and your dad share a passion for a particular football team? Did you and your mother spend time each summer canning tomatoes? Make these happy memories the foundation for new, shared activities.

11. Be honest about who you are and what you want. Maybe there are things about your growing up that your parents regret. But as long as you don't regret it, they have to adjust. Be clear about who you want to be, and help your parents accept you on your terms.

12. Look for common activities. Baking, shopping, hiking, skiing, carpentry, etc. At any age, sharing a common task or activity is a great way to build closeness.

13. We know your hot buttons. Do not allow parents to channel guilt at you. If your parents are the type to complain about you never calling, never visiting, forgetting an uncle's birthday, not sending enough pictures, or whatever irks them that day, don't take the bait and feel guilty—unless you honestly regret the oversight. In which case, apologize immediately and seek a way to make amends. Otherwise, let it roll off your back. You have no obligation to play parent-child guilt games. You are a mature, independent adult, and act on your own volition.

SOURCES: Tom Swanson, PhD, director of support services education at VistaCare, a hospice care provider in Scottsdale, Arizona; Tina B. Tessina, Ph., a licensed psychotherapist in Long Beach, California, and author of *It Ends With You: Grow Up and Out of Dysfunction* and *The 10 Smartest Decisions a Woman Can Make Before 40*.

Who Knew?
WHAT PARENTS ARE REALLY THINKING

....

These real parent/child text message volleys from the website *Crazy Things Parents Text* say it all.

Money
> Me: Dad, my bank account has ten dollars in it!
> Dad: Oh good, our plan to get you to contact us succeeded.

Job
> Me: I was offered a job!
> Dad: Accept it before they realize their mistake.

Tech Help
> Dad: What is IDK?
> Me: I don't know.
> Dad: Oh, do you know who does?

Love
> Me: I love you.
> Mom: I tolerate you.

Birthdays
> Me: Happy 49th, Dad! I love you so much!
> Dad: It's 48! You ruined my day.

Relationships
> Mom: Come downstairs and talk to me please. I'm lonely.
> Me: Isn't Dad there?
> Mom: Yes, but I like you more.

WHAT YOUR NANNY WON'T TELL YOU

Here are top things even *The Nanny Diaries* didn't bring to light.

1. Treat your nanny with respect and as an equal, and you will have a loyal friend for life. Most of us become lifelong friends of the babies we helped raise, as well as their parents.

2. When you're hiring a nanny, don't just rely on references; go with your gut. If you really like—or don't like— a candidate when you first meet her, trust that instinct.

3. Don't come home drunk or on drugs, wake up your children to play with them, and then wake me up to put them back to bed.

4. Don't treat me like a maid. Respect that I'm here to do an important job—watch your children—so don't expect me to start doing your errands and cleaning non-kid messes.

5. Nannies from other cultures need orientation. Tell me which foods are fancy gourmet foods to be used sparingly and which are everyday foods. I kept eating up the best caviar and spitting it out in the trash, thinking it had gone bad.

6. Ask tons of questions when you're interviewing. How would she deal with a child who won't stop crying? Has she ever been fired from a job? Seeing how she reacts under tough questions will give you answers you need to know and an idea of how she responds to pressure.

7. Don't misrepresent yourself to an agency. If you don't have an extra room for the nanny, say so. Don't claim to have a bedroom and bathroom for her, and then ask her to sleep with your child.

8. Pay us well. Value your child a little more and cut corners elsewhere.

9. I am not paid enough to be a substitute parent for your child all the time. If you do not have the time or patience to raise a child, don't have one.

10. I have my own family. Many of us have kids in other countries. We'd like to see them, but we need vacation time.

> 🔒 TOP SECRET! We're appalled when you feed your children junk. Seriously—give your kids a vegetable once in awhile! If you don't keep junk food in your house, your kids can't eat it. You can give them choices without hurting their health.

11. If you want to save a little money, try hiring a nanny in training. They are eager to please and probably have a lot of background babysitting.

12. If your child bites me, don't reward her. One parent actually said, "Oh honey, are you hungry?" to her child while ignoring my bleeding face.

13. Start off with a trial basis. That way if you don't get along, or anything isn't to your liking, your not locked into an agreement.

SOURCES: Nannies or former nannies in Boston, New York, Seattle, Pennsylvania, and Los Angeles. (Including playwright Lisa Ramirez—whose off-Broadway play, *Exit Cuckoo*, deals with nannying—and an English nanny who worked for a Hollywood couple).

Be An Instant Expert

10 Healthy After-School Snacks

Equip the nanny with these hungry-kid tamers.

* Frozen grapes
* Rice cakes
* Veggie sticks
* Fruit salad
* Whole grain toast or crackers and peanut butter
* Popcorn
* Yogurt
* Hummus and pita chips
* Light string cheese
* Chocolate-dipped bananas

10 Things to Keep On Hand

Make sure the nanny knows where all these things are, and everyone will be happier.

* List of important phone numbers
* Replacement batteries/chargers
* Spare keys
* First aid kit for kids and adults
* Well-stocked craft box
* Movies she and the kids will enjoy
* Music everyone can dance to
* Backup on all the essentials, like diapers
* Emergency kit with flashlights
* Extra cash for the unexpected

WHAT YOUR KID'S TEACHER WON'T TELL YOU

What really happens behind the classroom door? Find out the truth and how you might be helping—or not!

1. We know if you've been "helping." We can tell the difference between parents helping their children with homework and doing it for them (especially when they're clueless in class the next day). Please stop doing everything for your children and allow them to make mistakes. How else will they learn? Kids are not motivated to succeed if they feel their parents will bail them out every time.

2. The truth is simple: Your kid will lie to get out of trouble.

3. Please, no more mugs, frames, or stuffed animals. A gift card to Starbucks or Staples would be more than enough. A thank-you note: even better.

4. We know what your kids really want, and it's not what you think. Parents give their kids the pricey gadgets and labels, but what kids really crave is for you to talk to them. They want to know you're interested in their lives.

5. We're sick of standardized testing and having to "teach to the test."

6. We don't arrive at school 10 minutes before your child does. And we don't leave the minute they get back on the bus. Many of us put in extra hours before and after school.

7. Encourage your child to keep reading. That's key to success in the classroom at any age.

🔒 **TOP SECRET!** Kids dish on your secrets all the time—money, religion, politics, even Dad's vasectomy.

8. My first year of teaching, a fifth-grader actually threw a chair at me. I saw him recently, and he told me he just graduated from college. *That's* what makes it all worthwhile.

9. Teaching is a calling. There's not a teacher alive who will say she went into this for the money. Guys who dribble a ball for a couple of hours a game can make up to $20 million a year. We educate future leaders and make about $51,000 a year. And while having the summer off is great, many of us have to take on extra jobs—teaching summer school, tutoring—to make ends meet.

10. We get jaded, too. Teaching is not as joyful as it once was for many of us. Disrespectful students and belligerent parents take a toll on us.

11. We spend money out of our own pockets. Teachers often buy things our students need, such as school supplies and even shoes.

12. Please help us by turning off the texting feature on your child's phone during school hours.

13. You do your job, I'll do mine. I have parents who are CEOs come in and tell me how to run my classroom. I would never think to go to their offices and tell them how to do their jobs.

SOURCES: American Federation of Teachers; interviews with elementary and middle-school teachers in California, Connecticut, Georgia, Iowa, Minnesota, New York, and Texas.

Great Advice
BEAT BACK-TO-SCHOOL STRESS

The challenge with school stress is that kids don't always know how to talk about it—so you don't always know what's up. Here are expert tips from *USA Today* and the website *Shine* that are sure to help both of you out.

1. **Listen.** Try to casually find out what's going on with them. Even if they aren't talking, watch for non-verbal cues and trust your instincts if your kid just doesn't seem himself or herself. Begin the conversation by offhandedly asking about school while you're driving home, at the supermarket, or doing a chore around the house together. Don't pressure them, and refrain from pressing for answers.

2. **Talk about homework.** If they're new to homework, discuss the work with them before they sit down to work. Talk about what is due when and help them plan how to get the work done. Don't focus on grades, but rather focus on completion and understanding the concepts of the assignment. Learning to manage their workload efficiently will help them succeed not only in school, but also in the workforce.

3. **Establish a routine.** Set a breakfast and morning routine that works for everyone. Try to make mornings calm and be enthusiastic about what's planned for the day. Lead by example by happily sharing the plans that you have for your day.

4. **"Un-Schedule" kids.** Extracurricular activities are great, but it's just as important that kids take time to relax and have some unscheduled time at home or outdoors. Keep one week-day after school as a "free day," and stick to that schedule for the school year. It's easier to be relaxed and prepared for the rest of the week when your child has had proper downtime.

WHAT YOUR KID'S CAMP COUNSELOR WON'T TELL YOU

You might not want to know how much fun your kids are having without you!

1. They're not as homesick as you think they are. For the first week, the cries of the homesick are almost unbearable. After that: "Mom? Who's Mom?"

2. Your kid is a lot less shy and a lot more competent than you think.

3. Your son may go without showering for weeks and will shun clothing.

4. We don't always know where your kids are. As long as he or she is eventually found, we're not going to tell you about all the times we had to call a search-and-rescue for your child.

5. Some of us are hungover every morning and rigidly enforce afternoon naptime not because the kids need the rest but because our heads hurt.

6. Even if it's not a coed camp, your teen is going to learn more about the opposite sex (accurate or not) than you want them to know.

7. **If they want to eat peanut butter and jelly for weeks** in a row, there's really nothing we can do about it.

8. **We confiscate the "illegal" candy you send** and eat it ourselves. For your kid's own good, of course.

9. **Your kids will be plunged into icy water,** submitted to exotic "tortures," and scared witless countless times—just because we think it's funny. . . . Oh, and they'll love it.

10. **Camp builds self-esteem.** The typical camper return rate is about 60 percent, according to the American Camp Association (ACA), and 92 percent of campers surveyed say the people at camp "helped me feel good about myself."

11. **Your child is going to speak in incomprehensible camp slang** for weeks after coming home. And they'll pine for people named Lunchmeat, Fuzzy, and Ratboy.

12. **We actually do this because we love your kids**—and we'll probably do it again next year. According to the ACA, the average return rate for staff is 40 to 60 percent. Camp is even more fun as a counselor than it is as a camper.

TOP SECRET! Don't think labeling their stuff means things will make it home. Everything's going to get hopelessly mixed up.

13. **Learning to make wallets may seem silly,** but the real value is the self-confidence kids get when they make something they can actually use.

Great Advice

GIVE YOUR KIDS A GREAT CAMP EXPERIENCE— WITHOUT BREAKING THE BANK

1. **Make a rough list.** With a sense of your kids' interests—do they want a general camp or one for sports, arts, academics, or other interests—search for accredited local camps through the American Camp Association (find.acacamps.org) and pick some affordable options. Then call camp directors and ask how they operate, how long they've been around, and whether they offer financial aid. Even better, take the kids to visit, if you can.

2. **Ask about discounts.** While some camps offer financial aid, many more have discounts for early registration, multiple and returning registrations, as well as for getting others to sign up. But as with many potential money-savers, you won't know unless you ask. Also find out if there are extra fees or expenses (like uniforms, equipment, or field trips), and how refunds work.

3. **Get creative.** If everything but the price sounds perfect, and discounts aren't working out, consider a shorter stay—maybe four weeks instead of all summer.

4. **Mine your affiliations.** If traditional summer camp is out of your budget, being affiliated with certain groups might mean more affordable alternatives. If your kids are members of a scout troop or council, Boy or Girl Scout camps may be only $100 to $300 a week. Some camps allow non-scouts to participate. Don't overlook church, school, or community camps. And if your kids are on a school or community team, there may be summer training or team-building opportunities.

WHAT YOUR MALL SANTA WON'T TELL YOU

It turns out that Santa has a few requests of his own when it comes to managing this holiday tradition.

1. Some of us get bonuses for making our daily photo quota. So please forgive me if I try to move things along.

2. Never force your screaming kid onto my lap. Just bring him close and give me a few minutes.

3. Want to have more than just a few seconds with me? Skip the mall. Let's meet at your kid's preschool or a photo studio that invites Santa in for special portraits.

4. Between October and December, most of us work about 40 ten-hour days and listen to 30,000 children.

5. You're ruining the fun. I've noticed a lot of you have started telling your kids the truth about me a lot younger than you used to. Sometimes you spoil things before your child even asks the question, just because you're worried he'll hear it from someone else. Please stop.

6. I'm not an orthodontist, either. Don't ask me to tell your child why she needs to stop sucking her thumb.

7. As a matter of fact, I did go to school for this. Topics of study: how to hold children, manage sticky conversations, and care for my hair and beard.

8. I don't have total recall. Don't come back after a few minutes and ask what your kid requested. Stand close enough to listen.

9. It's hard not to sweat in our heavy wool suits. To make sure we smell nice, some of us sprinkle baby powder in our beards; others use evergreen-scented colognes and sprays. And we're always sucking on breath mints.

TOP SECRET! I love the kids, but my favorites are the old ladies in nursing homes. When they sit on my lap (which they love to do!), they turn into kids themselves, and their favorite Christmas memories come pouring out.

10. Please take your barely potty-trained two-year-old to the restroom before you get in line. Soil my suit, and it's coal for you, buster.

11. Those of us with real beards think we're superior. But the best of the rest of us pay as much as $3,000 to wig makers to make us authentic-looking whiskers.

12. I see you vigorously nodding your head, but even so, I will never, ever promise anything to a child.

13. I've been kicked in the shins, hit in the groin, scratched, bitten, and peed on. But there's a reason I keep doing this year after year: This is the best work I've ever found.

Great Advice

TEACH YOUR KIDS THE TRUE VALUE OF "STUFF"

1. **Show them money going in, not just out.** If your kids only see you with drawing those $20 bills from the ATM, they're going to think machines hand out money. Make sure they also see you depositing funds.

2. **Teach them to set goals and save for them.** Label a jar with a set amount of money to be used for something specific. Start small—say, $5 to buy some ice cream and sprinkles. Keep this money separate when you go to the store, so your child can buy the ice cream himself with the cash.

3. **Differentiate between wanting and needing.** You *need* shoes, but you *want* the trendiest brand. Apply this rule to anything you buy and to any of their requests for "stuff."

4. **Make choices, not sacrifices.** Instead of saying, "We can't afford that," "That's too expensive," or just saying no, substitute a comment that expresses an intentional choice. Examples: "I want to stay home and visit state parks this year so we can save for a special vacation next year." Instead of feeling that "no" means sacrifice, scarcity, or embarrassment, children learn that life is about making choices.

5. **Show them you're planning for the future.** In addition to using a change jar to save for special treats, let your kids hear you talk about saving for a new roof, paying off the car, saving for their education, and paying bills on time.

6. **Give to others.** Along with that jar for ice cream, label another jar for charity. Make sure your children put a fixed percentage of their earnings and allowance in it. Make sure they see you giving to others.

WHAT YOUR DOG ISN'T TELLING YOU

Your best friend would tell you these 13 things if he could.

1. If I have short hair, use a brush, not a comb, to groom my coat. Don't forget the tail and legs. Use a fine comb through feathery hair on the legs and tail.

2. For a long coat, hold the hair down at the roots so you don't tug the skin. Just like you, I don't like it when you yank at the knots. Be patient.

3. Brush and comb me before you try the bath thing. And only bathe me when I'm dirty or need a flea bath. Too much bathing leaves skin dry and flaky.

4. Put a rubber mat in the tub so I don't slip, please. Use lukewarm water to wet me from head to tail. Shampoo hind legs, tail and rear end, then the body, chest and front legs. After that, carefully wet my head and shampoo. Cover ears and eyes so no lather gets in.

5. Nails are softer after a bath, so that's the time to trim them if necessary. Don't cut them down to the "quick," the pink area inside the nail. That's living tissue with blood supply and nerves. (And yes, I'll complain about that.)

6. Reward me for good behavior, rather than punishing me when I do the wrong thing.

7. Be consistent. Apply the same rules at all time, using the same commands and the same rewards.

8. If I have lots of energy and you're trying to teach me something, let me burn off a bit of that energy in the backyard before going for a walk.

9. Learning to sit is pretty easy. Here's how to teach us: Face the dog with a treat in your hand and, as the dog trots toward you, hold it over the dog's head. Keeping the eyes on the treat, the dog will back up and sit down. As they do, say, "Sit!" Reward with the treat.

10. To stop me from jumping up, don't make eye contact and don't touch or talk to the dog. If a dog is ignored, he learns that this isn't the way to get attention and that it's calm behavior that wins rewards.

> 🔒 **TOP SECRET!** My attention span just isn't that long. Short but regular training sessions are more effective than one long one.

11. Keep me calm in a storm. Kathy Diamond Davis, author of *Therapy Dogs*, has some recommendations: Some dogs like to be cuddled; they may really fear being left alone as it thunders. For other dogs, distraction works. If they're having fun, they're less likely to focus on the storm. And lots of background noise can help, so try turning on a fan. If your pet is so frantic that she tries to escape or is destructive, keep her in a crate or other confined space, if that calms her.

12. I like a little background noise while you're gone. If you leave the radio on, I'll be a lot happier when you're out picking up biscuits for me.

13. Having my own safe spot makes me feel better when I'm stressed. A crate is like a cave for me, and I love it. My own little bed is another thing I'm thrilled to have.

Great Advice

DOGGIE TRAINING DOS AND DON'TS

Cesar Millan, the Dog Whisperer, is a canine shrink with an uncanny ability to turn even the most aggressive pooch around. Millan reveals how to bring out the Lassie in your Brutus:

Wake up and walk. Most dogs are wired to be active. When they're not, pent-up energy leads to whining and chewing. It's a must to take your dog on a 45-minute walk or run before work. If you can, hire a dog walker for midday. "A dog that's tired doesn't bite, dig holes, or bark."

Touch, but never hit. Don't be afraid to use touch to tell a dog he's broken the rules: Millan pulls at the tuft of the neck and gives a gentle nudge—not to hurt the dog, but to surprise and correct.

Be the boss. "Everybody wants to be a dog's best friend, but dogs don't follow friends; they follow a leader," says Millan.

Establish leadership from the get-go: head and shoulders up. "Remember the popular people in high school? They walk in the room and people move—act like that." Walk ahead going out the door; only let him bound ahead if you give the okay. And be firm. Dogs need consistent structure and routine.

Go to the pros. If your dog bites or is overly aggressive, seek help from a dog trainer.

WHAT YOUR CAT ISN'T TELLING YOU

What really goes on between that furry head and active tail?

1. We don't generally like to go face to face at first. Nose-to-nose greetings between cats are unusual, as it puts both in a vulnerable position. However, cats who know each other well but have been apart for a while feel safe enough to do this to confirm visual recognition and gain information about how the other cat is, where he has been, and what he has been doing.

2. Purring usually means we are content. But a deep purr can also indicate pain. If you know your cat well you will be able to tell the difference in his demeanor.

3. We learn how to purr quickly. Cats start to purr at one week old and can do so continually as they inhale and exhale.

4. Young cats purr in a monotone, while older ones do so in two to three resonant notes.

5. Scientists still do not know exactly how the purring sound is made—and, of course, we're not telling. Although some believe that it originates in the cardiovascular system rather than the throat.

6. Like dogs, cats can also get sick or die from eating chocolate.

7. We like to nap rather than sleep but if relaxed enough to enter a deeper sleep, cats produce the same brain wave patterns that humans do when dreaming.

TOP SECRET! **We talk kitten to you but are much more grown up with our peers. Cats appear to retain their kitten vocal signals to communicate with their owners, but they use an adult repertoire of sound with other cats.**

8. We blink and narrow our eyes when we accidentally make eye contact. To make friends with an unfamiliar cat, blink and look away when you catch his eyes.

9. A cat's pulse is between 160 and 240 beats per minute, depending on the age of the cat (the younger he is, the faster the heartbeat).

10. We don't understand punishment. Cats must be praised and rewarded for desired behavior instead.

11. Some of us can learn a trick or two, besides coming at the sound of a can opening. Fetch is a favorite of ours, but if you tell the dog, you're finding a present in your favorite shoe.

12. Giving us a strip of raw meat everyday to chew on will keep our gums and teeth in good condition. Suitable meats include poultry, rabbit, or beef that has been deboned.

13. If your cat appears to be able to tolerate heat very well this is because the ancestors of cats were originally desert-living animals.

Great Advice
HOW TO GIVE A CAT A PILL

Some cats happily take medication. Others think you're out to poison them, so giving them pills requires patience and determination.

To try the easy way, buy pill pockets (available from vets), which many cats love. If that fails, wrap your cat in a towel and sit on the floor with them between your legs. Calmly wrap your dominant hand around the head so your fingers are under the cheekbone. Tip the head back; the lower jaw should slacken. Use your middle finger to ease the jaw down, and place the pill near the back of the tongue. Release the head and stroke the cat's throat to encourage it to swallow. Watch in case the cat spits the pill out.

Big Advice

LIFE'S 25 TOUGHEST QUESTIONS ANSWERED!

· ·

Reader's Digest's "Ask Laskas" columnist, Jeanne Marie Laskas, answers what you've been wondering about your friends, family, and more.

1. **Can love really last a lifetime?**

   Absolutely—but only if you chuck the fairy tale of living happily ever after. A team of scientists found that romantic love involves chemical changes in the brain that last 12 to 18 months. After that, you and your partner are on your own. Relationships require maintenance. Pay a visit to a nursing home if you want to see proof of lasting love. Recently I spoke to a man whose wife of 60 years was suffering from advanced Alzheimer's disease. He came to sit with her every day and hold her hand. "She's been my best friend since high school," he told me. "We made a promise to stick together." Now, that's a love story.

2. **Why do married folks begin to look like one another?**

   Watch any two people who like each other talking, and you'll see a lot of mirroring. One smiles, and so does the other. One nods or raises her eyebrows, and so does the other. Faces are like melodies with a natural urge to stay in sync. Multiply those movements by several decades of marriage, all those years of simultaneous sagging and drooping, and it's no wonder!

3. **Can a marriage survive betrayal?**

   Yes. It takes time and work, but experts are pretty unanimous on this one. In her book *The Monogamy Myth*, Peggy Vaughan estimates that 60 percent of husbands and 40 percent of wives will have an affair at some point in their marriages. That's no advertisement for straying—but the news is good for couples hoping to recover from devastating breaches of trust. The offended partner needs to make the choice to forgive—and learn to live with a memory that can't simply be erased. Infidelity is never forgotten, but it can gradually fade into the murky background of a strong, mature marriage.

4. Why does summer zoom by and winter drag on forever?

Because context defines experience. As Albert Einstein once said: "When you are courting a nice girl, an hour seems like a second. When you sit on a red-hot cinder, a second seems like an hour."

5. Do animals really have a sixth sense?

Or seventh or eighth! A box jellyfish has 24 eyes, an earthworm's entire body is covered with taste receptors, a cockroach can detect movement 2,000 times the diameter of a hydrogen atom, and your dog's sense of smell is up to 100,000 times greater than yours (some dogs have been known to smell human cancers). It's safe to say that animals experience a much different world than we do.

6. Why does the line you're in always move the slowest?

Because you're late for your kid's band practice, and you curse your luck and envy those speeding by. Conversely, when you're in the fast line, unfettered by stress, you don't even notice the poor schlubs in the slow lane. Good luck rarely commands one's attention like bad luck.

7. By what age should you know what you want to do with your life?

Any moment now. This used to be a question the young asked. The Bureau of Labor Statistics reports that younger baby boomers abandoned the American ideal of picking a job and sticking with it. Between the ages of 18 and 36, these boomers held an average of 9.6 jobs. That's a lot of exploration. The wisdom of elders in all cultures seems to be this: There's nothing to do with a life but live it. As Gandhi pointed out, "Almost anything you do will be insignificant, but it is very important that you do it."

8. Where do traffic jams come from?

Scientists are hard at work on this one, studying computer models of the physics of gridlock and inventing all new traffic-light algorithms. Some of them postulate that the rhythms of automobile traffic are influenced by the same cyclical forces that cause waves in the ocean. For the average commuter, though, it may be helpful to think of it this way: congestion. There are just too many darn people trying to do the same thing at once. (Flush every toilet in a single office building simultaneously, and see what happens.) All of this is a way of saying: Buy a newspaper, load up some favorite tunes on your MP3 player, and take the bus.

9. When is your future behind you?

When you stop chasing dreams. So don't stop!

10. Do you have to love your job?

No. Love your children, your spouse, and your country. Love your parents, your neighbor, and your dog. Loving is too important an emotion to attach to the way you make a living. But it's OK to strive for satisfaction. According to a recent Harris Poll, across America 59 percent of workers say they are extremely, somewhat, or slightly satisfied with their jobs, but a depressing 33 percent feel as if they've reached a career dead end. If you're among the latter and thinking about a new job, consider the fact that employees in small firms said they felt more engaged in their work than did their corporate counterparts.

11. Can a man and a woman ever just be friends?

For a short time perhaps. Making the friendship last requires that you find each other at least vaguely repulsive. Good luck!

12. When do you take away Grandpa's car keys?

Twenty-two states currently require frequent testing for senior drivers. The American Medical Association and the AARP, however, say safe driving has more to do with functional ability than age. True, seniors are more at risk for reduced vision, hearing loss, and impairments associated with arthritis—but all of these conditions depend on the individual. So when it seems to you that Pop is becoming a danger to himself and a danger to others, tell him straight. Point out that his reactions have slowed or his judgment is losing its edge. Suggest he not drive any-more. Be firm, but at the same time, don't treat him like a child. Allow him his dignity. Offer him a ride.

13. Do siblings who fight really end up liking one another?

I surveyed my older sisters, both of whom have vivid memo-ries of how I tripped, pummeled, and whacked them with various large plastic dolls (hey, they started it—they teased me!), and both confirmed my suspicion that nowadays they like me just fine. I sure like them. All the experts will tell you that fighting among siblings is normal. The key is how parents handle it. Rule number one: Don't take sides. Never get into a discussion of who started what or what is more fair. Stop fights with a time-out for all offenders. My mother would send us to separate rooms. So we invented string phones and a pulley system to transport necessary treats and toys. And whatever we were fighting about was forgotten.

14. How do you know when to end a friendship?

As soon as you get that sneaking suspicion that it never really began.

15. Why do we turn into our parents when we swore we wouldn't?

Because really, when all is said and done, we admire them.

16. Can a half-empty person become a half-full person?

A current theory is that people have an "emotional set point." Some folks are just made happier than others. Pessimists will see this as bad news, believing it really doesn't matter what you do—they are never going to be any happier. But there is hope—as any optimist will see! Happiness has more to do with how you construe the events in your life than the actual events themselves.

17. When do kids become adults?

Biologically, it's happening earlier; emotionally, it seems to be happening later. Nowadays puberty occurs in females between ages 8 and 14, between 9 and 15 in males. A generation ago, when you turned 18, you were out the door and on your own.

Now we see kids in the Boomerang Generation coming home to Mom and Dad after college, hoping for a hand with bills, laundry, meals, and other responsibilities of adulthood. It's cute for a while, less adorable the older the kid gets.

18. Can a mother be friends with her teenage daughter?

No. Most teens aren't ready for anything close to a mature friendship. According to current research, the brain continues to develop into a person's twenties. Mothers often want to befriend their daughters; fathers, their sons. But this is not in anyone's best interest. Teenagers need to form identities distinct from their parents. That means: lots of privacy, even some secrets. It's usually easier for a teenage girl to befriend the friend of her mother, and it's usually best for the mother to leave it at that.

19. Does money really buy happiness?

No. Because happiness isn't for sale. Many people get tripped up by this one, amassing wealth only to find themselves cycling into a bottomless pit of insatiable yearning. Turns out, joy and misery are not that far apart when it comes to very big wads of cash. Consider the case of a Kentucky couple who won $34 million in 2000. Thrilled to be released from the demands of their boring old jobs, they frittered their fortune away on fancy cars, mansions, all the usual stuff—losing everything that mattered in the process. They divorced, he died of an alcohol-related illness, and she died alone in her new house just five years after cashing the winning ticket. When it comes to happiness, only people you love, and who love you, can bring it. If you have enough dough to buy yourself a luxurious yacht, but no real friends to sail with, you're sunk.

20. Can spenders and savers stay married?

Sure—and they won't run out of things to talk about either. Disagreements over money are a leading cause of divorce, so experts advise lots of work around this issue if, financially speaking, you've found yourself married to your opposite. Tip: Always talk in terms of "ours" instead of "mine" or "yours," and work your strengths. The saver should be allowed to draft the budget; the spender gets to be in charge of vacations, celebrations, and ordering extra toppings on the pizza.

21. Is money the root of all evil?

No. Greed is. Elvis nailed this one when he said, "Sharing money is what gives it its value."

22. What do you do if you see a parent berating a child?

Cringe. Take a deep breath. If you truly believe you can help the situation, approach as someone showing sympathy—not as an accuser or member of the parent police. Empathize with the overstressed parent. Suggest that he take a deep breath. Tell him it worked for you.

23. Why is it so hard to say you're wrong?

Because it often involves saying, "I'm sorry," which is even harder. Throughout history people have found it easier to stop speaking to one another, punch, slander, shoot, and bomb rather than apologize. Tip: Next time just say, "Whoops," and see what happens.

24. When should you reveal a secret you said you wouldn't?

It's a matter of damage control. Is the person who asked you to keep the secret in danger of hurting himself or others? If so, intervene. Otherwise, mum's the word.

25. Does the toast really always fall buttered-side down?

Scientists in the Ask Laskas Kitchen conducted a study for which they first toasted an entire loaf of bread, one slice at a time. They buttered each slice, and dropped it from a variety of heights ranging from tabletop to ceiling. Among their findings: A dropped piece of toast never lands on its edge; stomping your foot and yelling "Darn!" does not change a thing; and the floor in the Ask Laskas Kitchen is not nearly as clean as we'd like. Well, life's like that. Never as neat as you'd like it to be. But keep buttering your toast. And savor every slice you've been given.

Part Five

WHAT YOU DON'T KNOW ABOUT
YOUR LOCAL BUSINESSES

Our lives depend on local services—or at least our quality of life can! They fill our day-to-day needs for everything from keeping us on the go, to cleaning our clothes, to supplying our parties. We see these neighborhood merchants every day, but what do they see?

Some businesses aren't really hiding things from you, but knowing what happens on the other side of the cash register—including what really sells and what they're trying to push on you—can help you get exactly what you need . . . maybe even with a discount. Whether you're getting a transmission overhaul or an anniversary card, here's what every consumer should keep in mind.

WHAT YOUR CAR DEALER WON'T TELL YOU

Here are some tips that will put you in the driver's seat for new-car negotiations.

1. That car we advertised at the unbelievable price? It's a stripped-down model with a manual transmission and crank windows. Ever wonder about those ads that promise a minimum $3,000 trade-in value for your clunker? Those dealerships also pad the sales price to make up for the difference.

2. The best time to buy is at the end of the month, and it's best to negotiate the trade-in separately. Negotiate up from the invoice price (what we paid for the car, easy to find on the Web), not down from the sticker price.

3. Please do the math. You can't get a $40,000 Tahoe for $250 a month for 72 months! Even at zero percent, $40,000 divided by 72 months is $555 before tax, title, and license fees.

4. Despite the stories you've heard about sleazy car dealers, plenty of us are honest folks frustrated by the guys who give the rest of us a bad name.

5. Kelley Blue Book, Edmunds, and NADA (National Automobile Dealers Association) all offer guides for car values. We're the experts who do this every day and can evaluate what a 2008 Honda Accord EX is really worth in our market.

6. Don't expect retail for your trade-in and wholesale for our car. We have to recondition your trade, advertise it, warranty it, and pay interest on the amount we have in the car, then sell it for less than we want after it sits on the lot for months.

7. To get a great price with minimal haggling, call and ask for the Internet manager or fleet manager.

8. Go in armed and educated. Study the pricing of the car you like and have your financing lined up. If you walk in with nothing, you're not a customer—you're a victim.

9. Never pay the VIN-etch fee. It's a $250 optional add-on that's almost pure profit for us. And if you want us to tint your windows, apply rustproofing, or paint a pinstripe on your truck, I'll probably charge you two or three times the cost of doing it elsewhere.

10. Forget the overall cost of the car. Let's talk about what you want to pay each month. Then I can build in profit generators such as extended warranties and credit insurance, and you won't even notice. Watch out for this!

11. Once you've agreed on a price, you think you're done—but we're just getting started. I'll promise you just about anything to get you to sign on the dotted line. But if I don't put it in writing, I may not remember the next day.

TOP SECRET! Once I'm sitting behind the desk, you'll feel like I'm in control and may be willing to pay a little more. (We learn this during training.)

12. Banks almost never require you to buy a particular warranty or a particular add-on to get the loan. If the finance officer tells you otherwise, ask to speak to someone at the bank.

13. If your auto credit score is under 600, expect to get an interest rate higher than 16 percent and to put 20 percent down. If your score is under 550, we may put a tracking device in your car that will shut it off if you don't make a payment.

SOURCES: Car dealers in Florida, Ohio, North Carolina, and New York; Sarah Lee Marks, a Las Vegas–based personal car buyer who sold cars for almost a decade; and Jeff Ostroff, president and CEO of carbuyingtips.com.

Be an Instant Expert

8 Easy Ways to Extend the Life of Your Car

1. **Do not race your car's engine during start-up.** This is a quick way to add years of wear to your engine, especially if it's cold outside.
2. **Accelerate slowly when you begin your drive.** The most wear to the engine and drive train occurs in the first 10 to 20 minutes of operation.
3. **Warming the engine by letting it idle in the driveway is not a smart idea.** The engine doesn't operate at its peak temperature, resulting in incomplete fuel combustion, soot deposits on cylinder walls, oil contamination, and ultimately damaged components.
4. **Put less strain on your engine and automatic transmission by shifting to neutral at red lights.** Otherwise, the engine is still working to push the car even while it's stopped.
5. **Avoid driving at high speeds and accelerating quickly,** especially when it's very hot or very cold outside. Such driving behavior will result in more frequent repairs.
6. **When turning your steering wheel,** don't hold it in an extreme right or left position for more than a few seconds. Doing so can damage the power-steering pump.
7. **Consolidate your short driving trips.** Most of the wear and tear—as well as the pollution your car generates—takes place in the first few minutes of driving. Doing several errands at once, during low-traffic hours if possible, will keep your engine happier longer.
8. **Don't fill up if you see the tanker.** If you happen to see a gasoline tanker filling the tanks at your local gas station, come back another day or go to a different station. As the station's underground tanks are being filled, the turbulence can stir up sediment. Sediment in your gas can clog fuel filters and fuel injectors, causing poor performance and possibly necessitating repairs.

WHAT YOUR GAS STATION DOESN'T WANT YOU TO KNOW

You can make fill-ups less frequent with these simple strategies.

1. Gas price increases usually take effect in late morning. Retailers also tend to raise prices on weekends, especially holiday weekends, so midweek is better.

2. Always park so that you can pull forward rather than waste gas backing up. This can improve your mileage by 25 percent (some experts say this number might even be underestimated)!

3. The speed limit also limits pump visits. The U.S. Department of Energy says that by following the speed limit and swearing off aggressive driving, drivers can improve mileage by anywhere from 12 to 55 percent. Edmunds.com found that using cruise control improved mileage by an additional 7 percent.

4. Modern cars don't become fully efficient until the engine is warmed up, so if you plan on running a series of errands, drive to the farthest location first and then work your way back—a series of short stop-and-start trips will never allow your car to reach maximum efficiency.

5. Rapid acceleration and hard braking, completely avoidable actions, just throw gas away. Instead of braking hard at a red light, coast from a distance. Come to stops slowly and gradually (if there is no one behind you, coast to the red light if you can).

6. Lace up your sneakers and get some exercise doing errands while you save gas. A bicycle can help you rack up car-free miles even faster. Or nix trips to the store altogether and do your errands online, including banking, buying stamps, and paying bills.

7. Banking your trips means fewer gas station stops. Need to pick up a prescription, mail a package, and go to the bank? Instead of spreading these tasks out over a few trips, do them all at once. Park in a central spot and walk from place to place.

> 🔒 **TOP SECRET!** Cutting out idling leads to mileage improvements of up to 19 percent. If you're going to be at a standstill for 10 or more seconds, it's better to cut the engine.

8. Extra driving time means wasted gas, so figure out where you're going before you leave. Use a GPS or a website like MapQuest.com to get exact directions. Try to avoid making left-hand turns where you will spend more time idling your car.

9. Check the air in your tires. The less air, the more difficult to drive.

10. A clean engine means fuel will be more efficient, so change your oil every 3,000 miles.

11. Car pools are a great way to save on time and gas. Instead of picking up your kids from school every day, ask a neighbor with kids in the same school to help. You can each take turns picking up the tykes.

12. Drive the small car. Do you own an SUV and a fuel-efficient sedan? Take the smaller car on any long trips you can.

13. For every 30 pounds of extra weight your car carries, miles per gallon decreases by anywhere from one-tenth to one-hundredth of a percent. That may not seem like much, but mile after mile it adds up.

Great Advice
3 TIPS TO KEEP YOUR CAR IN TOP CONDITION

1. **Lighten up your key chain.** Does your car key share a chain with a dozen or more other keys? That's a pretty heavy load hanging off the car key when it's in the ignition. The weight, combined with bouncing while you drive, can wear out the tumblers inside the ignition and eventually lead to ignition switch failure.

2. **Keep an auto log.** Keep a pad and pencil in the glove compartment, and use them to record your gas fill-ups and mileage. If you notice that your gas mileage worsens, mention it to your service person. It may be an early warning sign that something is wrong with your car.

3. **Top off your brake fluid.** Check brake fluid monthly. Wipe dirt from the master cylinder lid before you open it. If you need fluid, add the type recommended by your car's maker. Never substitute other fluids, such as transmission or power-steering fluid. And don't use brake fluid from a previously opened container. Once exposed to air, brake fluid absorbs moisture and contaminates easily.

WHAT YOUR CAR MECHANIC WON'T TELL YOU

Real mechanics have revealed the top 13 ways to avoid an auto-repair scam.

1. Watch out for scare tactics. Admonitions like "I wouldn't drive this another mile" should be viewed with suspicion.

2. Check their credentials. Look for ASE (National Institute for Automotive Service Excellence) or AAA (America Automobile Association) certification, as well as a state license. Reputable shops are proud to display them.

3. Ask, ask, ask. Get recommendations and find out years in business, warranties offered, licenses, and the type of equipment used. Look for a clean garage. A floor cluttered with empty oil cans, worn tires, and dirty rags is a red flag.

4. Never sign a blank authorization form. Always get a signed work order with a specific estimate for each job and warranties that apply.

5. It's nuts to take a car with engine problems to a shop without a good engine analyzer and scan tool. Any mechanic who says "I don't need fancy equipment" should be avoided.

6. When you go for a second opinion, don't tell the mechanic what the first diagnosis and price were.

7. **Coolant flushes and power steering flushes are very common gimmicks** at quick lubes. Check your owner's manual; many cars have fluid that is designed to go 100,000 miles. And cleaning fuel injectors is a waste of time and money. There are additives on the market that do a great job. Transmission flushes are another one of the biggest scams going. Manufacturers don't recommend them, and your car almost never needs one.

> 🔒 **TOP SECRET!** Don't bring your car in on Friday afternoon. The mechanics might rush the job to get out for the weekend.

8. **Always ask for OE (original equipment) brake pads** or at least equivalent material. A $49.95 brake job will usually get you the worst friction material you can buy—it's the difference between stopping short and causing a pileup on the way to work.

9. **The market is being flooded with cheap parts from China.** Request a name-brand replacement and ask to see its box. Then get your old parts back. This way you'll know they've been changed, and you can tell if they were worn out.

10. **Beware of a mechanic who shows you a transmission pan** with metal particles in it and recommends a major job. The shavings are usually a sign of normal wear.

11. **Know what your state's tread specifications are** before buying new tires. Then have the mechanic measure the old tread with a gauge. Ask about your new tire's "build date." If you're getting an unusually good deal, you might be receiving three-year-old treads, especially risky for snow tires.

12. **Lifetime mufflers?** What would ever make you think a muffler will last a lifetime? Yes, they'll give you free replacements, but they'll hit you over the head for expensive pipe repairs.

13. **Consult your dealer before you have work done** on a catalytic converter or emissions parts. Some of these items carry a very long warranty, and free replacement is often required by law.

SOURCES: Domenic DiSiena, manager, Bedford (New York) Shell; Gary Montesi, owner, Montesi Volkswagen, North Haven, Connecticut; Bob Sikorsky, automotive writer, Tucson, Arizona; anonymous mechanics in Minnesota and New York.

Be an Instant Expert

4 Tips to Keep Your Car Battery Running

1. **Aspirin.** If your car's battery has given up the ghost and there's no one around to give you a jump, you may be able to get your vehicle started by dropping two aspirin tablets into the battery itself. The aspirin's acetylsalicylic acid will combine with the battery's sulfuric acid to produce one last charge. Just be sure to drive to your nearest service station.

2. **Baking Soda.** Eliminate the corrosive buildup on your car's battery terminals. Scrub them clean using an old toothbrush and a mixture of 3 tablespoons of baking soda and 1 tablespoon of warm water. Wipe them off with a wet towel and dry with another towel. Once the terminals have completely dried, apply a bit of petroleum jelly around each terminal to deter future corrosive buildup.

3. **Epsom Salt.** Is your car battery starting to sound as if it won't turn over? Give your battery a little more life with this potion. Dissolve about an ounce of Epsom salt in warm water and add it to each battery cell.

4. **Soda.** Yes, it's true, the acidic properties of soda pop will help to eliminate corrosion from your car battery. Nearly all carbonated soft drinks contain carbonic acid, which helps to remove stains and dissolve rust deposits. Pour some soda over the battery terminals and let it sit. Remove the sticky residue with a wet sponge.

Who Knew?

WEIRD THINGS THAT WORK TO KEEP YOUR CAR CLEAN

Cooking spray removes brake dust. You know that fine black stuff that collects on the wheels of your car and is so hard to clean off? That's brake dust—it's produced every time you apply your brakes and the pads wear against the brake disks or cylinders. Next time you're shining your wheels, give them a light coating of cooking spray. The brake dust will wipe right off.

Mayonnaise takes road tar or pine sap off your car with ease. Slather some mayonnaise over the affected area, let it sit for several minutes, and wipe it away with a clean, soft rag.

Socks make a perfect hand mitt for buffing the wax on your car.

Vinegar removes bumper stickers. Saturate the top and sides of the sticker with undiluted distilled vinegar and wait 10 to 15 minutes for the vinegar to soak through. Then use an expired credit card to scrape it off. Use more vinegar to get rid of any remaining gluey residue.

Vinegar also keeps frost from forming. Wipe or spray the outsides of the windows with a solution of 3 parts white vinegar to 1 part water. Each coating may last up to several weeks.

Dryer sheets are great for picking up pet hair that's stuck to your upholstery. Take a used fabric softener sheet and swipe it across the fabric. Even tenacious hair will get sucked right off the material, and the sheet will even leave behind a clean scent.

WHAT YOUR CAR DETAILER WON'T TELL YOU

Keep your car looking brand-new—
inside and out—with these secrets.

1. Paint does more than make your vehicle look great. It's also the first line of defense against rusted body panels. The best way to protect the paint is to park the car in a garage. If that is not possible, park in the shade or purchase a car cover. The sun's ultraviolet rays break down paint and cause it to fade.

2. Touch-up paint won't adhere well to rust. So be sure to keep some matching touch-up paint on hand so you can touch up any minor nicks, often found around door edges and keyholes.

3. A cracked taillight or turn signal cover can be much more serious than it seems. If left alone, your light compartment could fill with water and cause some real damage. A good short-term fix is to tape over the crack. Use the red or orange tape that's available at auto parts stores and that's made for this.

4. Take your car to a windshield repair shop when the windshield has a rock chip, crack, or ding. For far less cost than replacing the windshield, they can fix chips and cracks, even quite long ones. The repairs not only keep the chips and cracks from spreading and restore structural integrity, but they also improve clarity.

5. **Cracked washer/de-icer fluid tanks are fairly common** once a car is of a certain age. Until you can buy a new tank or find one at the junkyard, insert a plastic freezer bag into the tank and fill it with the washer fluid.

6. **Protect your car's roof from scratches with an old blanket** before tying lumber, bicycles, or luggage to your roof rack.

7. **The beginning of the end for the finish on many cars and trucks is a poorly stowed load.** It's the same for wagon and hatchback interiors. Invest in the appropriate racks for bicycles, cargo, and luggage. To keep tall objects from sliding around in a pickup truck bed, use a shower curtain rod (or two) as a brace. Just push the cargo against the front wall of the truck bed and install the rod behind it. Twist to secure. Cargo nets will also help keep objects from banging around and damaging a truck bed.

8. **Wheel-well splashguards are often flimsy, but they're important.** They help keep water and winter's salty slush from splashing up into the engine compartment, where it can damage sensitive electrical components. Unfortunately, these guards tear off easily, so check for damage when you wash your car. Resecure with the appropriate fasteners or replace as needed.

> 🔒 **TOP SECRET!** Running your windshield washer system once you suspect there's no more fluid in the tank could damage the washer fluid pump.

9. **The fastest corrosion occurs when the temperature repeatedly rises above and then falls below freezing.** Washing is more important in the winter than any other time of the year. All that sand, slush, and ice mixed with road salt is exactly what makes your car rust—especially the undercarriage.

10. **New self-adhering urethane films have been developed** to protect the most vulnerable painted areas on your car from stone chips and other minor abrasions. You can wash and wax these surfaces, just as you would the rest of the paint job.

11. **Too much pressure will scratch the clear plastic lenses on your dashboard.** Use a soft damp cloth to lightly

wipe the dust off. Too many scratches can make it difficult to read your gauges under certain lighting conditions.

12. **Wipe a rubber protectant (such as Armor All)** or silicone on door and window weather stripping to keep it in good condition. Don't use an oil-based product, such as WD-40, because the oil will damage the rubber. Bad weather stripping should be fixed immediately.

13. **All manner of food bits and liquids can accumulate under a baby seat,** where they can permanently stain the upholstery. Place a sheet of heavy plastic and an absorbent towel under the seat to prevent damage, and resecure the seat according to the manufacturer's directions.

Be an Instant Expert
4 Tips for the Perfect Wax Job

* Liquid and spray waxes are tempting to use—they make the car shiny with less work than rubbing in paste wax. But there's still no beating paste wax for the hardest, longest-lasting finish. Look for paste with a high carnauba wax content.
* Apply a thin, even coat of wax to the car's surfaces with a damp sponge or sock. Avoid applying too much, or it will be difficult to remove and some residue will inevitably mar your finish.
* To avoid fine scratches, use a clean, soft cotton or microfiber cloth to remove wax once it has dried.
* Apply an extra coat of wax to the nose and hood. The wax film in these areas wears away quickly.

Great Advice
MAKE CAR TIRES LAST LONGER

Keep the caps on. You step out into driveway ready to start your morning commute only to discover a flat tire. How in the heck did that happen overnight? If the tire valve is missing its cap, the culprit might be a leaky valve. Those little caps keep out dirt and moisture that can cause leaks, so be sure to keep caps on all your tire valves. Another tip: When you replace tires, remind the tire shop that you expect new valves with the tires.

Maintain proper inflation. Under-inflated tires are a tire salesman's best friend. They create excessive heat and stress that can lead to tire failure. If you want to get every last mile out of your tires, get yourself a tire pressure gauge and use it at least once a month (more in hot weather) to keep your tires inflated to the recommendation in the vehicle's owner's manual. Check tires when they are cold (driven for less than one mile) for an accurate reading.

Beware the wet thumb. If you top off your tires at a service station, check to see if there's moisture coming from the air pump. Simply depress the pin inside the inflator valve with your thumbnail. If your thumb gets wet, advise the station manager that his tanks need to be drained and go to a different station. Moisture, trapped inside a tire, can cause pressure variations and corrode rims.

Check for uneven wear. Check tires for uneven wear. If you've maintained tire inflation properly, uneven wear may indicate the need for a wheel realignment. It can also mean improperly operating brakes or shocks, a bent wheel, internal tire damage, or worn bushings.

Check tread for safety. Most states require tires to be replaced when they have worn down to $\frac{1}{16}$-inch (1.5 mm) of remaining tire depth. Tires sold in North America are required to have "wear bars" molded into them to make it easy to see when tire replacement is legally required. However, if you'll be driving in the rain, you should change your tires when there is ⅛-inch (3 mm) of tread left. Otherwise, water may not escape from under your tires fast enough and you risk hydroplaning—a dangerous situation in which your car loses traction and literally floats on the water. Stick an American quarter between the treads in several places. If part of Washington's head is always covered, you have enough tread to drive in the rain. If you drive in snow, you'll need at least 3/16-inch (5 mm) of tread to get adequate traction. Stick an American penny between the treads. If the top of the Lincoln Memorial is always covered, you're ready for winter driving.

Rotate your tires. Rotating your tires helps to distribute tire wear evenly and ensures that you'll get the maximum road life out of them. The first rotation is especially important. Your owner's manual should specify both rotation period and pattern. If not, rotate your tires every 6,000 to 7,500 miles (9,700 to 12,000 km)—your tire dealer should know the correct pattern of tire rotation.

When temperatures affect tire inflation: When outside temperatures drop or soar, tires tend to lose pressure. A drop of 10°F (6°C), in fact, will decrease a tire's air pressure by 1 or 2 pounds. Tires can lose even more air in hot weather. Under-inflated tires can result in accelerated wear and poor driving performance. If you live in a place where temperatures vary a lot, check your tire pressure often and add air as needed.

WHAT YOUR HAIR STYLIST WON'T TELL YOU

After reading these secrets, you'll know exactly what to say, do, and tip in the salon to get a style you love.

1. I work hard to make you happy, and I want you to like it. After you leave my salon, I worry about what you think. (I work on people, not on cars on an assembly line.) And if you feel like calling to tell me how happy you are with my work, you will make me smile.

2. You represent me. So it's in my best interest for you to look good.

3. I'm a beautician, not a magician. I can give you Gisele Bündchen's haircut, but I can't give you her face.

4. Come at least five minutes early. If you're running late, please call ahead. Show me some basic respect. This is a business, not fun and games.

5. Don't ask me to squeeze you in. If I'm already booked, I'd be taking time and effort away from other clients. You wouldn't like being treated that way.

6. My work takes time. When a client says she's in a rush, I tell her she needs to schedule her time better. Keep in mind that trim is not "just a trim." It requires my expertise, skill, knowledge, and time. Would you say to your dentist, "It's just a tooth," or to your doctor, "It's just a leg"?

TOP SECRET! Kids' haircuts aren't child's play. Why do you think a child's haircut should cost less than yours? Kids don't sit still. Kids kick. It's an intense experience.

7. If you cancel at the very last minute, that's lost money to me. I can't fill that appointment with little or no notice.

8. We see women at their worst. Their hair is wet; they have foils on their hair; they have no makeup on. There's nothing for them to hide behind. So they tell us everything.

9. Layers are the magic remedy. Some women think that if they keep their hair all one length the way it was in high school, everyone will think they're still in high school. Guess what? You're not. As you get older, you need to soften the lines around your face.

10. Bodies and hair change as hormones change. If your hair is dry, listless, or brittle, or if it's not holding your color or style the way it used to, see a doctor. If your hair isn't overprocessed, you could be pregnant (surprise!) or menopausal (yes, I can tell).

11. A dollar bill doesn't buy anything anymore. For stylists, tips should be 15 to 20 percent of the total cost of your bill. They are a significant portion of my pay. If you stiff me, I'll remember. Salon owners who style hair do appreciate tips and want them. And that single bill you stuff into the shampoo person's hands isn't doing her any favors. Tip at least $3—more if your hair is long.

12. Take a picture. Some clients will say, "Cut my hair just like you did last time." That always baffles me. The average time between appointments is six to eight weeks. I have hundreds of clients. How am I supposed to remember exactly how I did your hair the last time? If you want a carbon copy of a cut and style you loved, take a picture and show me.

13. Spend a little money on the right products. Your hair wants to be healthy. Just help it a little. Let it do its thing.

Great Advice

6 WAYS TO GET GORGEOUS HAIR WITHOUT PRICEY PRODUCTS

As much as we might all wish for it, there is one basic truth about hair care: the wash-and-go cut, simple-and-easy hairdo is essentially a myth. To keep your hair looking good, you have to spend a little time on it. The good news is that you don't have to spend a lot of money.

1. **Wash, rinse, repeat—not!** Washing your hair twice in one session is an old marketing trick designed to make you use up your shampoo twice as fast. Double-shampooing strips all the natural oils out of your hair as effectively as paint thinner. Hair should never be "squeaky clean" because that's the same as "super-dry." In fact, one of our top experts, a partner and senior stylist at an upscale New York salon, recommends using shampoo on your hair not twice in one wash, but only every second wash.

2. **Use baking soda.** Your hair will look shinier and bouncier if you remove all traces of styling products and conditioner every six weeks or so. You don't need a clarifying shampoo. Just mix 1 tablespoon of baking soda with 2 tablespoons of white vinegar, work it into your hair, then rinse thoroughly.

3. **Timing is everything.** Don't use any clarifying product if you have just colored your hair, because it can remove some of the color. But it's a great idea to use a clarifying shampoo just before you color your hair. Removing all traces of buildup allows the hair to take the color much better, so the color will last longer.

4. **Sleep like a princess for rapunzel-like locks.** Your hairstyle rumples less if you sleep on a satin pillowcase. Cotton pillow covers (yes, even those 400 thread-count sheets) roughen the cuticle more; satin allows the hair to slip smoothly over the surface as you roll and turn in your sleep.

5. **Baby those tresses.** Don't pay premium prices for high-end shampoos that are specially formulated for colored or permed hair. An inexpensive bottle of baby shampoo will treat your hair just as gently and will also allow the color or perm to last much longer.

6. **Give it a natural shine.** To bring out your highlights, use an astringent rinse while washing your hair. For lighter-colored hair, combine ¼ cup of lemon juice with 1 cup of warm water and pour it over your hair. To bring out the highlights in darker hair, mix ¼ cup of white vinegar with 1 cup of warm water.

WHAT YOUR DRY CLEANER WON'T TELL YOU

These tips will let you take your clothes—but not your wallet—to the cleaners.

1. Lots of "dry" cleaning isn't. As much as 24 percent of garments are cleaned in water. Perspiration doesn't come out otherwise.

2. It's not your gender, it's your clothes. Women's clothes—silk, special trims, buttons, slacks without a crease—can take more work and cost more, too.

3. Yes, we use perchloroethylene (perc). It's a probable carcinogen, but it's the best thing we have right now. If you can smell it on your clothes, they weren't cleaned correctly.

> **TOP SECRET!** If a dry cleaner claims "all work done onsite," they're either lying or incompetent. Only ten to fifteen percent of dry cleaners have the equipment and expertise necessary to handle everything that comes in for cleaning.

4. Don't get too excited about so-called "organic" cleaning. Among the most common perc replacements is the petroleum-based solvent DF-2000, made by ExxonMobil. Because it's hydrocarbon-based, to a chemist—and almost no one else—it's considered an "organic" compound. The EPA cites risk of neurological damage and skin and eye irritation in workers using it, and since it doesn't clean as well as perc on its own, dry cleaners often end up adding pretreatment chemicals.

5. People never remember to pick up their comforters. That's why this place sometimes looks like a Bed Bath & Beyond.

6. You blame us for damage, we blame your clothes. Instead of court or the Better Business Bureau, we'll suggest the International Textile Analysis Laboratory, run by our trade association. It's independent (honest!), and both sides get a report.

7. Certifications aren't everything. The Drycleaning and Laundry Institute (DLI) offers certifications for dry cleaners who pass an official examination, including Certified Professional Dry Cleaner (CPD), Certified Professional Wetcleaner (CPW), and Certified Environmental Dry Cleaner (CED). Those who meet even more stringent requirements may also attain DLI's "Award of Excellence." While some kind of certification is better than none, it's not the ultimate arbiter of skill or knowledge.

8. Your lost clothes are probably in someone else's closet. We'd really prefer not to write you a check. And if we say we have to get in touch with our insurance company, we could be stalling, hoping the clothes will turn up.

9. Many of us will reuse your intact hangers. (Thanks.)

10. We're not raking it in. The machinery is expensive. The people who press your silk shirt get up to $20 an hour. It's a skill.

11. Things happen. We've heard stories about dry cleaners who borrow a customer's dress for a weekend.

12. Clean your leather before you need it. Better to bring it in during the spring or summer. Leather cleaning specialists do about half their business in three months in the fall so jobs brought in then will typically not get the same attention or may take longer to return.

13. Quality knows quality. The best clothing store in town can recommend the best dry cleaner in town.

SOURCES: Steve Boorstein a former dry cleaner who dispenses clothing care advice on his website, www.clothingdoctor.com; and Chuck Horst, president of Margaret's Cleaners in La Jolla, California.

Be an Instant Expert
Treat Household Stains with One Kitchen Ingredient: Vinegar

* **To eliminate a fresh grease spot on a suede jacket or skirt,** gently brush it with a soft toothbrush dipped in white vinegar. Let the spot air-dry, then brush with a suede brush. Repeat if necessary. You can also generally tone up suede items by lightly wiping them with a sponge dipped in vinegar.

* **Lift out many water-soluble stains**—including beer, orange and other fruit juices, black coffee or tea, and vomit—from your cotton-blend clothing by patting the spot with a cloth or towel moistened with undiluted white vinegar just before placing it in the wash. For large stains, you may want to soak the garment overnight in a solution of 3 parts vinegar to 1 part cold water before washing.

* **Older, set-in stains** will often come out in the wash after being pretreated with a solution of 3 tablespoons of white vinegar and 2 tablespoons of liquid detergent in 1 quart (1 liter) of warm water. Rub the solution into the stain, then blot it dry before washing.

* **Cola, hair dye, ketchup, and wine stains** on washable cotton blends should be treated as soon as possible (that is, within 24 hours). Sponge the area with undiluted vinegar and launder immediately afterward. For severe stains, add 1 to 2 cups of vinegar to the wash cycle, as well.
  Remove a rust stain from your cotton work clothes by moistening the spot with some full-strength vinegar and then rubbing in a bit of salt. If it's warm outdoors, let it dry in the sunlight (otherwise a sunny window will do), then toss it in the wash.

* **Remove deodorant stains** from your washable shirts and blouses by gently rubbing the spot with undiluted vinegar before laundering.

* **Get crayon marks off kids' clothes** by rubbing them with a recycled toothbrush soaked in undiluted vinegar before washing them.

WHAT YOUR COMPUTER TECH WON'T TELL YOU

Rebooting really works! Here are some other secrets that will help you be your own IT person—sometimes.

1. Turn it off, turn it back on. Nine times out of ten, rebooting your computer—and any equipment that connects to it—will solve the problem.

2. Check the cables. People are always shocked that a cable came loose. Of course, everything that needs power is plugged into an outlet, right?

3. Google will not solve everything. Google is an amazingly helpful tool where you can find most answers to your tech questions by searching yourself . . . BUT I know which solutions are true and which are not. I can do a Google search for something and weed out all the illegitimate answers and know which ones make sense, which ones work, and which ones will cause more problems. The average user can't do that.

4. Sometimes it's easier to accomplish certain things using home-based technology than the big corporate office technology. For example. Gmail vs. Microsoft Exchange. Gmail is simple and easy to use, while Exchange is super complicated.

5. Use "strong" passwords. Combine letters and numbers—but not your birth date—to create a "base" password, and add a unique suffix for each site you use. If your base password is your spouse's initials and your anniversary date (say, SP061789), your Amazon password might be "SP061789AM."

6. Make sure you have current antivirus and anti-spyware protection, and set it to update at least once a day and run a full-system scan at least once a week.

> 🔒 **TOP SECRET!** If you can't get online, call your Internet service provider first. Connection problems can often be checked and fixed for free.

7. There's no free lunch. Downloading free music, movies, and games from file-sharing sites can open holes in your system for others to exploit.

8. Remember: Public Wi-Fi is public. If you don't have a compelling reason to check your e-mail or bank account while sipping a latte at the mall, don't do it. While you're on a public network, a nearby hacker can capture your passwords.

9. Give it a rest. Turning off your computer when it's not in use saves energy and clears out the RAM, or temporary memory, which would otherwise slow your machine over time.

10. I can't make a four-year-old computer fast. Computers naturally slow down with age. Hard drives wear out and slow down. I'll try to fix it, but sometimes new is just better.

11. Keep it clean. On a PC, run Disk Cleanup and Disk Defragmenter at least once a month. After about four years, your computer is elderly. If you're shelling out for a blazing-fast Internet connection, pony up for a new model.

12. Got neighbors? If you do, protect your home wireless network with a password. If a person knows what he's doing, getting into a computer on a non-encrypted network is easy.

13. You backed up your data, right? External hard drives with lots of memory now sell for under $200, and automated programs like Cobian Backup or Apple's Time Machine make regular backups a no-brainer.

SOURCES: Derek Meister, Geek Squad; Aaron Schildkraut of myhometech.net; anonymous posters on TechRepublic.com; techcomedy.com.

Who Knew?
NATURAL WAYS TO CLEAN YOUR COMPUTER GEAR

Your computer, printer, fax machine, and other home office gear will work better if you keep them clean and dust-free. And vinegar may be your best cleaning solution. Before you start cleaning, make sure that all your equipment is shut off.

Mix equal parts white vinegar and water in a bucket.
Dampen a clean cloth in the solution—never use a spray bottle; you don't want to get liquid on the circuits inside—then squeeze it out as hard as you can, and start wiping. Keep a few cotton swabs on hand for getting to the buildups in tight spaces (like around the keys of your keyboard).

If you have a mouse with a removable tracking ball,
use a 50/50 vinegar-water solution to clean it. First, remove the ball from underneath the mouse by twisting off the cover over it. Use a cloth, dampened with the solution and wrung out, to wipe the ball clean and to remove fingerprints and dirt from the mouse itself. Then use a moistened cotton swab to clean out the gunk and debris from inside the ball chamber (let it dry a couple of hours before reinserting the ball).

WHAT YOUR BABY STORE WON'T TELL YOU

You really don't have to have all those products we want to sell you. Here's what you can live without.

1. You don't need a Diaper Genie. The idea of keeping a dirty diaper, compacted or not, in a kid's room for an extended period of time isn't terribly appealing. Just throw all the dirty diapers into the trash and take it out daily. The really stinky ones go straight to the outside garbage.

2. The Wee Block may be a better concept than a reality. The sales pitch: "Just cover baby before diapering, and let the soft, absorbent dome catch your little guy's geysers." The reality: Accidents still happen, and it's just another thing to constantly wash.

3. Use a pot of boiling water or the dishwasher instead of a counter-space-consuming bottle sanitizer.

4. And you can scrap the bottle warmer, too. If you're willing to wait a few extra minutes (the bottle warmer is supposed to be faster), that same pot of boiling water can be used to warm your baby's milk.

5. Hold baby wipes in your hands for a few seconds and you've done the job of a Wipe Warmer for free—and you've saved electricity, too.

6. **Baby powder smells great,** but doesn't seem to serve a big purpose. Plus, powders containing talc can be dangerous if inhaled.

TOP SECRET! Receiving blankets can be cumbersome. They're too big to be used as burp cloths and too small to swaddle the baby. If you have blankets and changing pads, these may just end up in the dresser drawer.

7. **Long-sleeved shirts are great stand-ins for mittens.** If your baby scratches himself, mittens are tempting. The trouble: Sometimes they barely stay on for more than 30 seconds. The better alternative: Long-sleeved shirts like the ones your baby wears in the hospital. The sleeves fold over your baby's hands.

8. **Nix the baby food processor.** If you already have a food processor, you really don't need another one just for your baby.

9. **A video baby monitor is not really a must.** The picture quality of these isn't great, and all you really need to do is hear your baby.

10. **Your child may be Einstein—but a DVD series won't help.** It's no surprise that watching Baby Einstein DVDs won't turn your child into a genius. She won't become a connoisseur of classical music or fine art either. Disney admitted as much when the company offered refunds on the videos and DVDs. Instead, try reading, singing, talking, and playing with your baby.

11. **Shopping cart covers are just another thing to carry around.** As germ-laden as shopping carts are, there's no evidence that a cover will protect your kid from getting sick. If you're worried about germs, like most of us are, wash your baby's hands often and use a baby wipe to clean your cart.

12. **Unless you are an incredibly organized person,** you probably won't have any use for a diaper caddy.

13. **A good diaper bag is worth it.** This will be your home-away-from home station for everything you need from bottles to wipes to medicine to toys. Oh, and diapers!

SOURCE: Dina El Nabli from ReadersDigest.com

5 SMART USES FOR BABY WIPE CONTAINERS

1. **Organize your stuff.** Fill washed and dried containers with everything from sewing supplies, recipe cards, coupons, and craft and office supplies to small tools, photos, receipts, and bills. Label the contents with a marker on masking tape, and you're set!

2. **Make a first-aid kit.** Gather up your own choice of essentials, such as bandages, sterile gauze rolls and pads, adhesive tape, scissors, and triple-antibiotic ointment, and use a rectangular baby wipes container to hold it all. Before you add your supplies, give the container a good washing—and rub the inside with alcohol on a cotton ball after it dries.

3. **Use as a decorative yarn or twine dispenser.** A clean cylindrical wipes container makes a perfect dispenser for a roll of yarn or twine. Simply remove the container's cover, insert the roll, and thread it through the slot in the lid, then reattach the cover. Paint or paper over the container to give it a more decorative look.

4. **Store your plastic shopping bags.** Do you save plastic shopping bags for lining the small wastebaskets (or perhaps for pooper-scooper duty)? If so, bring order to the puffed-up chaos they create by storing the bags in cleaned, rectangular wipes containers. Each container can hold 40 to 50 bags—once you squeeze the air out of them.

5. **Hold workshop towels or rags.** A used baby wipes container can be a welcome addition in the workshop for storing rags and paper towels—and to keep a steady supply on hand as needed. You can easily keep a full roll of detached paper towels or six or seven good-sized rags in each container.

WHAT YOUR TV SALESMAN WON'T TELL YOU

You can save big on your next TV purchase if you know when the sales are—and what the gimmicks are.

1. Buy your new TV in September or January. That's when the new models come out and the prices go way down on discontinued models. Another time to get a deal: Black Friday, if you're willing to brave the crowds.

2. Shoppers' questions boil down to this: LED, LCD, or plasma? LEDs and LCDs use the same technology, but LEDs are thinner and more expensive. LEDs can also be too reflective in a bright room. Plasmas offer the best picture for your money, especially if you're watching at an angle, but they're thicker than the others, and ghost images can be an issue.

3. Which brands do I recommend? For LCDs, LG, Panasonic, Samsung, and Sony have consistently been among the best in rankings by *Consumer Reports*. Among plasmas, Panasonic tops the list.

4. Our margins on TVs are so thin that they're almost nonexistent. The prices are designed to get you in the store, and then we try to sell you the expensive cords, accessories, and, of course, the extended warranty.

5. Don't spend a lot of money on a fancy HDMI cable. The one you can buy for $10 online is as good as the $100 one in the store.

6. Flat screens have beautiful pictures, but the sound from most is pretty awful. If you can't afford an expensive audio system, get external speakers

7. Want a great deal? Buy a refurbished set, a TV previously opened or returned. Check the warranty, though.

8. We've had customers put a tilt mount for a 50-inch television on the wall, miss a stud or two, and then have the thing come crashing down. These TVs weigh more than 100 pounds. Unless you're a licensed contractor, pay for the professional install.

> **TOP SECRET!** Thinner is not always better. If you're setting your TV on a piece of furniture, why are you paying a premium for the thinnest technology?

9. Televisions in the store are set at their brightest levels to attract your eye. Adjust yours when you get home or the colors will be distorted.

10. Don't expect your flat screen to be around forever. You'll be lucky if it lasts five years. Today's TVs are made to be replaced.

11. Always have your TV installed the day it's delivered. If it's out of our possession and it doesn't work when you turn it on, we may try to say that you caused the problem.

12. If you're connecting your TV to the Internet, think twice before you go wireless. Interference is still a big issue, especially if you live near an airport or another location with a lot of radios. To minimize headaches, hard-wire the TV to your modem.

13. A contrast ratio of 50,000 to 1 may sound impressive, but because every manufacturer measures it differently, it's really a meaningless number. And unless you're watching a lot of Blu-rays, you don't need a resolution of ultrafine 1080p.

SOURCES: David Davis of Davis Audio & Video in Chicago, Illinois; Dennis Sage, owner of Dennis Sage Home Entertainment in Phoenix, Arizona; a former TV salesman in Chicago, Illinois; and Consumer Reports.

Who Knew?
WHY ARE TV ADS SO LOUD?

We all have been knocked off the couch by a blaring commercial that came on right after a tender TV moment. How do advertisers always manage to break those sound barriers?

Advertisers like it noisy. Commercials crank every sound level to maximum volume in a bid to get your attention. "In commercials, everything is equally loud—the voices, the music, the sound effects," says Brian Cooley, editor-at-large at the technology review site cnet.com.

"The peak levels of commercials don't exceed the peak levels of programming," admits Spencer Critchley, a communications consultant in California. "But the experience is similar to having a spotlight shining in your eyes all the time versus a flashbulb go off every now and then." In other words, an entire commercial can be broadcast at the same level as an extra-loud (but fleeting) explosion on 24.

And contrast counts. If you're watching a tender moment unfold on a soap opera just before a raucous ad for a monster-truck rally, the spot will be startling—making an already loud commercial seem even louder.

To combat the problem, you can purchase a TV sound regulator for about $50. Unfortunately, many aren't compatible with HDTV or TiVo, but higher-tech relief is on the way. In Japan, some televisions now come with built-in technology that automatically balances sound levels, and the technology should appear stateside soon. For now, though, you'll have to strike a deal: Whoever wields the remote must also monitor the mute button.

WHAT YOUR SHOE SALESMAN WON'T TELL YOU

These secrets make shoe shopping—and wearing—far less painful for everyone.

1. I may be kneeling at your feet, but I'm not your servant. Lose the 'tude, dude.

2. No one cares how big your feet are. Don't ask for a size 7 if you're a 9 (though we all appreciate a little foot powder, if it's not too much trouble).

3. There's more to measuring than you think. Shoes should be as wide as your feet and longer than your feet. It's not just the distance from the heel to the end of the big toe that matters. It's also the distance from the heel to the ball of the foot.

4. Please don't try on two different sizes and slip one shoe from each size into the box you're buying without telling me. A lot of people have feet that are a half or whole size different. Let me know if you're one of them up front.

5. Don't try on sample shoes if they're not your size. People smash their feet into shoes that are three sizes too small, and then I have sample shoes that have been stretched.

6. Please don't keep me waiting for ten minutes while you talk on your cell phone. What if I did that to you?

7. If we don't have exactly what you want, it may not exist. And I can't cobble it together in the back room while you wait either.

8. Leather shoes will stretch, so keep that in mind when you're buying them. If they're a little too tight you can probably break them in, but if they're really tight, they're not the right shoes for you, no matter what we say when we're pitching them to you.

9. There's a name for the metal gauge that measures the width and length of your feet. It's called a Brannock Device. Tell your kids it should stay flat on the floor and not go hurtling through the air toward my head. Many thanks.

🔒 TOP SECRET! Take our word for it if we tell you that a shoe isn't a good fit. Customers have been known to try on a shoe that's too small, and then they can't get it off.

10. Don't be a serial shoe returner. Once or twice, okay. But ten or twenty times a year? I don't think so.

11. I've spent thirty minutes with you, and then you tell me you need to get your wife's approval? News flash: She doesn't need yours. Next time, bring her along.

12. You get what you pay for. A $20 shoe isn't going to feel— or last—like a $120 shoe.

13. Do you really want to borrow one of the store's footies to try on shoes? The ones in that box? The ones that everyone in town has used? The ones that haven't been washed since I started working here? (I didn't think so.)

SOURCES: Shoe salespeople in New York, Texas, Pennsylvania, and Georgia.

Great Advice

12 SNEAKY TRICKS SHOPPERS SHOULDN'T FALL FOR

There are a lot of scams out there, but there are also a lot of ways to save money at your local shops and service stores. Spotting—and avoiding—these tactics will help you find real values and stave off buyer's remorse.

1. **Don't fall for prices ending in 9, 99, or 95.** These so-called charm prices make us think they reflect good deals, author William Poundstone tells Sonya Sobieski of *Psychology Today*. We also tend to round them down, reading a price like $5.99 as $5, a phenomenon known as the left-digit effect. Poundstone—the author of *Priceless: The Myth of Fair Value (and How to Take Advantage of It)*—also notes that markdowns don't often include these magic numbers. That's because when the discount is easy to calculate, we think it's a better bargain. Thus "Originally $20, now $15" works better than "Originally $20, now $13.97." You'll be more tempted to go with the former, even though the latter saves you more.

2. **Steer clear of 99-cent stores.** Not only are they loaded with charm-priced items, obviously, but they have a profit margin twice that of Walmart, Poundstone reveals. One exception: if you live alone or have a small family, reports shopsmartmag. org. These stores often sell pint-size packages of food, allowing those who consume less to avoid waste.

3. **You can expect to pay a premium if you're a lazy shopper.** From Dairy Queen to Starbucks, many food retailers have begun selling mini-size treats at prices that hardly make them a good value, notes *USA Today*. They know that many people would rather be seen as virtuous—eating fewer calories than a normal portion contains—than thrifty and that they're

willing to spend more if they don't have to actually dole out those portions themselves.

4. **Note the missing dollar signs.** According to a Cornell University study quoted at cbsmoneywatch.com, diners spent much less when menus used the word dollars or the dollar sign than when only numerals were used to indicate price.

5. **Know you're being tracked.** If you use a store loyalty card, your buying habits are being recorded and often used to lure you to buy more. According to the *New York Times*, retailers these days are successfully tricking consumers into spending more by determining their spending "sweet spot," based on previous purchases. So three 12-packs of Pepsi are marked at $12.99 at Stop & Shop because the grocer knows you'll buy at that price, even if you don't need it.

6. **Understand how certain phrases are used by retailers.** "For a limited time only" creates a sense of urgency, Yale marketing professor Ravi Dhar tells mainstreet.com. And retail analyst Amy Noblin theorizes in *USA Today* that the come-on "Buy one, get one 50 percent off" incites more people to buy than if the sign reads simply "25 percent off everything."

7. **See per-customer limits for what they are: a ploy.** As Vicki Morwitz of New York University's Stern School of Business explains to cbsmoneywatch.com, "[People] think, 'Oh, this is scarce, I should buy this,' when it's probably not."

8. **Beware new packaging.** Check the ounces on that newly packaged bottle of your shampoo, and you may find you're paying the same for less, says Poundstone. One way manufacturers hide this? A big dimple in the bottom of the container.

9. **Watch out for bogus "bargains."** If a retailer displays a cut-rate model that's clearly inferior to the one he wants you to buy, he's trying to influence you, says Poundstone.

10. **Look at what's displayed with what.** Research has turned up some very specific data on product adjacency that retailers use to get you to buy more, writes Martin Lindstrom in his book, *Brandwashed: Tricks Companies Use to Manipulate Our Minds and Persuade Us to Buy*. If you see prepaid calling cards set up next to the coconuts, assume it's for a reason. One grocery chain found that buyers of the former tended to buy the latter (because people who cook with coconuts tend to be from Asia or the Caribbean).

11. **Don't try on clothes you don't need.** A shopper who stops to chat with a store employee and tries something on is twice as likely to buy as a shopper who does neither, Paco Underhill, author of *Why We Buy: The Science of Shopping*, tells time. com.

12. **If you're a guy, shop alone.** According to a *Journal of Marketing Research* study reported by money.com, a full 56 percent of men shell out more if they hit the mall with a friend as compared with women, 4 percent of whom actually racked up bigger receipts when going solo. That's because when men shop, they like to show off their knowledge and status via their purchases.

WHAT **YOUR FLORIST** WON'T TELL YOU

Want to know the secret ways to get the freshest, cheapest blooms—and make them last? Here they are!

1. Sure, you can order flowers at 3 a.m. from 1-800-Flowers, FTD, or Teleflora. But they'll charge you an extra $15 and then just call us.

2. If you want more flowers for your money, find a florist in your recipient's town and call him directly. But it's harder than you think: Some florists in the yellow pages and at the top of your Google search are national businesses masquerading as local ones. They even buy local phone numbers. So make sure you look for a physical address in town.

3. Most flower shops restock on Monday mornings, so that's the time to place an order. Fridays and Saturdays are good days to ask what's on special.

4. Ask for a discount. We give one to senior citizens, professional groups, and customers we like.

5. Those stay-fresh packets really work. Our smartest customers ask for a bunch of them. Most of us will gladly give you extras. Out of preservative? Try this: one part 7UP, three parts water, and two or three drops of bleach. Do not use copper pennies.

6. Put away those scissors, which can crush the stem. Instead, use a sharp, non-serrated knife to cut a quarter of an inch off the bottom of stems, at an angle. While you're at it, cut off those leaves below the water line. They breed bacteria.

7. Change the water at least every other day.

8. Don't forget to wash the vase with soap when you change the water. Otherwise, the bacteria clinging to the sides will contaminate your new water.

9. How fresh is your rose? Look closely at the bottom of the blossom and see how many outside petals have been removed. The more ripped petals you see, the older it is.

10. How about thinking outside the box? Lots of women would love a vase filled with red tulips still in the bulb for Valentine's Day.

11. That cheap glass vase that came with your bouquet? Most of us will gladly recycle it if you return it.

> **TOP SECRET!** We didn't choose February. If it were up to us, Valentine's Day would be in the summer, when roses are actually in season.

12. Looking for a way to jazz up your red roses? Try pairing them with purple statice or heather. Or ask us: "What can you put in that that will really make her roses stand out?"

13. Believe it or not, weddings are not that profitable for most of us. This is primarily due to labor costs. But we're banking on your future business. Once we do a wedding for you and do it right, you're a customer for life.

SOURCES: Russ Schmitt of Schmitt's Florist in Louisville, Kentucky; Sharon McGukin, author of *Flowers of the Heart: A Bride's Guide to Choosing Flowers for Her Wedding*; Larry Novak of Novak's Flower Shoppe in Maple Heights, Ohio; Tina Stoecker of Designs of The Times in West Melbourne, Florida; Bob Wollam of Wollam Gardens, a commercial cut-flower farm in Northern Virginia plus florists in Atlanta, Cleveland, Louisville, and Florida.

Be an Instant Expert
Get the Biggest Impact from Just a Few Blooms

When you know how to choose flowers wisely and strategically place them—thanks to these tips from interior and floral designer Rebecca Cole—you don't need a whole florist's shop full of them.

* Place bud vases in high traffic home areas—with even just a few flowers. Any decorative glass from the kitchen will do.
* The kitchen table might be the best place for flowers, because it's where people gather.
* A bud vase with a simple cluster of flowers hidden in the center of a clear bubble bowl filled with potpourri is the perfect way to create a welcoming atmosphere in a guest room.
* For a contemporary look, group several vases together holding just one or two stems. If you're using your own container, be creative! Use champagne glasses, china pieces, or other items that fit the décor of the room.
* Old water pitchers, antique teapots, classic urns, or even tattered clay pots make fascinating containers for a casually placed flower arrangement.
* For an easy, elegant table decoration, set a series of crystal vases on a fabric runner. Place fresh flowers in each of the vases and surround them with greenery.
* Float two or three blooms, such as open roses or gerbera daisies, in a favorite crystal bowl.
* Flowers have different life spans. Once some flowers begin to fade, remove them, and transfer the longer-lasting flowers to a smaller vase to place elsewhere in your home.

WHAT YOUR FUNERAL DIRECTOR WON'T TELL YOU

Here are more than a few money-saving secrets funeral directors aren't taking to the grave.

1. Go ahead and plan your funeral, but think twice before paying in advance. You risk losing everything if the funeral home goes out of business. Instead, keep your money in a pay-on-death account at your bank.

2. If you or your spouse is an honorably discharged veteran, burial is free at a Veterans Affairs National Cemetery. This includes the grave, vault, opening and closing, marker, and setting fee.

3. You can buy caskets that are just as nice as the ones in my showroom for thousands of dollars less online from Walmart, Costco, or straight from a manufacturer.

4. On a budget or concerned about the environment? Consider a rental casket.

5. Running a funeral home without a refrigerated holding room is like running a restaurant without a walk-in cooler. But many funeral homes don't offer one because they want you to pay for the more costly option: embalming. Most bodies can be presented very nicely without it if you have the viewing within a few days of death.

6. Some hard-sell phrases to be wary of: "Given your position in the community . . . ," "I'm sure you want what's best for your mother," and "Your mother had excellent taste. When she made arrangements for Aunt Nellie, this is what she chose."

7. "Protective" caskets with a rubber gasket? They don't stop decomposition. In fact, the moisture and gases they trap inside have caused caskets to explode.

8. If there's no low-cost casket in the display room, ask to see one anyway. Some funeral homes hide them in the basement or the boiler room.

TOP SECRET! If I try to sell you a package that I say will save you money, ask for the individual price list anyway. Our packages often include services you don't want or need.

9. Ask the crematory to return the ashes in a plain metal or plastic container—not a stamped temporary container. That's just a sleazy tactic to get you to purchase a more expensive urn.

10. Sure, you can store ashes in an urn or scatter them somewhere special, but nowadays you can also have them crushed into a real diamond, integrated into an underwater coral reef, or blasted into space.

11. Shop around. Prices at funeral homes vary wildly, with direct cremation costing $500 at one funeral home and $3,000 down the street. (Federal law requires that prices be provided over the phone.)

12. Yes, technically I am an undertaker or a mortician. But doesn't funeral director have a nicer ring to it?

13. Never trust a funeral director who says, "This is the last thing you can do for your loved one." Always bring another person with you, ideally someone who's not as emotionally attached to the deceased.

SOURCES: Funeral directors in Illinois, New Jersey, Tennessee, and Washington; funerals.org; and Joshua Slocum, executive director of the Funeral Consumers Alliance and coauthor of *Final Rights: Reclaiming the American Way of Death.*

Great Advice
WHAT YOU NEED TO KNOW BEFORE THE SERVICE

. . . .

These tips will ensure you know what is going on behind the scenes, so you can make sure your loved one will look his or her best at the service.

If the deceased's favorite outfit is a size too small or a size too big, it can still be used. Part of the funeral director's job is making the clothes lie perfectly.

If you provide a photograph of the deceased to help the funeral home prepare the body, don't bring in your favorite picture from decades ago. Give them something nice but current, so they can work realistically.

If you opt for cremations, pacemakers will have to be removed because the batteries damage crematories.

It's usually less expensive if the body is not present for the funeral. This is especially true if the funeral home would have to do restorative work for an open-casket ceremony.

WHAT YOUR JEWELER WON'T TELL YOU

Use these rock-solid tips to figure out if a gemstone deal is too good to be true.

1. Think you got a great deal on that beautiful ruby? It may not be real. A number of jewelers nationwide have been caught selling "composite rubies," which are as much as 40 to 50 percent glass, for almost the price of the real thing.

2. A sure sign of poor craftsmanship: rough edges on the back of the piece. If it's not finished underneath, they've probably cut corners somewhere else.

3. If your favorite color is blue, I'm going to try to sell you the most expensive stone in that color, probably a sapphire. But many other stones—including spinel, tanzanite, and tourmaline—also come in blue. You just have to know to ask.

4. Seek out jewelers who are credentialed by the American Gem Society (americangemsociety.org), which holds them to a high standard of knowledge and a code of ethics.

5. When you tell me, "I never take it off," I can't help but think, *That's disgusting.* To leave it on when you clean the house, lotion up your hands . . . yuck. You should take it off.

6. Please don't lick or spit on your finger to get your ring off and then hand it to me.

7. **If you're buying a diamond on a budget,** don't get stuck on the clarity grade. You can come down several clarity grades and in most cases will see absolutely no difference with the naked eye, especially once it's set in a piece of jewelry.

8. **Here's a word to watch for** on that diamond's certification report: laser. If your diamond has a high clarity grade, but under "Comments" it says "laser path" or "laser," that means a laser beam was used to get rid of a flaw, and it should cost 15 to 40 percent less than an untreated diamond of the same grade.

9. **If your jeweler tells you that none of his emeralds are treated** in any way, he's probably either ill informed or dishonest. Almost all emeralds today are treated.

10. **Clean your gems in warm water with** a mild liquid detergent and a toothbrush.

11. **Extended warranties from jewelry stores** typically aren't worth the money. If you have a rider on your homeowner's insurance for your ring and it's lost, damaged, or stolen, or if a stone falls out, your policy will usually cover it.

12. **The "60 or 70 percent off" sales you sometimes see?** Not possible. There just isn't enough margin in what we sell today that you can discount like that and run a business and pay your bills.

> **TOP SECRET!** For some extra shine on your diamonds (as long as they're not fracture filled), spray a little Windex on them, then wipe it off. That's actually what a lot of jewelers use, even the ones who sell expensive cleaner.

13. **We like to say,** "If you don't know your jewels, know your jeweler." It really does come down to trust.

Who Knew?
CREATIVE WAYS TO STORE YOUR JEWELRY

Avoid tangles and morning "where-is-it?" hassles with these solutions.

Egg cartons and ice-cube trays. The compartments of egg cartons and ice-cube trays are just the right size for keeping jewelry separated, organized, and visible. They are especially good for keeping pairs of earrings together; just line them up side by side in a drawer.

Padded coat hangers. Put necklaces and bracelets around the neck of the hanger, then use the padding to hold pierced earrings and pin-on brooches. You could color-code hangers to hold jewelry to go with a range of outfits.

A coat rack. Draping necklaces and bracelets from the hooks on a coat rack mounted on the wall next to your dressing table is a smart idea. For one thing, your baubles are there when you need them; for another, they can add a nice decorative touch to an expanse of bare wall.

Plastic pill organizers. Clean plastic pill bottles or organizers are a great solution for traveling. The compartments are small, see-through, and perfect for holding earrings, rings, brooches, and bracelets separately. No tangling and no rooting through everything to find what you want.

WHAT YOUR MOVIE THEATER MANAGER WON'T TELL YOU

Find out what theater employees know about the food they serve you, the quality of the equipment, and what's really under those seats.

1. It smells so good because the popcorn has chemicals in it to make its aroma fill the theater.

2. "Extreme Digital" is actually lower quality than IMAX digital. We use it because it's easier to maintain.

3. Of course we're making money on concessions. A large percentage of ticket sales goes right back to the movie studios, and that number is highest on opening day. Theaters rely on concession stands to make money. That's why concessions are overpriced. Popcorn costs almost nothing to make.

4. I know all the methods you use to sneak in. I just don't always care enough to kick you out for it.

5. The only foods I trust are the popcorn, drinks, and boxed candy. I wouldn't eat the pretzels, hot dogs, or nachos.

6. If you complain to the manager and he sides with you, chances are he's just putting on a show to calm you down. The manager might pretend to yell at me for a minute, but he'll pat me on the back the moment you're out of sight.

7. Think you're saving calories by ordering a small popcorn? That "small" popcorn could have been a medium last month.

8. Stop getting angry that your food isn't ready. Microwaves can't cook frozen pizzas in 30 seconds!

TOP SECRET! Combination deals don't save you money at some theaters. You'd pay the same price if you purchased the items separately.

9. No, I can't give you extra cups. Everything is inventoried at the end of the night.

10. Your suspicions are correct. Sometimes I sweep excess food under the seats. Movies often end every few minutes. Sometimes, three or more screenings end at the same time. I don't always have time to clean everything up.

11. Yes, movies start late. But they almost always end on time—otherwise, the ushers wouldn't know when to clean up. Theaters have you come in early so you have time to watch commercials and previews.

12. If you really hate sitting through previews, and you're going to a large theater chain, you can sit down about fifteen minutes after the listed start time and still see the opening credits.

13. Popcorn keeps for a day or two. Many customers confuse warm with fresh.

SOURCES: Movie theater employees in California, Illinois, and Indiana.

Who Knew?

7 CHEAP WAYS TO WATCH MOVIES—NO SNEAKING INTO THE THEATER NECESSARY!

1. **Set up a workplace DVD exchange.** Science has proven time and again that the honor system works. Keep things simple and free by designating an area of the office for people to exchange DVDs that would otherwise collect dust at home.

2. **Visit your public library.** Movies are free. Bonus: Most libraries also carry DVDs of entire TV series. Even better, having your library card account number on hand will most likely let you order films your library might not have shelved. You can basically create a queue this way, and it costs a lot less!

3. **Find a Red Box.** If you can return discs on time, Red Box (find a location at redbox.com/locations) charges only a little over a buck to see new releases.

4. **Look up free screenings.** Google's your best friend here. Look up local libraries and check their event listings. Lots of libraries show new releases to patrons and guests. If they don't, ask if they can.

5. **Use Free On Demand.** If you have On Demand and don't know about the free movies section, you've just scored access to a handful of movies to consider the next weekend it rains.

6. **Head to Hulu.com** Certain titles are free. Some fans have even canceled cable to watch all their favorites for free on this site.

7. **Visit Goodwill.** Take a trip to your local Goodwill and see what DVDs it's selling. We're betting the cost is far less than watching a Pay-Per-View flick.

Big Advice

THE GUERRILLA GUIDE TO GETTING GOOD CUSTOMER SERVICE

· ·

As costs balloon and paychecks shrink, customers are chasing value while merchants are chasing profits. Naturally there are some nasty collisions. But good service is, in the end, good business—and it's something both sides want.

Usually this means you need to weave your way through the automated labyrinth and talk to a real, live person. These strategies can get you there, but before you call you need to ask yourself two questions: *Do I have a valid complaint? Am I expecting a reasonable solution?* If the answer to both questions is yes, you can use the tactics here to get satisfaction for almost any transaction.

Before you Begin

1. **All valid complaints start the same way.** You expect one outcome but get another. It's just like algebra class: x dollars = y service. If you're getting ½y, then you should have to pay only ½x. Or perhaps they can throw in z, where z is something you feel equals ½y. It's a simple matter of balancing the equation.

2. **Just how much time should you spend on the problem?** Calculate your income as an hourly wage. If your time is worth $30 an hour, don't spend all day chasing down a $25 refund. Life is short. Hold times are long.

3. **You may have to give customer service more than one shot.** Concisely and calmly explain your problem. If the first rep is stuck on no, call back and get a different one.

13 THINGS THEY WON'T TELL YOU

How to Reach a Real Person

1. **Push zero repeatedly, say "operator" or "agent,"** or simply stay on the line until the end of the options.

2. **Gethuman.com** lists hundreds of companies and the phone shortcuts to quickly reach someone.

3. **Try the back door.** Call sales, investor relations, or the main corporate headquarters line.

4. **Select the Spanish-only option.** You'll likely get a bilingual operator faster than an English-only agent.

5. **Call from a friend's phone** instead of the one registered to your account. In some companies, potential new customers leapfrog to the top of the queue.

6. **Call the company's international customer-service** number collect. Its incentive for keeping you on hold will drop dramatically.

Tried-and-True Tips for When You Need to Escalate Your Tactics

1. **Dictate the Options**

   How to Do It: Begin the call by saying, "I have a situation that you are going to fix for me today." Clearly state in a sentence or two exactly what you want them to do for you. Have your options figured out. It may help to write them on an index card and keep it in front of you.

   Why It Works: You set the tone and expectations from the outset. You'll skip the "if" of helping you and get right to the "how." You'll save time, and not just for yourself. Many call centers work on commission and incentives. It's a high-stress environment. The faster the rep completes his calls, the bigger his bonuses.

   In the past, it wasn't unheard of for AOL reps to hang up on customers if they tried to cancel their accounts. One insider revealed he took stress medications until he got acclimated to the job and its pressures. He became one of AOL's top guys when it came to convincing people not to cancel their accounts. His reward? Thousands of dollars a month in bonuses and an annual all-expenses-paid trip to Mexico. Not surprisingly, an AOL spokesperson says, "It is not our policy for representatives to achieve time targets by hanging up on customers. Such behavior could result in termination."

2. Threaten to Cancel

How to Do It: Tell the company that unless it solves your problem, you're taking your business to a competitor. It's helpful to cite the other company's enticing promotional offers. A deal-sealing phrase? "Give me a reason to stick around."

Why It Works: One study shows that if a business hangs on to an extra 5 percent of its customers, profits increase an average of 44 percent. In contrast, the cost of replacing you is five times the cost of making you happy. Some companies even have a special division—the "retention department"—with specialists trained to convince you not to leave, even if they must dangle credits and freebies in front of you.

3. Call the Executive Suite

How to Do It: It's a little-known secret, but many large companies like Bank of America, US Airways, Verizon, and Best Buy have a firewall of high-ranking customer-service personnel surrounding the executive offices. To reach them, find the number for corporate headquarters and the name of a top-ranking executive. The CEO works nicely. Call the main operator and ask in your most professional voice to be transferred to his or her office. Once there, quickly pitch your case to the assistant, who will likely hand you over to an elite squadron equipped with customer-service superpowers.

Why It Works: The job of the executive customer-service team is to solve all problems in their path. They like to make customers happy. They also like to keep you from bothering busy executives, complaining to regulatory agencies, and blabbing to the local news.

4. Launch an E-Mail Carpet Bomb

How to Do It: Figure out the company's e-mail address format. It's usually something like firstname.lastname @ companyname.com. You can find sample e-mail addresses in company press releases and SEC filings (sec.gov). Next, find the names of a number of top executives, plug them into the formula, and blast your complaint letter to as many as you want. For a list of potential targets, check out the company at google.com/finance and look under Management. The About Us or Investor Relations sections of a company website are also good places to find a high-level executive roster.

Why It Works: A top executive understands he won't have a company if there are no customers. Perhaps he read the study in the *Journal of Marketing* that found the stock of companies scoring high on the American Customer Satisfaction Index outperforms the general market. Plus, he's a bigwig. If you can convince him your cause is just and he tells his people to fix your problem, it will get done.

5. Become a Town Crier

How to Do It: As a last resort, try typing up a one-page flyer telling your true tale of customer disservice. Make copies and take them with you to the store. Inform the manager that unless he gives you what you deserve, you will stand outside the store and distribute flyers to anyone and everyone who walks by.

Why It Works: Now that it has your money, a store can afford to lose your business. But what about the business of the next ten customers?

Warning

These techniques are recommended only for sane people who can speak in reasonable tones and treat strangers like humans. Threatening an individual may result in a visit from the police. Causing a company to lose money may result in a lawsuit. The right to free speech does not exist on private property and may have to be exercised just beyond the owner's property line, which usually extends from the edge of the store to where the sidewalk meets the asphalt.

And know this: One year, Sprint fired 1,000 "professional" customers (that's right—customers). Some had called customer service dozens of times over six months, begging for credits. "These were the customers who had nothing better to do but call us every single day demanding credit," one insider revealed. "And they were getting it because customer care was exhausted from arguing with them. At the end of the year, we were literally paying these customers to use our service." You want to stand up for your rights, but there is a limit. When you break it all down, these professional customers were probably spending more in "time dollars" than they got back in credits.

Part Six

WHAT YOU DON'T KNOW ABOUT
YOUR MONEY

Get rich quicker? Be a smarter saver? There are tons of tricks that will help you hold onto your money and even multiply it when you're on the insider track. Find out why your bank is pushing you to open new accounts and what to turn down when your cell phone sales rep is pressuring you. Arm yourself to outsmart identity thieves—which we've made easier to do by interviewing people who've been convicted for that very thing. Absorb all this advice, and you'll get more of what you never have enough of: time and money.

In this part, you'll discover everything from the secrets of debt collectors all the way to what rich people know about saving money. Finances will be a snap once you discover everything they do!

WHAT YOUR BANKER WON'T TELL YOU

What you don't know about your bank can result in extra fees, extra hassles, and less protection against identity theft. We got bankers to open the vault and share their secrets.

1. It takes us three days to post checks to your account. Just because you deposited a check today doesn't mean you can start living it up tomorrow. (And why should we hurry? If you bounce a check, we collect around $30.)

2. Call or visit in person to resolve a problem. Filling out online forms will usually get you the by-the-book reply, but with a rep, you can get practically any fee waived if you ask.

> **TOP SECRET!** Banks don't always promote the accounts that have the highest interest rates. Why tell you about those when you're already willing to sign up for an account that pays less?

3. Small business loans are hard to get. Unless you're Wolfgang Puck, our loan officers have pretty much decided before you walk in that you're not getting a loan for your dream bistro. But they'll let you apply for one anyway. We're not crazy about lending to nonprofits and houses of worship, either. We don't want the bad publicity when we go after them.

4. Our tellers routinely press you into opening new accounts. Their jobs depend on it. Banks hire "mystery" customers who secretly test whether a teller is cross-selling services.

5. There are times when we help you out. Many banks will permit you to withdraw more money than you have on deposit at the ATM, but they'll charge you about $34 for the privilege.

6. Postdating a check rarely works. With stacks to process, we don't look at dates. If the check bounces, you're liable.

7. Please don't haul in plastic bags of loose change. We really don't have the time or manpower to count it.

8. Keep receipts for every ATM transaction. And please don't feed cash directly into the machine without first putting it into an envelope unless you are sure the ATM can handle it.

9. We know you hate itemized penalties, such as a bounced-check fee, but don't leave money in your checking at the expense of your savings account. Personal-finance writer Jason Zweig says, "Banks make a ton of money off this mental quirk since they would have to pay interest on the money if we left it in our savings accounts."

10. A bank has the right to pay itself back. Any fees that you owe can be deducted from your next deposit.

11. Online banking is pretty safe. But it could be better, according to researchers at the University of Michigan. They found design flaws such as banks redirecting users to less-secure sites.

12. Your ATM card isn't as secure as your credit card. If you're using your ATM card for debit transactions, ask your bank what kind of protection it offers if the card is stolen or lost.

13. Don't swallow the poison. If a bank-issued credit card has a universal default clause, run for the nearest exit. It allows the bank to look through all your credit accounts, and if it sees that you're late paying a bill on another card, it gets to jack up the interest rate on its card.

SOURCES: David Bach, author of *Fight for Your Money*; Jean Ann Fox, director of financial services, Consumer Federation of America; Jason Zweig, author of *Your Money & Your Brain*; anonymous bank employees in New York, Ohio, and Texas.

Great Advice
5 COMMON MISTAKES PEOPLE MAKE WITH THEIR MONEY

Even the savviest of savers sometimes overlook ways to keep and protect more of what they earn each year. Here are a few common errors from money.cnn.com and *Money* magazine that you can steer clear of so you're not one of the clueless.

1. **Failing to Check Credit**

   Everyone is entitled to one free credit report a year from each of the three major bureaus (Experian, TransUnion, and Equifax), yet John Ulzheimer of smartcredit.com tells *Money* that only 4 percent of those reports are claimed. Discovering errors could prevent you from paying too much for a loan or being denied a credit card or even a job.

2. **Missing College Aid**

   According to Mark Kantrowitz, publisher of finaid.org, a lot of people don't realize that if they applied for financial aid and were denied it for their first child, they can reapply and perhaps qualify once their second is ready for college. Missing the boat for aid and scholarships is another common mistake—different schools have different deadlines. To make sure you leave nothing on the table, reapply for aid annually, and start researching scholarships in the fall before your child enters college.

3. **Avoiding a Trust**

   If you assume that trusts are only for the wealthy, you assume wrong. Even if you don't have millions to bequeath, you can benefit from a revocable living trust, which will save your heirs time and money by keeping your assets out of probate. Once your lawyer sets up a trust, don't forget to transfer title of assets into it, says Justin Fulton, a financial advisor with Signature in Norfolk, Virginia.

4. Skipping Tax Implications

Investment gains are great, but they'll be reduced by the amount of your tax bracket, so they should be managed carefully, says Frank Armstrong, CEO and founder of advisory firm Investor Solutions. You can also offset capital gains by reviewing your portfolio in the fall and dumping any losers before year's end. By selling them for less than you paid, you can then deduct the loss from your capital gains to lower your taxable earnings.

5. Investing with Insurance

Beware of buying cash-value life insurance policies for retirement funding. While the tax-deferred saving feature might be tempting, the steep fees can eat away at so much of your returns that it may make more sense to invest the money on your own, says insurance consultant Glenn Daily.

WHAT IDENTITY THIEVES DON'T WANT YOU TO KNOW

It's easier than you think to steal an identity. At least according to these real thieves who coughed up their secrets. Here's how it happens—but not to you.

1. Watch your back. In line at the grocery store, I'll hold my phone like I'm looking at the screen and snap your card as you're using it. Next thing you know, I'm ordering things online—on your dime.

2. That red flag tells the mail carrier—and me—that you have outgoing mail. And that can mean credit card numbers and checks I can reproduce. And if a bill doesn't show up when it's supposed to, don't breathe a sigh of relief. Start to wonder if your mail has been stolen. Stealing mail is easy. Sometimes, I act like I'm delivering flyers. Other times, I just stand there and riffle through it. If I don't look suspicious, your neighbors just think I'm a friend picking up your mail.

3. Check your bank and credit card balances at least once a week. I can do a lot of damage in the 30 days between statements.

4. If you see something that looks like it doesn't belong on the ATM or sticks out from the card slot, walk away. That's the skimmer I attached to capture your card information and

PIN. If you use the same ATM every time, you're a lot more likely to notice if something changes on the machine.

5. I use your credit cards all the time, and I never get asked for ID. A helpful hint: I'd never use a credit card with a picture on it.

6. Thanks for using your debit card instead of your credit card. Hackers are constantly breaking into retail databases, and debit cards give me direct access to your banking account.

> 🔒 **TOP SECRET!** How much is your information worth? I can buy stolen account information—your name, address, credit card number, and more—for $10 to $50 per account from hackers who advertise on more than a dozen black market websites.

7. Sometimes I pose as a salesman and go into a small office. After I make my pitch, I ask the secretary to make me a copy of something. Since most women leave their purses on the floor by their chairs, as soon as she leaves the room, I can grab her wallet. I also check the top and bottom right-hand drawers of their desks, where I often find company checks.

8. Even with all the new technology, most of us still steal your information the old-fashioned way: by swiping your wallet or purse (thanks for writing your PIN number on that little slip of paper in your wallet), going through your mail, or Dumpster diving. I can dig through Dumpsters in broad daylight, and if anyone asks (but no one does), I just say my girlfriend lost her ring or that I may have thrown my keys away by mistake.

9. That's me driving through your neighborhood at 3 a.m. on trash day. I fill my trunk with bags of garbage from different houses and sort later, because you throw away the darnedest things—preapproved credit card applications, old bills, expired credit cards, checking account deposit slips, and crumpled-up job or loan applications with all your personal information.

10. One time I was on the run and needed a new identity so I went through a hospital Dumpster and found a statement with a Puerto Rican Social Security number for a Manuel Rivera. For a good two years after that, I was Manuel Rivera. I had his name on my apartment, on my paychecks, and, of course, on my credit cards.

11. Why don't more of you call 888-5-OPTOUT to stop banks from sending you preapproved credit offers? You're making it way too easy for me.

12. Is your Social Security number on your driver's license or your checks, or is it your account number for your health insurance? Dumb move.

13. When I send out e-mails "phishing" for personal information by posing as a bank or online merchant, I often target AOL customers. They just seem less computer literate—and more likely (I hope) to fall for my schemes.

SOURCES: Former identity thieves in Kentucky, Florida, Indiana, Virginia, and New York.

Great Advice

4 ONLINE SCAMS AND
HOW TO AVOID THEM

1. **Free Trial Offer! (Just Pay Forever)**

   How it works: You see an Internet offer for a free one-month trial of some amazing product—often a teeth whitener or a weight-loss program. All you pay is $5.95 for shipping and handling.

   What's really going on: Buried in fine print are terms that obligate you to pay $79 to $99 a month in fees, forever.

   Stay away: Read the fine print on offers, and don't believe every testimonial. Reputable companies will allow you to cancel, but if you can't get out of a "contract," cancel your card immediately, then negotiate a refund; if that doesn't work, appeal to your credit card company.

2. **The Hot Spot Imposter (He's Close—Really Close!)**

   How it works: You're sitting in an airport or a coffee shop and you log into the local Wi-Fi zone. It could be free, or it could resemble a pay service like Boingo Wireless. You get connected, and everything seems fine.

   What's really going on: The site only looks legitimate. It's actually run by a nearby criminal from a laptop. If it's a "free" site, the crook is mining your computer for banking, credit card, and other password information. If it's a fake pay site, he gets your purchase payment, then sells your card number to other crooks.

   Stay away: Make sure you're not set up to automatically connect to nonpreferred networks. Before traveling, buy a $20 Visa or MasterCard gift card to purchase airport Wi-Fi access (enough for two days) so you won't broadcast your credit or debit card information. And don't do any banking or Internet shopping from public hot spots unless you're certain the network is secure. (Look for https in the URL, or check the lower right-hand corner of your browser for a small padlock icon.)

3. Your Computer Is Infected! (and We Can Help)

How it works: A window pops up about a legitimate-sounding antivirus software program like "Antivirus XP 2010" or "SecurityTool," alerting you that your machine has been infected with a dangerous bug. You're prompted to click on a link that will run a scan. Of course, the virus is found—and for a fee, typically about $50, the company promises to clean up your computer.

What's really going on: When you click on the link, the bogus company installs malware—malicious software—on your computer. No surprise, there will be no cleanup. But the thieves have your credit card number, you're out the money, and your computer is left on life support.

Stay away: If you get a pop-up virus warning, close the window without clicking on any links. Then run a full system scan using legitimate, updated antivirus software like free editions of AVG Anti-Virus or ThreatFire AntiVirus.

4. Dialing for Dollars (with a Ring of Fraud)

How it works: You get a text message on your cell phone from your bank or credit card issuer: There's been a problem, and you need to call right away with some account information. Or the message says you've won a gift certificate to a chain store—just call the toll-free number to get yours now.

What's really going on: The "bank" is a scammer hoping you'll reveal your account information. The gift certificate is equally bogus; when you call the number, you'll be told you need to subscribe to magazines or pay shipping fees to collect your prize. If you bite, you will have surrendered your credit card information to "black hat" marketers who will ring up phony charges.

Stay away: Real banks and stores might send you notices via text message (if you've signed up for the service), but they never ask for account information. If you're unsure, call the bank or store directly. You can also try the Better Business Bureau, or Google the phone number to see if any scam reports turn up.

WHAT YOUR FINANCIAL ADVISOR WON'T TELL YOU

Is your financial planner making money for you—or for himself?

1. Do some digging before you hand me the keys to your future. Use BrokerCheck at brokercheck.finra.org to see if I've been in trouble.

2. If I work on commission, I typically make money whenever you buy a new product, and I've probably got monthly quotas to meet. That's why I always seem to call with something to purchase at the end of the month.

3. You aren't qualified. Let's face it—you pay a carpenter to redo your kitchen. You pay a plumber to fix your toilet and a tutor to help your kid get into college. Yet when it comes to the most important area of your life—your financial future— suddenly you think you're qualified for a do-it-yourself project?

4. Certified financial planners and NAPFA-registered (National Association of Professional Financial Advisors) advisors take a pledge to put their clients' interests ahead of their own, but traditional stockbrokers aren't held to the same standard, even if they've given themselves the title "financial advisor."

5. Be careful with annuities. They pay me big commissions, but they're not a good fit for many clients. And stay away from investments that have a fee to get back out. If you get married, get divorced, change jobs, or move, it can come back to bite you.

6. There have been ten recessions since 1953. I have no clue where the market is going, and neither does anyone else. So if someone promises a certain amount of growth, walk away.

7. Some of us can give discounts, but you may not get one if you don't ask.

8. Haven't heard from me in a while? Not a good sign. I don't like to be the bearer of bad news.

TOP SECRET! If you ask me, "How are you getting paid?" and I say, "Don't worry about that. My company pays me," that's not a good sign.

9. Sure, I can help you buy 100 shares of IBM. But why pay me, when you can do it on E*Trade for less than you'd pay for a large pizza?

10. I am your inside source. If you're getting your stock tips from Jim Cramer's *Mad Money* and CNBC, you're waaaay late.

11. Paying off your mortgage may be a great idea. But I'd rather get paid to manage that money for you.

12. You're paying me for financial advice. Please come to me before you invest a bunch of money in something you don't understand. I had a client last year who put $80,000 in a currency trading investment that was supposed to pay him $4,000 a month. Of course it was a Ponzi scheme that stopped paying after three months. If he had asked me up front, I could have told him it wasn't legit.

13. Despite what you've read about Bernie Madoff, I am not going to steal your money. Frankly, you just don't have enough. If I were going to risk my entire career and life, you'd need to have $100 million, not $500,000.

SOURCES: Dana Anspach, principal, Wealth Management Solutions, Scottsdale, Arizona; John Gugle, CFP, Charlotte, North Carolina; Geoffrey Hakim, founder, Marin Capital Management, San Rafael, California; Terri Hickman, financial consultant, Grand Junction, Colorado; Jim Joseph, certified financial planner, Rockville, Maryland; Mark Stein, CFP, president, AeGIS Financial Advisors, Phoenix, Arizona.

Great Advice
6 THINGS THAT ARE NEVER WORTH THE MONEY

1. **Credit Card Payment Insurance**
   For a monthly fee, many credit card companies offer an optional insurance policy: They'll cover your payments if you become disabled or unemployed. Financial advisors explain that most of these programs are rife with complex rules and restrictions and recommend using the money you would have spent on insurance to pay down your balance instead.

2. **Premium Gas**
   You may think that filling your tank with premium rather than regular will help your car run better and longer, but according to *Car and Driver* magazine, you'd be wrong. A recent study by the magazine revealed that high-octane gasoline had no effect, except on ultra-high performance vehicles.

3. **Unlimited Cell-Phone Minutes**
   You may think you need a cell phone plan with unlimited minutes, so you have the freedom to talk as much as you like without incurring extra fees. But most people don't exceed the number of minutes offered in even the least expensive plans from most carriers (about 700 per month for a family plan). Check your usage amount on bills for the past several months before choosing a pricier plan.

4. **Automobile Service Warranties**
   The manufacturer warranty you get when you purchase or lease your car is legit. The one you're offered via a postcard in the mail, in all likelihood, is not. According to an investigation by the Better Business Bureau of St. Louis (home to several warranty companies), nearly $3 million in repairs that should have been covered according to contracts were not. What's more, more than 90 percent of those who purchased such insurance found the process to be "misleading or improper."

5. Bottled Water

Contrary to what most bottled water producers would like you to think, much of what they're bottling came straight from a tap rather than a spring or well. Using a water filter will give you similar results for a fraction of the price. It's also kinder to the planet—most plastic water bottles end up in landfills, rather than at recycling facilities.

6. Lottery Tickets

Yes, $10 million probably will make your life wonderful, but almost anything is more likely to happen than you winning the lottery. The chance of winning most big-ticket lottery jackpots is well over 100 million to one, according to Moneyland.

WHAT PEOPLE WITH MONEY WON'T TELL YOU

They might not be making more; they may just be saving more. We got their best insider tips on how to save smartly.

1. Many department managers at stores can cut the price of goods you want—if there's a defect or the price is higher than you planned to spend. When one shopper told a manager about her budget for a side-by-side refrigerator, he sold her the $1,400 model she wanted for $1,000.

2. Stores often place coupons in newspaper circulars and magazines you may not get to see. Ask the cashier if there's a coupon you missed and whether you can have the same discount.

3. Sales are usually held at the same time each year. Mark up a calendar so you know in advance when they're coming up. If you buy too early at full price, you may be able to bring back the merchandise and your receipt and get the discount.

4. Make friends with helpful salespeople by taking their business cards and stopping by to see them when you're shopping. Eventually they'll call you to tell you about upcoming sales and specials, or they'll hold items for you.

5. The bigger the cart, the more you buy. If you're going to the supermarket to buy one item, refrain from getting a basket. If you're only buying three items, get a basket, not a cart. When you venture into the store knowing you're going to have to carry your purchases up to the counter, you probably won't make impulse buys.

6. Discount card scanners sound like they're working, even when they're not. If your discount card is on your key chain, be careful when you hand it to the clerk if more than one store's discount card is attached to it. If the clerk scans the wrong card, the machine may still beep as if it's going to give you the discount—but it never does.

7. Buy wine from not-so-famous regions—like Paso Robles, California, instead of Napa—and choose lesser-known grape varieties. Wine from warmer climates, like Spain, will be cheaper because the grape harvests are more reliable there, keeping prices down.

8. From medicines to bleach to spices, hundreds of generic items are just like their higher-priced cousins, except for packaging and price. If you ever buy a name brand when there's a cheaper and identical generic substitute available, you're wasting cash.

9. Saving is as easy as typing what you're looking for into a deals search engine, and plenty of times, a coupon comes up. Shopping without taking a few seconds to do that is silly.

10. Form a neighborhood co-op and split the cost of things like lawn mowers, ladders, chainsaws, and other rarely used items with one or more neighbors. You'll reduce both your cost and clutter by at least 50 percent.

11. Stop paying for things you don't use. Do you pay for premium cable channels you never watch? Health clubs you rarely visit? Magazines you don't have time to read? Do you still really need your telephone landline? Really pay attention to where your money is going and see if there's something you can live without.

12. If you leave the house with only enough cash to buy what you're shopping for, you're automatically unable to succumb to impulse buys, which often bust your budget. We're more likely to overspend with pieces of plastic than real money.

13. For 30 days, promise yourself that you won't make a single big-ticket purchase without waiting a full day. If you still want it 24 hours later, then it's yours to buy. Whether your weakness is shoes, gadgets, or candy bars at noon, this rule can save you big bucks.

SOURCES: Renee Barnett, a mystery shopper in Tennessee; Stacy W. Johnson, CPA and author of *Life or Debt 2010*; Beth Kobliner, author of *Get a Financial Life: Personal Finance in Your Twenties and Thirties* and BethKobliner.com; Anne Obarski, author of *Surprising Secrets of Mystery Shoppers.*

Who Knew?

BUY IT ONCE, KEEP IT FOREVER

. . . .

These items may cost a little more up front, but if you spend good money on good products, you'll save a lot of money by not having to buy them over and over. Plus, they'll be a pleasure to have and use.

Cast-Iron Pan

On a new cast-iron pan, the surface should be uniformly dull gray inside and out and uniformly rough in texture with small grains or "pores." Avoid pans with seams, cracks, or uneven sharp edges. Buy one that is all one piece—not one with a wooden handle. Avoid a ridged bottom; a flat surface conducts heat best.

Kitchen Knife

If you buy a good chef's knife and care for it properly, you should never have to replace it. Avoid knives that have a serrated cutting edge or those that claim to "never need sharpening." Good knives do need sharpening. Buy one that you feel comfortable handling. Also buy a honing steel and use it regularly to keep your knife honed.

Hand Tools

Good quality hand tools should last not just one lifetime, but for a couple of generations. Look for forged rather than cast metal, and plastic, fiberglass, or metal handles rather than wood.

Albums

Look for a baby book, photo album, or scrapbook with pages made from dye-free, pH-balanced archival paper. Affix your photos and memorabilia with picture corners or small mounting squares. Avoid plastic sheets, sticky-backed pages, and don't use regular tape.

WHAT YOUR TAX ACCOUNTANT WON'T TELL YOU

Reduce your tax bill? We can do that.
Sometimes. But you need to read this first.

1. We see many disastrous returns prepared by ill-trained preparers. Shop experience, not price. You get what you pay for. Some companies put their newly hired preparers through a six-week, evenings-only tax course and then turn them loose to prepare returns with very little oversight. In other words, the person preparing your return might have been styling hair or selling appliances six weeks ago.

2. A box full of receipts pretty much horrifies us. Nothing is more frustrating than when clients show up with a stack of receipts and forms and say "prepare my tax return." Organize your tax items into something we can use—like a spreadsheet. At the very least, write everything down so we know what is included.

3. Keep track of your donations. People often lose out on non-cash charitable contributions. If you make several trips to your local Goodwill or Salvation Army in a given year, keep good records of these donations.

4. When it comes to an audit, hire your CPA to go with you, as opposed to going yourself. I've had a few clients who went to the audit themselves, and they're now facing a huge liability because the auditor found their documentation to be insufficient. If you go yourself, you're probably more vulnerable. You can even authorize your accountant to go on your behalf.

5. When in doubt, throw the receipt in the tax file, and we can discuss it.

6. If you're self-employed, you need to set aside big money for taxes so you're not slapped with a massive tax liability at the end of the year. Independent contractors should be setting aside money for taxes equal to 35 percent to 45 percent of your gross pay and should be paying quarterly estimated tax payments for federal and state taxes. The self-employment tax is computed at 15.3 percent of your net income.

7. Please don't try to bargain down our fees based on the fact that you or your business had a bad year. The time and effort it takes to complete a tax return does not change in relation to your annual income or loss.

8. You don't need to spend $200 on a CPA if your return isn't complex. By "isn't complex" we mean you receive a W-2, you receive a couple of 1099s, you don't work in multiple states, you have no partnership income or other flow-through income, and maybe you itemize. If you have just a few issues, those can be easily researched on the Web.

🔒 **TOP SECRET!** Better records often mean lower taxes. Use Mint.com or Quicken to track everything you spend, and you'll maximize your eligible deductions, thus reducing your taxable income, which will lead to less tax due.

9. But don't overestimate your abilities. If you have complex returns, trying to save by doing the return yourself may cost you more in the long run, through missed deductions or dealing with subsequent IRS tax notices about missed income or misapplied deductions.

10. Just because they say it is deductible on TV or the radio doesn't make it so. Nearly every deduction or tax credit has limitations, exemptions, and exceptions.

11. If you show up after April 10 asking us to prepare your return, in all likelihood, you'll be going on extension. We rarely drop what we're doing for just anyone. If you wait until the last minute and come unprepared, don't even bother asking for it to get finished by the deadline.

12. If you get an extension, you still have to pay now. If you cannot file your return by the April 15 tax-filing deadline, you can file for an automatic six-month extension. However, the extension only extends the time to file your returns—not to pay your taxes!

13. If you pay too much with your extension payment, you can have the excess refunded or applied to the following tax year.

SOURCES: Dennis Coomes, CPA, Kansas City, Missouri, coomescpa.com; Anil Melwani, CPA, New York, New York, armeltax.com; Caleb Newquist, CPA and editor of the accounting blog goingconcern.com.

Great Advice

4 HELPFUL TIPS FOR TAX TIME

Here's how to make at least one painful moment in life a little easier to take.

1. **Make No Mistake.** Every year the IRS sends thousands of notices to taxpayers nationwide because of easily preventable errors including these:

   * Social Security numbers—wrong number, no number, and misplaced digits could really ruin everything.

   * Despite the use of computers, math can still be a source for errors. Especially if you're adding numbers on the side and inputting only the total on the return.

   * If you're filing electronically, you'll be signing your return electronically, too. But if you're not filing electronically, make sure you sign that return.

   * If you're paying by check, make sure you sign that, too.

   * Make sure you're using the right form. Using a simple form like an EZ might be fast, but be sure you wouldn't get a bigger refund with a 1040A or 1040.

2. **Paying for a Pro? Use Them.** When you decide against do-it-yourself software and enlist the service of a pro, you may not be accomplishing much other than creating a bigger bill. If you're going to pay a pro, ask as many questions as you can about strategies to minimize your taxes and get enough sensible, specific, actionable advice to offset the additional cost.

3. Don't Agree to a Tax Refund Anticipation Loan.

Every year Americans take out loans on their tax refunds . . . and every year tax preparation companies rake in millions in interest and fees. Need your money fast? Use this simple system to get it: 1) File electronically, it's much faster than paper. 2) Use direct deposit. Combining those two things can get you your return within eight to fifteen days. If everybody did this, refund loans would be obsolete. If you're getting big refunds, amend your W-4 to have less withheld on your paychecks.

4. Start Early.

Every year some of us wait until December 24 to do our Christmas shopping or the day before our anniversary to rush out and get a gift. Even though we knew of the occasion well in advance, we procrastinate. While that may seem acceptable, traditional, even cute when it comes to shopping, don't adopt that attitude when it comes to taxes.

Waiting until the last minute and rushing through your taxes is more than just stressful. It's dumb. Because if you miss potential breaks and deductions due to haste, what you might waste is thousands of dollars. Start early, take your time, do a little research, and see how less taxing your life can be.

SOURCE: Stacy W. Johnson, CPA and financial expert.

WHAT YOUR CELL PHONE SALES REP WON'T TELL YOU

We got cell phone salespeople to spill the beans about how companies get you to pay more, so you don't ever have to overpay again.

1. Resist the temptation to get a new phone the moment your contract expires. Wait a few weeks, and we'll start dangling all sorts of discounts and incentives in front of you.

2. Always come in at the end of the month when we're scrambling to make our quotas.

3. Don't let us gouge you with our ridiculously high 411 fees. Use a free service like 800-FREE411 or 800-CALL411.

4. That phone advertised for $29? You'll have to pay $129 for it, then fill out a bunch of paperwork to get a $100 rebate mailed to you. We make money because many of you won't go through the hassle.

5. Leaving your phone in the bathroom while you take a steamy shower is almost as bad as dropping it in the bathtub.

6. We've got all sorts of discounts—some as big as 28 percent off your monthly bills—that we can offer to employees of large companies and government agencies, credit union members, and more.

7. Trust me: You do want all the accessories and the unlimited-texts package. I make a lot of money off those, so I'll be much more likely to give you a discount on your phone or service plan if you get them. Then, if you don't want them, bring back the accessories the next day and call to cancel the text package.

8. Want out of your contract? Tell us you're moving somewhere we don't have service. Most of us don't require proof.

9. Another way out: Watch your bill. If we raise your non-regulatory taxes and fees without notifying you, we have to let you out. Maybe we sent you a notification by mail, but you didn't open it, or there was a text message you didn't read. Raise enough stink, and we'll let you go.

10. Thanks for buying our fancy rhinestone case for $25. You can get the same one at a flea market for $5.

11. When you see those commercials on TV urging you to "text now!" to get a free ring tone or your daily horoscope, don't do it. You're almost always subscribing to a service with monthly fees ranging from $2.99 to $29.99. And we can't get you out of it.

> **TOP SECRET!** Are you way over on minutes or text messages? If the billing cycle hasn't closed yet, call us and upgrade to the next plan. It can mean the difference between paying a whopping 35 to 45 cents for each extra minute or $5 to $10 for the higher plan.

12. If your phone gets a lot of static and seems about to drop the call, don't hang up! We track dropped calls to identify and fix dead spots. If you hang up, we won't know there was a problem.

13. You don't have to be related to take advantage of a family plan. You can team up with a group of trustworthy friends to get one. As an added bonus, most networks have free in-network calling, so if you sign up with the people you talk to most, you'll never go over your minutes.

SOURCES: Cell phone salespeople in North Carolina, Mississippi, and Michigan; and Jeff Brown, a "digital lifestyle coach" in Nashville.

Great Advice

NEW TECHNOLOGY AND PHONE ETIQUETTE

· ·

These are the new rules for being polite in a world full of rude devices.

Long "@" conversations on Twitter bore other followers. Take them to Twitter's Direct Message (DM) or send an e-mail.

Don't use cell phones in a waiting room, checkout line, restaurant, train, or (heaven forbid!) bathroom stall.

When instant-messaging, always ask if now is a good time to chat.

It's OK to piggyback on a neighbor's free Wi-Fi as long as you don't hog it and realize it's not secure.

RSVP to legitimate online invitations promptly.

Things not to do when e-mailing: "shout" in all caps, use colored fonts or clip-art emoticons, attach large files, forward an e-mail (unless appropriate).

You can e-mail thank-yous for party invitations and birthday gifts given in person as long as you send each of them separately. (No cc's.) For mailed gifts, letters of recommendation, and wedding presents, a written note is still preferable.

Work e-mails can be sent anytime, but business texts should be restricted to one hour before the start of the workday to two hours after it ends, according to *The Modern Gentleman*.

It's OK (and even advisable) to follow your boss on Twitter, but you shouldn't try to friend him on Facebook. Friends implies equivalency; followers, not so.

WHAT YOUR SALES CLERK WON'T TELL YOU

Learn how to get a deal—and what guarantees that you won't get—at all your favorite retail stores.

1. Many retailers count the shoppers who come in, then calculate the percentage who actually buy something. If I don't "convert" enough browsers to buyers, I hear from my district manager.

2. New merchandise goes at the front of the store, bargains at the back. The endcaps on the backside of aisles at Target, for instance, usually have items 15 to 75 percent off. If you want a deal, try to figure out when your favorite retailer does its markdowns. Some do them on Thursdays or Fridays, others at the end of the month.

3. Plenty of stores have great prices on Black Friday. Even if mine isn't one of them, you still line up and wait for us to open.

4. After you buy something, keep your receipt and pay attention. Most mainstream retailers promise a refund if the item goes on sale within a certain number of days after you buy it.

5. With savings clubs, e-mail deals, coupons, Internet discount codes, and other incentives, fewer and fewer people are paying full price.

6. This is not a garage sale. I can't give you a lower price just because you haggle.

7. If you start to throw a fit in front of other customers because I won't take a return, I'll probably give in and offer your money back. But I really want to kick your tush.

8. Most shoplifters aren't the people you'd expect. They're great customers who come in all the time, buy a lot of stuff, and are really nice to you. I guess they're thinking, *I'm a good customer, I deserve a little something.*

9. Our store sends out a birthday coupon to customers on our mailing list. When people redeem it, I often say, "Happy Birthday" as they walk away. Sometimes the customer will say, "you too." I know it's because they aren't really listening, but that cracks me up.

10. Everything gets marked down eventually. Watch and wait for the discount, then pounce.

11. Some of us will tell you anything to make the sale. Especially if you haven't been nice.

TOP SECRET! Outlet stores likely sell special outlet merchandise, and it's not the deal you expect.

12. If I'm $200 from my sales goal and having a tough day, and you ask me if it's going to be cheaper tomorrow, I may lie.

13. If you want some extra attention or you need something special, call ahead and see if the store will let you make an appointment for a private visit. In a lot of stores, especially upscale ones, clerks are willing to open a little early or stay there a little late for a loyal customer.

SOURCES: Retail sales associates in North Carolina, Massachusetts, New Hampshire, Texas, and Florida, and a clerk in the Pacific Northwest who blogs at blametheclerk.blogspot.com.

Great Advice
14 WAYS TO DRESS FOR LESS

Follow these top tips from financial expert and CPA Stacy Johnson of MoneyTalksNews.com to save big on what you wear.

1. **Buy out of season:** shorts and bikinis in January, coats and sweaters in July.

2. **Always check a coupon search engine first before you shop.** Think of it as an instant savings dispenser attached to your computer.

3. **Find it cheaper in the boy's or men's department.** If you're a woman shopping in a department store for something unisex like a T-shirt or sweatshirt, you might be able to spend less by shopping in the men's section. Apparently the sexist pigs who price clothing believe women will pay more for comparable clothes than men. Call 'em on it.

4. **Don't overwash your clothes.** It wears them out faster. Avoid dry-cleaning if possible, and when you do wash your clothes, avoid dryers. That lint in your dryer screen is made of little pieces of your clothes that get rubbed off. Hanging them on a rack or clothesline is better for them and your electric bill.

5. **Develop a hang-up.** How many times have you had to wash otherwise unsoiled clothing just because you threw it in a wad on the floor?

6. **Learn to sew.** My mother wouldn't let me leave for college until I'd mastered simple stitchery, like button-sewing. Next time you're in a fancy hotel, take the sewing kit.

7. **Use a budget.** This is a tip that works for everything. If you plan what you're going to spend, you'll spend what you plan.

8. **Use cash.** Cash, along with budgets, are the ultimate way to avoid impulse buys. Remember all that stuff in your closet that you never wear? That's where it came from.

9. **Use a list.** This applies to everything you shop for and is also effective at preventing impulse buys.

10. **Swap with your friends.** Have a small party and ask everyone to bring stuff they're not wearing. What doesn't get taken can be given to charity. Besides, your friends are going to borrow your clothes and not return them anyway . . . might as well get something back.

11. **Buy outfits, not items.** It doesn't do you any good to buy a shirt that doesn't go with any of your pants. Plan ahead. Build a wardrobe around a few key things and make sure new additions build on that foundation.

12. **Don't buy clothes to change your mood.** Don't shop for the high, to build your self-esteem, or to fight off depression or boredom. The good feeling you get by buying new clothes (and most other things) is temporary, ineffective, and expensive. Physical solutions have no effect on emotional problems.

13. **Shop alone.** If you really need someone's input, fine. But be aware that friends, especially when combined with our own ego, often result in purchases that we might not otherwise make.

14. **Buy the right size.** This almost sounds too obvious to mention, but even I've done it: "It's a little too small, but that's OK because I'm about to lose a few pounds." Who am I kidding? If I'm really about to change sizes, what the heck am I doing shopping now?

WHAT YOUR DEBT COLLECTOR WON'T TELL YOU

Here are the hard-knock and straightforward strategies they use to get you to part with your money and pay up.

1. The more money I get out of you, the bigger my bonus will be. Every month, we watch top performers get bonus checks of $10,000 or more.

2. We also have an astounding power to wipe out thousands of dollars of your debt. Most accounts have a one-time settlement rate that's preapproved.

3. They teach us that all debtors are compulsive liars, and no matter what you tell us, we're supposed to keep pushing. So we ask, "Can you take money out of your 401(k)? Can you pay it with another credit card?" All are horrible ideas that would make a good financial planner cringe.

4. We've heard every tale of woe. We may listen and act sympathetic, but in our notes, all those excuses are summed up as *HLS*, for "hard-luck story." You're wasting our time, and time is money.

5. A lot of agencies buy debt for pennies on the dollar, so always start your settlement offer low, maybe 25 cents on the dollar. Say something like "I have $200 that I can apply toward this debt. Will you accept that as payment in full?"

6. Sometimes when we're negotiating, I'll say I have to get a manager involved, and then I'll have another collector be the "bad cop." The theory is that just having another voice on the line will open up your wallet.

> 🔒 **TOP SECRET!** We love calling you at work because of the extra pressure it puts on you. If you specifically ask us not to, by law we have to stop, but we're not going to tell you that.

7. Like us or not, we're a vital part of keeping the cash flow going in this country. In 2010, more than 10,000 collection agencies collected more than $8 billion.

8. Always check whether the debt has passed the statute of limitations in your state (see a list at creditcards.com). If it has, we can't sue you or put it in your credit report. However, if you make any kind of payment or even acknowledge the debt, that usually starts the clock over.

9. If you decide to settle, I am trained to "take your application." In a bored voice, I ask for your cell number, your spouse's work phone, and so on, as if I'm filling out a form. But it's just a way to get the information we need to find you in case the settlement falls through.

10. Many times when we leave a message on your phone, it's just a recording of a made-up person. Our office uses the name Jim Taylor. When you call back and ask for him, we say he's out to lunch and offer to help you instead.

11. Don't ask for a manager. He or she will not help you.

12. If you are having a really bad time with one collector, you're better off just calling back and getting another person on the line.

13. If I threaten to have you arrested, use profanity, or call before 8 a.m. or after 9 p.m., report me to your state attorney general's office and the Federal Trade Commission. Those are violations of the Fair Debt Collection Practices Act.

SOURCES: Michelle Dunn, former owner of a debt-collection agency and author of *The Guide to Getting Paid*; Fred Williams, who worked as a debt collector for three months to write *Fight Back Against Unfair Debt Collection Practices*; and debt collectors in Florida, New Jersey, and Pennsylvania.

Who Knew?

HOW TO TELL IF YOU'RE A SMART SPENDER

Concerned about how much you're spending, how much you should be saving, and how much house you can afford? Use these easy equations to determine how fiscally healthy you are.

1. **The price of your home** should not be more than 2.5 times your annual gross household income.

2. **Your total monthly debt payments** (including mortgage, student loans, car, and credit card payments) should not be more than 35 percent of your monthly gross income. Some mortgage brokers will stretch this ratio up to 40 percent, but that leaves you very little budgetary wiggle room.

3. **Your nest egg,** if you want to retire comfortably, should be about 20 times what you want your annual income to be. If you anticipate needing about $75,000 a year to live on when you retire, you'll need a nest egg of about $1.5 million. Of course, this will vary if you retire early or continue to work longer than usual.

Big Advice

SMART, SIMPLE WAYS TO SAVE MORE MONEY FOR LIFE

No matter what the market does, you should know how to shore up your resources so you won't have to worry about every little hiccup. Here are time-tested strategies you can master—how to spend less, reduce your debt, make the most of your tax breaks, invest wisely, and finance your retirement. The idea, says William Speciale, a Boston-based advisor with the financial planning firm Calibre, is to focus on what you can control: "Little steps can really make a huge difference."

Taxes

Forget the short form. Most taxpayers—65 percent of us, to be specific—just take the standard deduction. But you may save money by itemizing your deductible expenses. It doesn't matter if you use an online program, a current tax guide, or a storefront preparer. Out-of-pocket health care charges, business expenses (including some for job searches), and charitable donations are just a few of the items you may be able to deduct. Fill out the long form, known as the 1040, and compare numbers. If your total deductions are greater than the standard deduction, you'll save money by itemizing when you file.

Your kids should file a tax return. The IRS doesn't care how old they are. If they earn more than $5,450 in a given year (in wages and/or interest income), they have to file—even if you claim them as dependents. And if they make less than that, they should still file because they'll get back all the money their employer withheld. Help them fill out the paperwork. It's a great learning experience that may earn them some extra cash.

Avoid a tax refund. You may feel giddy knowing you'll get a check from the IRS this spring, but you shouldn't. Getting money back means you're essentially lending money, interest free, to the government for the year. Better to have that cash in your account than lend it to Uncle Sam. So if you've been getting big refunds or have had a big life change (a marriage, a baby, a divorce, a radical increase or decrease in income), adjust the withholding allowances on your W-4 form. You can do that at irs.gov. Use the withholding calculator to determine the correct figure for you. Then print a new W-4, fill it out, and give it to your payroll department.

Avoid "rapid refund" programs. Sure, they sound great. After all, what can be better than getting your money fast? A tax-prep chain might try to get you to agree to one of these "instant" or "anticipation" options. Don't take the bait. This is not your refund. It's a loan—and a very high-interest loan at that. Some have been higher than 120 percent. If you file electronically, even if it's through a tax chain, the IRS will deposit your refund directly into your bank account within a week or two.

Checking and Savings

Make sure your free checking is really free. A lot of banks advertise it, but read the fine print. If the minimum balance is steep—thousands of dollars, in some cases—look for a bank with no minimum requirement. This could save $100 a year or more. Bankrate.com is a good site for comparing accounts. (And don't waste $2 on ATM withdrawals at another bank's machines.)

Bank online. You'll be surprised how easy it is to pay bills, transfer funds, save automatically, and keep track of it all. In fact, gathering records at tax time will be a cinch. And by setting up the automatic bill-payment option, you'll help protect your credit score. Banking online is actually safer than banking at a brick-and-mortar institution. Banks have spent a fortune to make sure their sites are among the most secure on the Internet.

Keep your money in super-safe places. Aim to amass at least six months of emergency expenses, in case you lose your job or become disabled. Where's the best place to keep it?

FDIC-insured bank savings, CD, and money market accounts are still three of the most secure places. Money market funds that invest in Treasury bills are super-safe, too, but low yielding. Internet banks and credit unions tend to pay higher interest rates, but go to fdic.gov and check to make sure they offer the same government-insured guarantee. Look into Series I bonds, or I bonds, which are just as safe and are guaranteed to keep up with inflation. They're also free from state and local taxes (and possibly federal tax, if you use them for college costs). The downside? You can't redeem them for at least a year. And if you cash them in before five years, there's a small penalty. Other savings options, including corporate and tax-exempt money market funds, are a bit riskier. Compare yields at cranedata.us.

Debt

Cut up your extra credit cards. But don't close the accounts. Yes, it's smart to reduce your temptation to splurge by destroying your cards. But if you actually cancel them, it could hurt your credit rating. Here's why: Lenders worry about how close you are to using all the credit available to you. If you close an account, you lose its credit line. As a result, you are using a greater portion of the reduced amount you can now borrow. How many cards do you need? While the average American household has nine, two or three active cards should be plenty.

Pay your bills on time. A single late payment means that you could pay a much higher interest rate on any future loans and on your existing credit card accounts. That's because even one missed payment can lower your credit score by as much as 100 points. That plunge means that lenders view you as a risky customer. If you're shopping around for a mortgage, you could end up paying as much as a full percentage point more. That's an increase that could ultimately cost you tens of thousands of dollars in interest. Set up automatic payments to make sure you're never late on your major bills. The sooner you can show lenders you're back on track, the better.

Pay $10 more each month. Most American households keep their credit balances at around $2,000, but about 10 to 15 percent carry balances that are $9,000 or higher. If you paid the minimum $224 required on that $9,000 balance each month, it would take you 31 years and more than $13,000 in interest to pay it off. Increasing your payment by just $10 a month, to $234, until you've paid off the balance would save you $8,900. And you'd get rid of the debt in five years. (To check your own balances, try the calculator at bankrate.com.)

Put your savings to work. Many people who are deep in debt usually have some savings stashed in a bank account. They argue that they don't want to use their hard-earned savings to pay off debt. But do the math: It would make sense to keep the money in savings only if the bank is paying you an interest rate higher than the one your credit cards charge. Paying off a card with an interest rate of 13 percent is the equivalent of earning 13 percent interest on your money after taxes. There are no savings or investment options with that kind of guarantee. Experts caution that you still want to keep emergency cash on hand. A good rule is to take 5 percent of your paycheck to pay off debt and put an additional 5 percent into savings.

Pay more on your mortgage. You may have heard that because the interest is tax deductible, a mortgage is a good debt. But even if you're getting a tax break, you're still paying interest—and the longer you've had the mortgage, the smaller the tax break (because you pay less interest each year). As with all debt, paying it off sooner is better. So once you've paid off your credit cards and other high-rate debt, go ahead and add an extra payment each year (or spread it out over 12 months). If you do that over the life of a 30-year fixed loan with a rate of 6 percent, you'll shave roughly 20 percent off the total interest you pay. On a $150,000 mortgage, that means saving about $26,000.

Reduce your credit card interest rate. It may be time to get nervy with the credit card companies. If you pay your bill on time and your credit card company still raises your rates or lowers your limits, call the company's toll-free number (ask for the retention department) and explain that you're thinking of taking your business elsewhere. You may reap a rate reduction. And credit crunch or not, banks are still motivated to keep good customers. And check your accounts often. These days, banks are increasing rates even on good customers.

Get your credit report for free. You're entitled to one free report from each of the three credit bureaus (Experian, TransUnion, and Equifax) every year. Beware, though. Many sites advertising "free credit reports" are actually fronts for companies trying to sell you services—credit monitoring, debt consolidation, credit repair—most of which you don't need. The reports are free, but you'll be automatically signed up and billed for these products. Get your reports from annualcreditreport.com, which is sponsored by the three bureaus and the Federal Trade Commission. You can purchase extras on this site, too, but just stick with the free reports. If you want to see your credit scores (a numerical representation of how good a credit risk you are), you'll have to pay $48 at myfico.com.

Insurance

Shop around for car insurance. An online search and a few phone calls can turn up vastly different rates in the same area. You'll also want to ask about lesser-known breaks. For example, even if your kids are grown and out of the house, they might be able to get a substantial discount if they insure their cars through the company you use.

Sign up for an FSA. Many employers offer flexible spending accounts as a way to set aside part of your salary for health care and child-care costs. You can pay for everything from Band-Aids to orthodontic work with pretax money, which translates into a discount of about 30 percent or more, depending on your tax bracket. But plan carefully. If you don't use all the money in your account within the year (at many companies, you have until March 15 of the following year to submit receipts), you lose whatever's left.

Keep grown kids on your health insurance policy. If you're going to end up lending (or giving) your children money for coverage, it's much cheaper to keep them on your policy as long as possible. In some states, you can do this until they are 26, whether they're still in school or not. (New Jersey will give you until they turn 30.) Some states require proof that they are single, without children, and that they live in the same state as you. For the rules where you live, go to statecoverage.net. Even if your state doesn't mandate extended coverage, your plan might, so call your human resources department for details.

Hold off on that long-term-care insurance. The soaring cost of extended nursing care has prompted many people in their forties and fifties to sign up for long-term-care insurance in order to lock in a rate. It's true that the premiums go up as you get older, but not by the huge amount you might expect. According to data collected by America's Health Insurance Plans, a 65-year-old may end up paying just $126 more a year than someone who bought a policy at age 55. During those ten years, that person would spend close to $19,000 on coverage, even though he or she probably won't need it until age 83 or so (if at all). Depending on your health, the best time to buy is between 60 and 65. Until then, make retirement savings the priority, not long-term-care insurance.

Sign up for disability insurance. It helps protect your income in the event you become unable to work for a long period. Ideally, you should have enough to replace 60 to 70 percent of your salary. If your company plan doesn't provide this much coverage, consider buying more on your own. It can be costly, but it's worth it. Visit affordableinsuranceprotection.com or unum.com for quotes.

Think twice about life insurance. If you don't have dependents, you may not need it. If you do have kids or other dependents, you're probably better off with term life insurance until, say, your children are grown and can take care of themselves. It's generally less expensive than whole-life or other types of policies that build up value until you die or cash them in. Agents will tell you that whole-life insurance is a good investment because your money builds up tax-free, but these policies often have very high fees. You're better off putting that money toward your 401(k) and IRA instead. To comparison shop for term life policies, try term4sale.com.

Write your will. Although no one likes to think about dying, you need to. A will doesn't have to be a fancy contract that teams of lawyers slave over. It's just a written record of whom you want to entrust your kids and assets to when you die. You can write one using a simple boilerplate form and then sign it in the presence of witnesses (usually two people who aren't named in the will). You'll also want to make sure all the beneficiaries on your life insurance policies and bank and retirement accounts are up-to-date.

Investments

Stay away from individual stocks. In spite of what you may hear from your cousin the broker, buying the stock of a single company is generally not wise. It's essentially putting all your eggs in one basket—and paying broker fees that could eat up your earnings. In fact, you don't really need a broker. Instead of buying individual stocks, invest directly in mutual funds, which spread your dollars among a group of stocks. It's usually safer, cheaper, and simpler. But remember, you should do this only with money you can invest long term and can afford to lose in the short term.

Stick with index funds. You'll want to go with a special type of mutual fund called an index fund, which buys a little piece of each of the companies that make up established market benchmarks like the S&P 500. One of the best-kept secrets of investing is that in the long run, index funds perform at least as well as the funds that charge high fees and have a professional stock picker making the choices. For a list of low-cost index funds, go to vanguard.com or fidelity.com.

Don't buy investment products from your bank. Banks sell a wide range of mutual funds, annuities, and individual stocks and bonds. These aren't FDIC-insured, and they tend to be more expensive than what you could get elsewhere because banks usually charge high sales commissions. Buy directly from mutual fund companies instead. Go with companies like Vanguard or Fidelity, which charge low fees and no commissions.

Build a portfolio. The rule of thumb is to put 50 percent of your long-term savings in stocks and 30 percent in bonds and keep 20 percent available in cash (that means in a savings or money market account where you can withdraw it at a moment's notice). In tough times especially, getting the right mix will depend on the risk you're willing to take and how soon you'll need your money. Stocks are generally more risky than bonds, but there are exceptions. For example, bonds issued by companies that are in questionable financial health—called junk bonds or, more euphemistically, high-yield bonds—are a lot riskier than, say, stock in utility companies.

Retirement

Contribute to your company's 401(k). If your company matches funds, sign up. This will be the best investment you can possibly make. Typically, a company will kick in 50 cents for every dollar you save, up to 6 percent of your salary. That's the equivalent of earning an immediate 50 percent return—a rate you can't get anywhere. Yet incredibly, one in three American workers who are eligible isn't taking full advantage of it. With the matching funds, you can more than double the size of your 401(k) in 20 years, even if the stock market remains flat. For a family making $44,000, your contribution may cost you as little as $30 a week, money you won't even miss after a while.

Put retirement savings ahead of college savings. This sounds crazy to parents who need to come up with tuition money well before it's time to retire. But because of the tax breaks and the flexibility of retirement accounts, you're much better off contributing to a 401(k) or an IRA and taking out loans for college. Many people don't realize that the contributions you put in Roth IRAs can be withdrawn free of penalties at any time. That's very different from the college savings plans, called 529s, that smack you with a significant penalty if the money is not used for college. Another plus: Most schools don't count money in your retirement accounts when assessing how much financial aid they'll offer you.

Say no to company stock. Think of Lehman Brothers, Bear Stearns, and Enron. All were once on top, but when they went under, many employees were left without jobs and with retirement accounts that were overloaded with worthless company stock. You already have a huge stake in the company because you depend on it for your paycheck. Don't risk your retirement money as well. If your employer offers company stock as a

401(k) option, don't take it. If you get company stock as part of your matching-funds plan, sell it as soon as you're allowed to, and switch that money into some other type of investment. Ask your HR representative for details.

Don't worry about Social Security. You've probably heard the dire predictions that anyone younger than 35 can't expect to collect Social Security. Even in bleak economic scenarios, though, Social Security will probably pay you 65 to 80 percent of your currently promised benefits. And with some fairly modest changes—like raising the retirement age or increasing payroll taxes for anyone earning more than $250,000 annually—the system can be shored up for decades to come. Make sure you're saving enough so you don't have to count on the program for your entire retirement income.

Part Seven

WHAT YOU DON'T KNOW ABOUT
YOUR JOB

What takes you from wannabee to gainfully employed and moving up the ladder? We pulled back the curtain and got headhunters and HR professionals to reveal the best and worst of what they see (and believe us, they've seen it all). Your coworkers told us what you're doing to annoy them, and your company spilled about how people wrangle higher salaries.

From first impressions that get you hired to bad moves that get you fired, the pros get frank about where you stand at the office. It's not always where you think.

WHAT YOUR HEADHUNTER WON'T TELL YOU

Here's what they're really saying about your résumé.

1. You're considered pretty much unemployable once you've been unemployed more than six months. We assume that other people have already passed you over, so we don't want anything to do with you.

> **🔒 TOP SECRET!** Résumés don't need color to stand out. When I see a little color, I smirk. And when I see a ton of color, I cringe. And walking in and dropping off your résumé is no longer seen as a good thing. It's actually a little creepy.

2. Who you know really does matter. No matter how nice your résumé is or how great your experience may be, it's all about connections.

3. Often the best thing to do is to avoid HR entirely if you're trying to get a job at a specific company. Find someone at the company you know, or go straight to the hiring manager.

4. People assume someone's reading their cover letter. I haven't read one in 11 years.

5. We will judge you based on your e-mail address, especially if it's something inappropriate like kinkyboots101@hotmail.com or johnnylikestodrink@gmail.com.

6. Don't put the year you graduated on your résumé if you're in your fifties or sixties.

7. Children and hobbies do not belong on a résumé. And never, ever say, "Now that my kids are in college, I'm ready to get back in the workforce."

8. There's a myth out there that a résumé has to be one page. So people send their résumé in a two-point font. Nobody is going to read that.

9. I always read résumés from the bottom up. And I have no problem with a two-page résumé, but three pages is pushing it.

10. We get résumés on fancy schmantzy papers. We get them with gold-pressed lettering. We get them in binders and in document protectors with ribbons. None of that sways me.

11. I had somebody list their prison time as a job. And once an exotic dancer called herself a "customer service representative."

12. Most of us use applicant-tracking systems that scan résumés for key words. The secret to getting your résumé through the system is to pull key words directly from the job description and put them on. The more matches you have, the more likely your résumé will get seen by a real person.

13. About 98 percent of the résumés we receive when we post a position on a big jobs site like Monster or Careerbuilder are junk that come from people who are nowhere near qualified. That's why we like posting jobs on websites that target specific industries.

SOURCES: Chris Ferdinandi, HR professional in the Boston area; HR director at a financial services firm; HR director at a health-care facility; HR manager in St. Cloud, Minnesota; HR professional at a midsize firm in North Carolina; Rich DeMatteo, a recruiting consultant in Philadelphia, Pennsylvania; Sharlyn Lauby, HR consultant in Fort Lauderdale, Florida; Shauna Moerke, an HR administrator in Alabama who blogs at hrminion.com; Cynthia Shapiro, former human resources executive and author of *Corporate Confidential: 50 Secrets Your Company Doesn't Want You to Know*; Michael Slade, HR director at Eric Mower and Associates, an integrated marketing communications agency.

Great Advice

7 THINGS CAREER CHANGERS NEED ON THEIR RÉSUMÉS

1. **Broader Skills**

   Reanalyze your skills and include every area of the business that you've been able to impact, says Jill Smart, chief human resources officer at Accenture, a management consulting and technology firm. "People changing careers need to make sure their résumé shows the full breadth of their skills—operations, leadership, management, communication," explains Smart.

2. **Summary Paragraph**

   Experts' opinions are mixed on the need for a résumé summary or objective if you're staying in your field, but it's an important feature for a career changer, says Bonnie Marcus, a New York-based business coach and founder of Women's Success Coaching. In the summary paragraph, tie "everything in the job description with everything you've accomplished in the past," she says.

3. **Relatable Job Title Descriptions**

   Adding a short descriptor after the official job title can help hiring managers easily identify your transferable skills. "For example, if your job title was 'software engineer,' but you want to transition to project management, consider writing the job title as 'Software Engineer (with a heavy emphasis on Project Management),'" résumé writer Robyn Feldberg explains. But, she adds, "You only want to use this approach if you can do it honestly."

4. **A Mixed Format**

   When working with career switchers, Feldberg creates a functional-style résumé on the first page and includes the traditional chronological format on the second page. "In other words, the first page looks like a glorified profile," says Dallas-based Feldberg, who runs Abundant Success Coach, a career coaching and résumé writing service.

5. A Little Name Dropping

Showing that you've been able to succeed and work with established industry leaders in your previous career shouldn't be saved for the interview, says Theresa Szczurek, chief executive of Radish Systems, a Boulder-based software firm.

6. Non-Work Related Experience

Include activities that relate to your desired role, like professional association memberships, volunteering, internships, or part-time consulting.

7. Natural Alignments

"Look for things about your current position that would have meaning to the person considering you for the new position," says Luke Tanen, who left the music industry to work as the director of the Chicago Innovation Awards. For example, Tanen's mention of closing sponsorship deals was similarly impressive in both fields.

WHAT YOUR HIRING MANAGER WON'T TELL YOU

Avoid these top mistakes on your next job interview, and you'll be as good as hired!

1. It's amazing when people come in for an interview and say, "Can you tell me about your business?" Seriously, people. There's an Internet. Look it up.

2. A lot of managers don't want to hire people with young kids, and they use all sorts of tricks to find that out, illegally. One woman kept a picture of two really cute children on her desk even though she didn't have children (hoping job candidates would ask about them).

3. Is it harder to get the job if you're fat? Absolutely. Hiring managers make quick judgments based on stereotypes. They're just following George Clooney's character in *Up in the Air*, who said "I stereotype. It's faster."

4. I once had a hiring manager who refused to hire someone because the manager was worried that the car the applicant drove wasn't nice enough.

5. I've seen managers not hire a woman because the environment is mostly male, and they're worried that no matter how smart or talented she is, she won't fit in.

6. If you've got a weak handshake, I make a note of it.

7. Someone might tell you to "Be yourself" in the interview. Don't be yourself. That's the worst advice ever. We don't want people who are neurotic and quirky and whatever else. All we care about is your skill and experience.

8. I once had someone send me forget-me-not seeds with their thank-you note. Yes, thank me for taking the time, that's great. But sending me seeds? That's weird.

9. One time a candidate sent—I love this—a thank-you card with a professional picture of herself, which quite honestly became the running joke for weeks. The picture was blown up and posted in my office with hearts drawn around it.

10. Don't ever tell me that you have to have this job because you're going to lose your house, your kids have nothing to eat, your mother has cancer. Companies aren't a charity.

> **TOP SECRET! I know a lot more about you when you walk in the door than you realize. I'll search for you on the web and often use my own personal network to do a pre-interview reference check.**

11. In interviews, everyone works well with others, and everyone learns quickly. Please tell me something else.

12. If you're a candidate and the hiring manager spends 45 minutes talking about himself, the company, or his Harley, let him. He's going to come out of the interview saying you're a great candidate.

13. Don't just silence your phone for the interview. Turn it all the way off.

SOURCES: HR director at a financial services firm; Hr manager at a medical-equipment sales firm; HR professional at a midsize firm in North Carolina; HR manager in St. Cloud, Minnesota; HR professional in New York, New York; Senior HR Executive in New York City; Sharlyn Lauby, HR consultant in Fort Lauderdale, Florida; Suzanne Lucas, a former HR executive and the Evil HR Lady on bnet.com; Cynthia Shapiro, former human resources executive and author of *Corporate Confidential: 50 Secrets Your Company Doesn't Want You to Know*; Laurie Ruettimann, HR consultant and speaker in Raleigh, North Carolina.

Great Advice
THE COVER LETTER YOU SHOULDN'T USE

. . . .

Templates are useful as ways to know what should be in a cover letter. But don't use the template outright. Frank Risalvato, a recruiting officer for Inter-Regional Executive Search Inc., is deluged with cover letters from different candidates that all obviously use the same template from the same career coaches.

"Some of these [cover letters] we see are very obviously not written by the individual," says Risalvato. "We get fifteen to twenty of these a month, and it sounds disingenuous and insincere, seeing these cover letters from Seattle one week, Chicago another, and it's all the same style."

Some career experts also warn against the tired stand-by opening lines in a cover letter. "Opening a letter with a passive and clichéd statement such as 'Enclosed please find my résumé highlighting my experience and skills that would help your company to grow and succeed,'" is a no-no, says Ann Baehr, certified professional résumé writer and president of New York–based Best Résumés. "It's best to use something catchy and more specific such as, 'If your company could benefit from the expertise of a hard-charging sales producer with a flawless record of success . . .'"

If you're uncomfortable with that approach, make your cover letter unique to you with insights about the company you're applying to, advises Darrell Gurney, Los Angeles–based founder of career coaching site Careerguy.com and author of *Backdoor Job Search: Never Apply for a Job Again!* Prove you understand their business.

"Put in a note saying something like, 'I've been following your company's progress in the last year and in February and I noticed your company was mentioned in the Journal of such and such,'" Gurney says.

WHAT YOUR HR PERSON WON'T TELL YOU

The truth about who really gets hired—and who stays happily employed—may surprise you.

1. I have better things to do than deal with who slept with who, or who's talking about you behind your back. Sometimes I feel like a high school guidance counselor.

2. Even in jobs where you test applicants and those with the top scores are supposed to get the job, I've seen hiring managers fix scores to get the people they like.

3. I was asked by one CEO to hire the long-legged girl with the long dark hair even though she didn't have the right skills. Another time, I was instructed not to hire anyone with children because the company had too many people leaving for soccer games. That kind of thing happens all the time.

4. Networking does not mean using Facebook or LinkedIn. It means going to events, getting your face in front of people, and setting up informational interviews.

5. My LinkedIn profile is for myself, a way for me to find another job. It's not a way to find a job with me.

6. If it's been a week or two and I tell you "I don't have an update yet," that often means there's a better candidate we're talking to, but we can't tell you that in case they decide not to take the job.

7. If you call to check on the status of your résumé and I ask, "What job did you apply for?" and you don't know, you're done.

8. If we ask you to travel for your job or attend a conference, it's not really a question. Say no, and it can be career-ending.

9. When we had someone go out on disability and we knew he was faking it, we didn't want to go to court to prove it. So we put him on an assembly line in a job where we knew he wouldn't succeed. Eventually, we were able to fire him.

10. I know many of you met your spouse at the company. But the thing is, for every one of you, there are five people it doesn't work out as well for. And your office romance can and will be held against you.

11. Many people think, *If I work extra hard, I'm going to get noticed.* But it doesn't work that way. If you want to advance, some of the responsibility falls on you to toot your own horn. Make sure your supervisor and your supervisor's supervisor are well of aware of what you're contributing.

12. Don't stalk me. If you have a question, come to my office. Don't corner me in the bathroom.

13. You're right to be paranoid. The company is always watching you, and there's a record of everything you do: every phone call, every text, every tweet and instant message. At most companies, they save that data forever.

> 🔒 **TOP SECRET!** The number one thing in job security is your relationship with your boss. Even if he says, "I'm sorry I really wanted to keep you, but they made me lay you off," that's almost never true. He probably made that decision.

SOURCES: Kris Dunn, chief human resources officer at Atlanta-based Kinetix and who blogs at HRcapitalist.com; HR pro at a mid-level staffing firm; HR professional at a midsize firm in North Carolina; a human resources professional in New York, New York; HR representative at a Fortune 500 financial services firm; HR representative in the manufacturing industry; recruiting consultant Rich DeMatteo, Philadelphia, Pennsylvania; Laurie Ruettimann, HR consultant and speaker in Raleigh, North Carolina; Cynthia Shapiro, former human resource executive and author of *Corporate Confidential: 50 Secrets Your Company Doesn't Want You to Know*; Michael Slade, HR director at Eric Mower and Associates, an integrated marketing communications agency.

Who Knew?
SCARY BUT TRUE OFFICE ANTICS

Sometimes, you'd really rather not keep your job. *Please Fire Me*, by Jill Morris and Adam Chromy, collects dozens of hilarious vents from anonymous clock punchers forced to put up with various forms of crazy nine-to-five. Some doozies:

Last week a coworker asked me, "What day is Black History Month?"

Our HR girl overheard me describing the plot of *The Road* to a coworker, you know, the book about survivors of nuclear Armageddon who are being chased across a deserted America by anarchist cannibals. She asked, "Was that based on a true story?"

I just caught my old boss copying down my goals from last year's review and noting them as his own for this year.

My team leader took a digital picture of everyone's face and pasted it to an animal cutout. Now each employee is a different animal on the "productivity" board. Whoever does the most work each week gets one step closer to the piece of meat that person's animal likes to eat, which is glued to the other end of the poster. I'm the bison.

WHAT YOUR IT DEPARTMENT WON'T TELL YOU

Ever wonder what the computer whizzes really think about solving other people's problems all day long? Find out what it's like to be on call all the time and how you can rise to the top of their priority list.

1. Just because we're "buddies" at work, don't expect me to come running every time you've got a problem. I've got a slew of IT problems to fix.

2. We use the word "corruption" when we don't have a real answer. Occasionally, when trying to fix a problem, something goes wrong and some part of the system breaks or stops working, or more damage happens. I was helping a customer a couple weeks ago move e-mail over from one system to another and accidentally lost all of his calendar items. Of course I didn't tell him it was my fault.

3. It drives me crazy when you just ignore the work I've done to explain something. People will ask me how to do simple tasks that I have spent time documenting for them. Read the document. I'm taking screenshots and writing instructions to make things easier for you.

4. E-mail me. I would love to talk to you on the phone, but it's not efficient. E-mail me a list of your problems and questions, and it's a lot easier for me to respond to them all.

5. If you travel with your laptop, get a lock. One survey by the Computer Security Institute found that 50 percent of respondents had a laptop or other mobile device stolen in the past year. A simple cable lock (starting at about $20) lets you physically secure your laptop anywhere you go.

6. If your company owns the computer, they own what's on it, too—even your e-mail in some cases. Act accordingly.

7. You can't hide anything from us. Think trashing cookies and clearing your Web history are keeping you invisible? Think again. Everything still goes through my firewall, which sees all traffic when you connect to the Internet. It goes from your computer to a device that directs the traffic out. That's why we can use things like content filters that block sites like Facebook, YouTube, and pornography.

> **TOP SECRET!** Sometimes we talk about you—in code. If you hear "HKI error" (for human-keyboard interface) or "PEBCAK" (problem exists between chair and keyboard), we're insulting you.

8. Sometimes we're asked to get dirt on employees a company wants to fire. I was once asked to sniff out all of an employee's traffic and show what sites she went to and how much time she spent surfing.

9. You're right. Sometimes we make five-minute jobs last an hour.

10. If you don't understand me, I'm not doing my job. Confusing tech jargon is a sign of insecurity, not intelligence.

11. We're like Santa: We know if you've been bad or good. Fessing up to what really happened right before the system crashed is going to save time—and I'm going to figure it out anyway.

12. Urgency is based on priority. Just because you say your problem's urgent doesn't really mean it's urgent to me. Your e-mail not working is not as important as another customer's server being down.

13. We didn't create the problem; we're just trying to help you fix it.

Who Knew?

TOP IRRITATING PHRASES TO AVOID IN E-MAIL

When Lifehacker.com asked readers which e-mail phrases they'd like to see banished—or at least improved—they got a flood of responses. Here's a choice selection of the best:

1. **"We need to . . . "** Translation: "XYZ needs to be done, but . . . I'm not actually going to come out and directly tell any of you to do it."

2. **"Cheers"**—especially when used outside British pubs or the U.K. in general.

3. **"Thanks in advance"**—as opposed to thanks from the past?

4. **"Touch base."**

5. **"Circle back."**

6. **"To be honest."**

7. **The worst: "Please consider the environment before printing this e-mail."** I'll print it if I need to, whether you nag me or not!

WHAT YOUR COWORKERS WON'T TELL YOU

Are you hearing office snickers but don't know why? Here's how to guarantee they won't be about you.

1. Using a speakerphone at full volume to go through your voice mailbox is the definition of annoying. Don't use a speakerphone unless you're in your office and holding a meeting that's being attended by someone remotely.

2. Popping up and "prairie dogging" above someone's cubicle is just weird. Don't hold a conversation as a disembodied head.

3. Stop microwaving stinky foods in the lunchroom.

4. "Hello" is the word that greases many squeaky wheels. Get into the habit of smiling and greeting your colleagues. It's really amazing how fast this little courtesy can thaw chilly workplace relations.

5. Many helpful alliances are born at the office bowling league or softball games. These are great ways to get exercise while you get to know your coworkers in an informal setting.

6. Keep your cell phone out of the conversation. When talking to someone in person, don't glance down at your cell phone to see who's trying to reach you.

7. People love to be asked their opinion, so go out of your way to ask, "What do you think belongs in this report?" or "How do you think I should handle this situation with client X?"

8. Office gossip can stop with you. When a coworker sidles up to you bearing a juicy tidbit of gossip about Betty's office romance or Bill's impending firing, respond with, "Really?" and then change the subject or get back to work. If you don't respond, the gossiper will move on—and you'll retain the trust and respect of your colleagues.

9. If you're dealing with a difficult coworker, pretend your kids are watching. This neat little visualization will help you keep a cool head. After all, you've taught your children to be mannerly. With them "watching" you, it will be difficult to stoop to the level of your infuriating colleague.

10. You're saying "you're unimportant to me" if you ignore people's e-mails and phone messages. Return them promptly.

> 🔒 **TOP SECRET! If you want to** annoy people, make them read three paragraphs into your e-mail before you get to the point. If you want to rise in the company, state your purpose in the first sentence or two and then get to the why and how of the matter.

11. Make it clear that you would never ask anyone to do a level of work you wouldn't be willing to take on yourself. Always work at least as hard as anyone working with or for you.

12. When you don't end e-mails with a suggestion or a request for action, nothing is likely to happen. You might end with something like, "I will call you on Monday at 10 a.m. to discuss this" or "When can we get this done?"

13. Some companies are well managed; some are managed by idiots. On the outside chance executive management is not a bunch of idiots, did you ever think that maybe, just maybe, they know more than you do? Try a little experiment: If you experience an issue or two and it changes when you jump companies or groups, then you were probably in a dysfunctional workplace. But if it doesn't change, if it's always the same, then it's probably you. You might want to see somebody about that.

Great Advice

HOW TO RUN A MEETING PEOPLE WON'T DREAD

"If you had to identify, in one word, the reason the human race has not achieved, and never will achieve, its full potential, that word would be meetings." So said humorist Dave Barry, and many of us would agree. But it doesn't have to be this way. Some tips for having a good one:

Start and end strongly. Running a productive meeting isn't rocket science. As Denver-based consultant Teri Schwartz notes, much of it boils down to opening and conducting every meeting with a purpose and closing it with a plan for "going forward." Problems arise when people forget this. "It's like flying a plane," says Schwartz. "Most crashes happen at takeoff and landing."

Pick a leader. Four years ago, Cleveland's KeyCorp bank adopted a new principle: Always assign someone to lead. "The worst thing you can do is go into a meeting with no one in charge," says the bank's senior EVP and chief risk officer, Charles Hyle. "It turns into a shouting match."

Think small. Be realistic about what you can accomplish. "You can't solve world hunger in an hour," Schwartz says. By the same token, keep the number of attendees manageable to stimulate discussion. "When you have too many people in the room," says Hyle, "everyone clams up."

Direct, don't dominate. "People hate it when they can't get their work done because they have to go to somebody else's meeting," says Michael Feiner of Irving Place Capital. So encourage others to speak up and get involved, especially junior staffers. "They need to believe it's not his meeting or her meeting, but 'our' meeting," Feiner says.

WHAT YOUR PAYROLL MANAGER WON'T TELL YOU

Don't negotiate for a salary or raise without these insider tips.

1. There's one website that will drive you and the company crazy: salary.com. It supposedly lists average salaries but if you look up any job, the salary it gives you always seems to be $10,000 to $20,000 higher than it actually is.

2. On salary, some companies try to lock you in early. At the first interview, they'll tell the HR person to say, "The budget for this position is 40K to 45K. Is that acceptable to you?" If the candidate accepts, they'll know they've got him or her stuck.

3. You think you're all wonderful and deserve a higher salary, but here in HR, we know the truth. And the truth is, a lot of you aren't very good at your jobs, and you're definitely not as good as you think you are.

4. Be careful if a headhunter is negotiating for you. You may want extra time off and be willing to sacrifice salary, but he is negotiating hardest for what hits his commission.

5. I once hired someone, and her mother didn't think the salary we were offering was high enough, so she called me to negotiate. There are two problems with that: 1) I can't negotiate with someone who's not you. 2) It's your mother. Seriously,

I was like, "Did that woman's mother just call me, or was that my imagination?" I immediately withdrew the offer.

6. Never accept the job immediately. Think about it overnight. Once you sign on the dotted line there's no room for negotiation.

7. Some companies do everybody's raises on their anniversary dates. I'm not a fan of that because if the budget comes out in January, those poor people hired in December get, "Oh sorry, we'd like to give you more, but we gave a huge increase to Bob so you're just going to get 2 percent."

8. Yes, the HR person has access to everyone's salary, but, says one, "I don't look unless I have to. There's nothing worse than having to reprimand someone, and then seeing they make $60,000 more than me."

9. Unlimited sick days usually benefit the company. When people are told they have a set number of sick days, they end up taking them all because they don't want to lose a day off. If given unlimited sick days, they may take none at all.

10. Protocol is still important. When introducing people, name the person of greater status first: "Mrs. CEO, I'd like you to meet the mail guy, Ron."

11. Your group gets no respect. IT is always getting dumped on. Sales and marketing has it easy. Guess what? The other group probably feels the same way.

> **TOP SECRET!** If we ask "What salary are you looking for?" say you're flexible or it depends on the responsibilities of the job. Try not to name a salary unless it's required, because that gives us a leg up in the negotiating.

12. Being on time shows you respect other people's time. Being late over and over again will definitely get noticed.

13. If you're accused of sexual harassment, even if you're found to be not guilty, people will always look at you funny afterward. It can kill your career.

SOURCES: Ben Eubanks, HR professional in Alabama; HR director at a public relations agency; HR professional in New York, New York; HR professional at a midsize firm in North Carolina; Suzanne Lucas, a former HR executive and the Evil HR Lady on bnet.com.

Great Advice

THE BEST WAY TO ASK FOR A RAISE

1. **Do your homework.** Do some market research to determine what others in your industry currently earn at your position and poll your friends and colleagues in similar positions—as long as you work for different companies.

2. **Know your employer.** Many companies have official policies for discussing salary increases. If your employer offers salary reviews once a year, that's probably the best time for you to negotiate a raise. If the company's practices are more flexible, take the pulse of the financial situation of your department and the corporation as a whole when considering the timing of your discussion.

3. **Show them what you're worth.** Keep a journal, list, or spreadsheet of your daily tasks and accomplishments. Use this documentation as evidence to support your assertion that you're worthy of a salary increase.

4. **Have a number in mind.** Based on your industry research, your responsibilities, and your accomplishments, determine the salary you feel you deserve in advance of a meeting with your boss.

5. **Come prepared.** When you meet with your boss, be ready to back up your request with specifics about your performance and accomplishments, as well as goals for the future and additional responsibilities you're willing to take on. Keep the meeting professional and avoid discussing any personal reasons you feel you need a higher salary. Beware of using tactics such as a competitive job offer to get a raise—they may backfire on you.

WHAT PRODUCTIVITY EXPERTS WANT YOU TO KNOW

Your company's food service would love you to come in for a cookie or three when the afternoon slump hits, but there are better ways to perk back up.

1. Ten minutes outdoors is practically prescription-strength. When the slump hits, head outside and sit in the daylight for 10 minutes. Better still, have your lunch outside and divide your break between eating and a walk. It will help reset your biological clock, keep down the amount of melatonin (the sleep hormone) your body produces during this circadian dip, and give you a valuable boost of beneficial vitamin D, reducing your risk of osteoporosis, as well as various cancers.

2. A green salad sprinkled with low-fat cheese, a hard-boiled egg, and some sliced turkey wins over a pasta salad. Basically, protein will give you energy, while carbs may sap it. So a tuna salad without the bread is a better choice than a tuna sandwich. The change can really make a difference.

3. Teatime can soothe and energize. A mid-afternoon cup of tea is a good step toward beating the afternoon doldrums thanks to that little bit of a caffeine burst and the few quiet minutes it entails. Keep a selection of exotic flavored teas (preferably caffeinated) in your office and an aesthetically pleasing cup just for tea.

4. Your desk and e-mail inbox can pick you up—if you clean them out. Cleaning them out is a relatively mindless task that doesn't require great amounts of concentration or clear thinking, and both will leave you feeling more energized because you'll have accomplished something visible, as well as having reduced energy-sapping clutter.

5. Put a drop of peppermint oil in your hand and briskly rub your hands together, then rub them over your face (avoid your eyes). Peppermint is a known energy-enhancing scent.

6. You don't even have to leave your desk to gain energy. Simply roll your shoulders forward, then backward, timing each roll with a deep breath in and out. Repeat for 2 minutes.

> **TOP SECRET!** An "I was thinking of you" phone call works wonders. A five-minute keep-in-touch call to your wife, child, siblings, parents, a friend, or a retired colleague will lift your spirits for hours and reinvigorate you to get your work done.

7. Consider a morsel of dark chocolate. Unlike milk chocolate, dark chocolate is truly a healthy food, closer to the category of nuts than sweets given the high levels of healthy fat and antioxidants it contains. Plus, it has abundant fiber and magnesium. Additionally, it provides a little caffeine, as well as a satisfyingly decadent feeling. Just stop at one square.

8. Chewing gums with strong minty flavors are stimulating, and the mere act of chewing is something of a tonic to a brain succumbing to lethargy. Plus, chewing stimulates saliva, which helps to clear out bacteria responsible for cavities and gum disease from lunch. Just be sure to choose sugar-free gum.

9. If you often work on your own, try to organize work involving others at the time of day when your concentration might otherwise be waning. We are social animals, and interactions always rev us up. But make sure it's an interesting, interactive activity. Sitting in a room listening to someone else drone on and on will just send you snoozing.

10. You can get your blood moving and feel more energized even in a meeting. Isometric exercises involve nothing more than tensing a muscle and holding it. For instance, with your arm held out, tense your biceps and triceps at the same time and hold for 5 to 10 seconds. You can do this with your calf muscles, thigh muscles (front and back), chest, abdomen, buttocks, shoulders, and back.

11. Not only will sharing your space with a plant—a live, growing thing—provide its own mood boost, but also studies find the scent of rosemary to be energizing. Whenever you need a boost, just rub a sprig between your fingers to release the fragrance. Or, if you're really wiped out, rub a sprig on your hands, face, and neck.

12. Have an afternoon snack designed to get the blood flowing. That's one that combines protein, fiber, and complex carbohydrates (such as whole-grain crackers or raw vegetables) to raise your blood sugar levels steadily and keep them up.

13. Keeping manageable items on your to-do list will keep you motivated. Checking off tasks you've completed makes you feel productive and ready for the next job. Be sure to keep routine items that you are always accomplishing on your list so you can have the satisfaction of checking them off.

Great Advice

7 WAYS TO FEND OFF WORKPLACE STRESS

1. **Take breaks throughout the day.** It will help clear your mind and relieve pressure. Something as simple as going to the water cooler for a drink may do the trick.

2. **Enroll in a noontime or an after-work exercise class.** This will give you a chance to unwind, which helps relieve stress.

3. **To help your workday go smoothly, try pacing your activities:** Do more demanding work in the morning, when your energy level is higher, and leave the easier work for later in the day.

4. **Try listening to white noise recordings,** such as a pounding surf or songbirds, to help you relax.

5. **Get to work early or stay late once a week.** You may be able to accomplish more when you vary your routine.

6. **If your stress comes from job insecurity, take stock of yourself.** Update your résumé, and remind yourself of your skills and strengths. Also, make sure you keep up with new developments in your field. This will make you valuable to employers.

7. **Don't let work rumors, which are usually false, cause you worry.** A coworker may just be thinking out loud about worst-case scenarios.

WHAT THE **COMPANY NURSE** WANTS YOU TO KNOW

Here are some great—and easy—ways to stay healthy and happy while on the job so you don't find yourself becoming a regular in the nurse's office.

1. Breathe easily. "Breathing from your diaphragm oxygenates your blood, which helps you relax almost instantly," says Robert Cooper, PhD, the San Francisco coauthor of *The Power of 5*, a book of five-second and five-minute health tips. Shallow chest breathing, by contrast, can cause your heart to beat faster and your muscles to tense up, exacerbating feelings of stress.

2. How do you know if you're truly breathing deeply? Place your hand on your abdomen just below the navel. Inhale slowly through your nose and watch your hand move out as your belly expands. Hold the breath for a few seconds, then exhale slowly. Repeat several times.

3. Say cheese. Smiling is a two-way mechanism. We do it when we're relaxed and happy, but doing it can also make us feel relaxed and happy. "Smiling transmits nerve impulses from the facial muscles to the limbic system, a key emotional center in the brain, tilting the neurochemical balance toward calm," Dr. Cooper explains. Go ahead and grin. Don't you feel better already?

4. Stop gritting your teeth. Stress tends to settle in certain parts of our bodies, the jaw being one of them. When things get hectic, try this tip from Dr. Cooper: Place your index fingertips on your jaw joints, just in front of your ears; clench your teeth and inhale deeply. Hold the breath for a moment, and as you exhale say, "Ah-h-h-h," then unclench your teeth. Repeat a few times.

5. Soothe your eyes. Rub your hands together vigorously until they feel warm, recommends David Sobel, MD, of San Jose, California, author of *The Healthy Mind, Healthy Body Handbook*. Then cup them over your closed eyes for five seconds while you breathe deeply. The warmth and darkness are comforting.

6. Switch to decaf. Wean yourself slowly, or you might get a caffeine-withdrawal headache that could last for several days, cautions James Duke, PhD, the Fulton, Maryland, author of *The Green Pharmacy*. Subtract a little regular coffee and add some decaf to your morning cup. Over the next couple of weeks, gradually increase the proportion of decaf to regular until you're drinking all decaf. You should also consider switching from regular soft drinks to caffeine-free ones or sparkling mineral water.

7. Shake it up. Loosen the muscles in your neck and upper back with this exercise from Dr. Sobel: Stand or sit and stretch your arms out from your sides. Shake your hands vigorously for about 10 seconds. Combine this with a little deep breathing, Dr. Sobel says, and you'll do yourself twice as much good.

8. Munch some snacks. Foods that are high in carbohydrates stimulate the release of serotonin, feel-good brain chemicals that help induce calm, says Dr. Cooper. Crackers, pretzels, or a bagel should do the trick—but the whole bag can create an energy-sapping cycle of remorse. So try this trick when you know you will be satisfied with just a little bit.

9. Get your vitamins. Make sure you're getting the vitamins you need. That may require you to take a multivitamin. But skip the stress formulas, which often contain large amounts of randomly formulated nutrients, such as the B vitamins, but little or nothing else, says Elizabeth Somer, RD, author of *Food and Mood*.

10. Fall for puppy love. In a study of 100 women conducted last year at the State University of New York at Buffalo, researchers found that those who owned a dog had lower blood pressure than those who didn't. If you don't have a pooch, visit a friend's. Petting an animal for just a couple of minutes helps relieve stress, researchers have found.

11. Stretch. Muscles tighten during the day, and when we feel stressed out, the process accelerates. Stretching loosens muscles and encourages deep breathing.

> 🔒 **TOP SECRET!** Wash your hands really well, and keep hand sanitizer at your desk. Offices swarm with germs, and the best way to keep them out your system is to keep them off your hands.

12. Don't slouch. When people are under stress, they slump over as if they have the weight of the world on their shoulders. "Slumping restricts breathing and reduces blood and oxygen flow to the brain, adding to muscle tension and magnifying feelings of panic and helplessness," Dr. Cooper explains.

13. Sit up straight. Straightening your spine has just the opposite effect. It promotes circulation, increases oxygen levels in your blood, and helps lessen muscle tension, all of which promote relaxation.

Become an Instant Expert
Say Yes to Acupressure

Breathe deeply and apply firm, steady pressure on each of these three points for two to three minutes.

1. **The Third Eye,** located between the eyebrows, in the indentation where the bridge of the nose meets the forehead.
2. **The Heavenly Pillar,** on the back of the neck slightly below the base of the skull, about half an inch to the left or right of the spine.
3. **The Heavenly Rejuvenation,** half an inch below the top of each shoulder, midway between the base of the neck and the outside of the shoulder blade.

Big Advice

THE BEST WAYS TO MANAGE A STRESSFUL DAY AT WORK

Sometimes work can be tough and we react by getting stressed out. We don't always have control over what happens to us, says Allen Elkin, PhD, director of the Stress Management Counseling Center in New York City. Yet that doesn't mean we have to react to a difficult, challenging situation by becoming frazzled or feeling overwhelmed or distraught. Instead, use these easy, natural methods to overcoming anxiety when it hits.

Mental Relaxation Techniques

Visualize calm. It sounds New Age-y, but at least one study, done at the Cleveland Clinic Foundation, has found that it's highly effective in reducing stress. Dr. Cooper recommends imagining you're in a hot shower and a wave of relaxation is washing your stress down the drain. Or try this routine, recommended by Gerald Epstein, MD, the author of *Healing Visualizations*: Close your eyes, take three long, slow breaths, and spend a few seconds picturing a relaxing scene, such as walking in a meadow, kneeling by a brook, or lying on the beach. Focus on the details—the sights, the sounds, the smells.

Do some math. Using a scale of one to ten, with one being the equivalent of a minor hassle and ten being a true catastrophe, assign a number to whatever it is that's making you feel anxious. "You'll find that most problems we encounter rate somewhere in the two to five range—in other words, they're really not such a big deal," says Dr. Elkin.

Be a fighter. "At the first sign of stress, you often hear people complain, 'What did I do to deserve this?'" says Dr. Cooper. The trouble is, feeling like a victim only increases feelings of stress and helplessness. Instead, focus on being proactive. If your flight gets canceled, don't wallow in self-pity. Find another one. If your office is too hot or too cold, don't suffer in silence. Call the building manager and ask what can be done to make things more comfortable.

Put it on paper. Writing provides perspective, says Paul J. Rosch, MD, president of the American Institute of Stress in Yonkers, New York. Divide a piece of paper into two parts. On the left side, list the stressors you may be able to change, and on the right, list the ones you can't. "Change what you can," Dr. Rosch suggests, "and stop fretting over what you can't."

Count to ten. Before you say or do something you'll regret, step away from the stressor and collect yourself, advises Dr. Cooper. You can also look away for a moment or put the caller on hold. Use your time-out to take a few deep breaths, stretch, or recite an affirmation.

Just say no. Trying to do everything is a one-way ticket to serious stress. Be clear about your limits, and stop trying to please everyone all the time.

Admit it. Each of us has uniquely individual stress signals—neck or shoulder pain, shallow breathing, stammering, teeth gritting, queasiness, loss of temper. Learn to identify yours, then say out loud, "I'm feeling stressed," when they crop up, recommends Dr. Rosch. Recognizing your personal stress signals helps slow the buildup of negativity and anxiety.

Schedule worry time. Some stressors demand immediate attention—a smoke alarm siren or a police car's whirling blue light. But many low-grade stressors can be dealt with at a later time, when it's more convenient. "File them away in a little mental compartment, or make a note," Dr. Elkin says, "then deal with them when the time is right. Don't let them control you."

(Continued on the next page.)

Time-Outs That Help You Focus Later

Space out. Look out the window and find something natural that captures your imagination, advises Dr. Sobel. Notice the clouds rolling by or the wind in the trees.

Take a walk. It forces you to breathe more deeply and improves circulation, says Dr. Cooper. Step outside if you can; if that's not possible, you can gain many of the same benefits simply by walking to the bathroom or water cooler, or by pacing back and forth. "The key is to get up and move," Dr. Cooper says.

Soak it up. "When I have the time, nothing is more stress relieving for me than a hot bath," Dr. Weston says. "But when I don't have time, I do the next-best thing: I wash my face or even just my hands and arms with hot water. The key is to imagine that I'm taking a hot bath. It's basically a visualization exercise, but the hot water makes it feel real."

Dial a friend. Sharing your troubles can give you perspective, help you feel cared for, and relieve your burden.

Make plans. "Looking forward to something provides calming perspective," Dr. Elkin says. Buy concert tickets, schedule a weekend getaway, or make an appointment for a massage.

Goof off. It temporarily removes you from a potentially stressful situations. Esther Orioli, president of Essi Systems—a San Francisco–based consulting company that organizes stress-management programs—keeps a harmonica in the drawer for when she's feeling stressed out. Bonus: Playing it promotes deep breathing.

Part Eight

WHAT YOU DON'T KNOW ABOUT
YOUR
VACATION

Life isn't a day at the beach for the people who get you to the shore (or the slopes or the plains) and check you in when you arrive. But if you know what they're up against, you can use a little compassion and some insider info to turn even tough travel situations to your advantage.

Knowing how the systems work lets you take advantage of huge travel deals, avoid lines, and save big bucks at your destination without feeling like you're pinching every single penny. Sometimes it's knowing where to go, and sometimes it's knowing when. Veteran globetrotters, travel agents, and pilots all have unique information that will round out your expertise to make you a travel-savvy vacationer, so read this before you hit the road!

WHAT TRAVEL AGENTS WON'T TELL YOU

Use these tricks and your next trip may add up to a lot less money—and seriously better stories—than you thought it would.

1. It's a rare day when a $20 bid on priceline.com won't get you an economy rental car anywhere.

2. Sometimes airlines really are playing tricks on you. But there are ways to get around it. You're shopping for a flight on the Web, and the flight prices Seem to keep going up, not down. Why is that? Many Internet sites install "cookies" on your computer when you visit. A "cookie" is a collection of information that will include your user name and the date and time you visited the site. Sometimes travel websites use this information to increase their prices if you repeatedly run the same searches for airlines or hotels. If you price a flight, and go back to the site a few hours later only to find that the price has increased, it's probably a cookie at work. Before you buy a ticket, erase the cookies from your computer.

3. Not all islands are hurricane prone. Hurricanes not only do major damage, but they also scare the heck out of tourists. So what to do? The best places for a Caribbean vacation are the ABC islands: namely, Aruba, Bonaire, and Curaçao. They all lie outside the path that hurricanes have been following for hundreds of years. So next time you book that summer getaway, be sure to sneak a peek at these less-traveled gems.

4. Nobody uses traveler's checks anymore. If you have been faithfully ordering traveler's checks every time you hit the road, give up the habit. These days, the most economical way to manage money in a foreign country will probably be withdrawing currency from local ATMs as needed with a bank card.

5. But be sure to ask your bank in advance what fees are charged for international transactions and whether there are any no-fee ATM withdrawal arrangements with any banks at your destination. To lower the impact of a significant flat fee, make larger, less frequent withdrawals during your trip.

6. Advance tickets to the Magic Kingdom can pay off. A seven-day parkhopper pass costs about $250 (at the time of this writing) and expires after two weeks, but for an extra $75 or so, you can get a pass that doesn't expire. This is a good idea because it allows you to get some of your travel arrangements out of the way now; you can work on the scheduling later. Also, Disney ticket prices go up every single year. If you know you'll be heading down there eventually, you could spend now and save big later.

7. There's a way around exorbitant hotel dry-cleaning bills. A product called Wrinkle Releaser spray is an inexpensive solution to hotel laundering. You just hang up your clothing, spray it, smooth out the wrinkles with your hands, and let it air dry. Or you can try making your own by mixing 1 tablespoon of fabric softener and ¼ cup of unscented rubbing alcohol with 1 cup of distilled water. Put it in a travel spray bottle and gently mist the garment about a hand's length away.

8. There are secret words that can get you upgrades. If you're willing to spend a little extra money, it's worth asking the agent to "split the difference" on the price of the first-class ticket. If first class isn't booked, which usually happens on less-traveled routes on off-peak travel days, the agent has some discretion when it comes to moving people into first class. Some airlines also let you use your frequent-flier miles to "purchase" an upgrade.

9. Sometimes we can get resort fees waived. The extra $10 to $15 per day they try to charge you as a "resort fee," supposedly to cover such amenities as the swimming pool and fitness club, is nothing but a ruse to make a hotel's rates appear lower at the time you are scouting for a room, say industry insiders. At the time of booking, scan the fine print of your agreement and ask the hotel about any fees that are not included in the quote. If you're surprised by such fees at the registration counter, call your credit card company after checking in and ask it to get the fee waived.

🔒 **TOP SECRET!** Cruise lines love repeat customers. All cruise lines have loyalty programs, and the more you vacation with one company, the better the perks will get—they could be anything from $100 cruise vouchers to private cocktail parties or free bottles of wine.

10. Cab drivers are our best friends. "I always depend on the taxi drivers," says Mark Zwick, one of the partners of PhillyTrips.com. "They always know the places to go, the things to See."

11. Many times a taxi driver works in tandem with bars and restaurants and will have special coupons for his favorite places. He'll be more than happy to let you have them. Why? Because he gets a kickback from the establishments. So let those taxi drivers take you to some places where they get a little something extra, because most of the time you'll be getting something extra as well, in the form of discounted meals or drinks.

12. We pretend we're traveling solo. Airline search engines mess with your head a little when it comes to booking your family's travel. The truth is, sometimes you'll get a cheaper rate by booking seats individually, because single seats can easily go unsold (especially middle seats in the back of the plane). Airlines jump at the chance to get rid of them. See what happens when you book seats individually.

13. We think trains, not planes. While traveling by train in North America is not the most popular choice, it's the way to go when traveling abroad, especially in Europe. If you really want to become an expert at this type of travel, you must go to www.seat61.com. It's the most comprehensive site out there when it comes to trains the world over.

HIT THE ROAD EQUIPPED WITH THESE KIDS' GAMES

If you don't have a travel-friendly DVD player, or you want your vacation to be spent away from the screen—bring along these games and ideas for young kids:

Create your own scavenger hunt, challenging young passengers to spot license plates identifying as many states as possible. For an educational boost, *Kids' Road Atlas* (ages 6–12) from Rand McNally is a colorful U.S. atlas offering a kid-friendly map, state symbols, and games that describe each state's history, geography, or folklore. Young travelers learn how to read a map by using a legend, scale, and coordinates.

Give kids a map and a highlighter, and have them follow the route you take.

Bring along a sketch pad and lots of pencils. If you want to get a little fancier, a laptop coloring desk is a great way for kids to keep occupied and make postcards to send to friends and family.

Play 20 Questions. You think of a person or object, and your opponent(s) asks you 20 yes-or-no questions to try to figure out who or what you're thinking of.

Try the Memory Game. "I'm going to the World's Fair, and in my trunk I packed . . ." Players take turns adding a new item to the list. Beginning with A, the first letter of each new item must start with the next letter of the alphabet.

Hold a Sound Contest in which kids imitate the noises they hear in places such as home, street, farm, or zoo. After 20 minutes of that, you may want to try the Quiet Contest—whoever can be quietest the longest wins a prize.

Pack a deck of cards. Popular games like War, Rummy, or Go Fish can keep kids busy for hours.

Keep a family vacation scrapbook. It doesn't have to be an elaborate production; in fact, the simpler, the better. A spiral-bound sketchbook or individual pages saved in plastic sheet protectors and kept in a loose-leaf binder work well. Bring along some crayons, colored pencils, or washable markers. Along the way, collect mementos of your trip—restaurant menus or place mats, ticket stubs from zoos, parks, and museums (and hopefully not speeding tickets!). Each day have the kids draw a picture of something or someone they saw. Older children can include written memories. The finished journal will make the vacation easy to revisit and share with friends and family.

WHAT **YOUR PILOT** WON'T TELL YOU

Most of us never get the chance to talk the pilot, but who hasn't wondered what's going on in the cockpit during all those hours of flight time?

1. We miss the peanuts, too.

2. I'm constantly under pressure to carry less fuel than I'm comfortable with. Airlines are always looking at the bottom line, and you burn fuel carrying fuel. Sometimes if you carry just enough fuel and you hit thunderstorms or delays, then suddenly you're running out of gas and you have to go to an alternate airport.

3. We tell you what you need to know. But we don't tell you things that are going to scare the pants off of you. So you'll never hear me say, "Ladies and gentlemen, we just had an engine failure," even if that's true.

4. We'd like to wait, but we can't. The Department of Transportation has put such an emphasis on on-time performance that we pretty much aren't allowed to delay a flight anymore, even if there are 20 people on a connecting flight that's coming in just a little late.

5. The truth is, we're exhausted. Our work rules allow us to be on duty 16 hours without a break. That's many more hours than a truck driver. And unlike a truck driver, who can pull over at the next rest stop, we can't pull over at the next cloud.

6. Some FAA rules don't make sense to us either. Like the fact that when we're at 39,000 feet going 400 miles an hour, in a plane that could hit turbulence at any minute, flight attendants can walk around and serve hot coffee and Chateaubriand. But when we're on the ground on a flat piece of asphalt going five to ten miles an hour, they've got to be buckled in like they're at NASCAR.

7. The two worst airports for us: Reagan National in Washington, D.C., and John Wayne in Orange County, California. You're flying by the seat of your pants trying to get in and out of those airports. John Wayne is especially bad because the rich folks who live near the airport don't like jet noise, so they have this noise abatement procedure where you basically have to turn the plane into a ballistic missile as soon as you're airborne.

8. I'm not the best person to ask for directions to the airport. We're in so many airports that we usually have no idea.

TOP SECRET! At some airports with really short runways, you're not going to have a smooth landing no matter how good we are: John Wayne Airport; Jackson Hole, Wyoming; Chicago Midway; and Reagan National.

9. We really do know the weather. This happens all the time: We'll be in Pittsburgh going to Philly, and there will be a weather delay. The weather in Pittsburgh is beautiful. Then I'll hear passengers saying, "You know, I just called my friend in Philly, and it's beautiful there, too," like there's some kind of conspiracy or something. But in the airspace between Pittsburgh and Philly there's a huge thunderstorm.

10. Your plane isn't truthfully labeled. You may go to an airline website and buy a ticket, pull up to its desk at the curb, and get onto an airplane that has a similar name painted on it, but half the time, you're really on a regional airline.

11. The regionals aren't held to the same safety standards as the majors. Their pilots aren't required to have as much training and experience, and the public doesn't know that.

12. How you land is a good indicator of a pilot's skill. So if you want to say something nice to a pilot as you're getting off the plane, say "Nice landing." We do appreciate that.

13. You really are getting there "early" more often. No, it's not your imagination. Airlines really have adjusted their flight arrival times so they can have a better record of on-time arrivals. So they might say a flight takes two hours when it really takes an hour and 45 minutes.

SOURCES: 17 pilots from across the country, including an AirTran Airways captain from Atlanta; Joe D'Eon, a pilot at a major airline who produces a podcast at flywithjoe.com; a US Airways pilot from South Carolina; Jack Stephan, US Airways captain based in Annapolis, Maryland, who has been flying since 1984; Jim Tilmon, a retired American Airlines pilot from Phoenix, Arizona.

Great Advice
TOP WAYS TO AVOID JET LAG

· ·

Acclimate. If you're going to be gone longer than a couple of days, begin acclimating your body to the new time zone by altering your eating schedule three days before your plane takes off. If you're heading west to San Diego from Boston, for example, three days before you leave, eat an hour earlier each day. Flying from San Diego back to Boston? Help reverse the acclimation and get back on home time by eating an hour later each day for three days.

Chug. Stay hydrated with bottled water. Avoid alcohol during your flight. It can dehydrate your body, mess up your internal clock, and exaggerate jet lag symptoms.

Hit the linguine. Or any other carb-dense food at dinner on the night before your flight. Scientists have been arguing for some time about whether or not this decreases jet lag and increases your potential for normal sleep, but recent research on has uncovered subtle effects that indicate carbs boost your ability to sleep— particularly when you fly westward. No one's quite figured out how they help, but they do know that carbs provide your brain with a source of tryptophan, from which it can make the sleep-inducing neurotransmitter serotonin.

Refrigerate. If you're flying during what would be night hours at your destination, try to get some sleep on the plane. Use earplugs to eliminate noise, an eyeshade to kill the light, and turn the air-conditioning valve on high. Another cue your body uses to set its internal clock is temperature. A lower temperature lowers your body's core temperature and signals it's time for sleep. To keep from getting too chilled, bring along one of those silk blanket-and-pillow sets that are sold through airline and online travel catalogs.

Avoid airline food. Your body also uses food to set its internal clock. Since airline food is served onboard according to the time at your home base, eating it can sabotage efforts to reset your clock to the time zone to which you're traveling.

Consider melatonin. No, you don't need a prescription. But since it has the ability to really mess with your brain chemicals, consult with a doctor anyway—especially if you're taking another medication. It's not as strong as a sleeping pill, but it directly affects your body's internal clock and nudges it toward sleep. But the safety profile of melatonin has not been seriously investigated, so it's not, experts agree, for long-term use until studies verifying its safety over the long haul have been done.

Have the eggs benedict. A protein-rich meal the morning after you arrive will give your brain what it needs to produce neurochemicals to increase your alertness throughout the day.

Stay on home time. If you're going to be away from home for only a couple of days, stay on the same eating and sleeping schedule while you're away as you would at home.

Or switch immediately. If you're away for more than just a couple of days, don't just set your watch to local time when you arrive—help reset your internal clock by eating, going to bed, and waking at the local time as well.

Bring your workout gear. Schedule a 30-minute workout each day you're on the road. You'll feel and sleep better.

WHAT YOUR FLIGHT ATTENDANT WON'T TELL YOU

The bathrooms really *are* that gross, your over-sized suitcase isn't helping anyone, and other insights from the travel experts who've seen—and dealt with—it all.

1. Want to start off on the wrong foot with me? Put your carry-on in a full overhead bin, leave it sticking out six inches, then take your seat at the window and wait for someone else (me!) to come along and solve the problem you just created.

2. We're not just being lazy. Our rules really say we aren't allowed to lift your luggage into the overhead bin for you, though we can "assist."

3. Yes, passengers are incredibly rude. But stealing a beer, cursing out passengers, and jumping out of a plane is not the way to handle it. You disarm an unruly passenger by introducing yourself, asking his name, and saying something like "I've been incredibly nice to you for three hours. Why are you treating me like this?" Generally that gets the other passengers on your side—and sometimes they'll even applaud.

4. Don't ask us if it's OK to use the lavatories on the ground. The answer is always yes. Do you think what goes into the toilet just dumps out onto the tarmac?

5. Do not poke or grab me. I mean it. No one likes to be poked, but it's even worse on the plane because you're sitting down and we're not, so it's usually in a very personal area. You would never grab a waitress if you wanted ketchup or a fork, would you?

6. I hate working flights to destinations like Vail and West Palm Beach. The passengers all think they're in first class even if they're not. They don't do what we ask. And the overhead bins are full of their mink coats.

7. If you're traveling with a small child and you keep hearing bells, bells, and more bells, please look to See if it's your child playing with the flight attendant call bell.

8. The lavatory door is not rocket science. Just push.

> 🔒 **TOP SECRET!** If you're traveling overseas, do yourself a favor and bring a pen. You would not believe how many people travel without one, and you need one to fill out the immigration form.

9. If you have a baby, bring diapers. If you're diabetic, bring syringes. If you have high blood pressure, don't forget your medication. That way, I'm not trying to make a diaper out of a sanitary pad and a pillowcase or asking over the intercom if someone has a spare inhaler.

10. If you hear us paging for a doctor or See us running around with oxygen, defibrillators, and first aid kits, that's not the right time to ask for a blanket or a Diet Coke.

11. You really expect me to take your soggy Kleenex? Or your kid's fully loaded diaper? I'll be right back with gloves.

12. Just in case you hadn't noticed, there are other people on the airplane besides you. So don't clip your toenails, snore with wild abandon, or do any type of personal business under a blanket!

13. I'm sorry it's taking forever to get you a wheelchair, but that's one thing you can't blame the airline for. The wheelchair service is subcontracted to the cities we fly into, and it's obviously not a top priority for many of them.

Great Advice
HOW TO FLY COMFORTABLY

You can get in and out of the airport faster—and with a lot less stress.

Fly early in the day. At airports scheduled to capacity, any delay in the morning means there will be at least that much of a delay for every flight thereafter.

Leave a day early. Depart a day in advance for crucial trips, such as a key business meeting or a wedding.

Check the delay statistics for your flight. Use websites like bts.gov (Bureau of Transportation Statistics) or flightstats.com to See how often that flight is more than 15 minutes late on a scale of 1 to 9 (the lower the number, the more often it's late)—before you book your tickets. If the number is 5 or below and time is of the hereessence, consider another flight.

Skip the lines. Sign up for the registered traveler program to take some of the pain out of the preflight experience. Travelers who pass a voluntary background check can use special lanes to whisk through security at certain U.S. airports.

Don't let it drop. If you have a truly terrible experience, write a reasonable letter afterward to the airline CEO, explaining what happened and asking for compensation. Refer to the contract of carriage listed on the airline's website; it explains the compensation policies. It's up to the airline whether to remedy a passenger's bad experience. If you used plastic to buy your ticket, your credit card company can challenge the airline for violating its contract with a customer.

WHAT YOUR HOTEL DESK CLERK WON'T TELL YOU

Here's the real deal on upgrades, lower rates, and what we talk about when you can't hear us.

1. The 1-800 reservations number will probably send you to a central office with set rates. If you call the hotel directly instead, you can negotiate.

2. Hotels can pay a commission of up to 30 percent to online booking sites. So offer me 20 percent less than the online price, and we both come out ahead.

3. Independently owned hotels are far more likely to give you a discount. Some chains balk at dropping the rate.

4. Don't ask me for an upgrade when other guests are within earshot. Want a more spacious room without paying more? Request a corner room or a handicapped one.

5. If you request a king bed, there's no guarantee. No matter how confident the reservations agent sounds, call the hotel directly and make the request again a few days before you travel. Then do it again on the day of. If we still don't have one when you get there and you're nice about it, we may comp your breakfast or upgrade you to a suite.

6. Most of us are happy to help. If you ask us to, we'll tell callers you're not registered at the hotel, or tell you where to park so you can't See your car from the interstate. But we're also talking behind your back about what you might be hiding.

7. Some concierges get kickbacks for sending you to pricey tourist traps. If you want an unbiased recommendation, ask the clerk.

8. Sometimes my boss makes me lie, like when the elevator's not working and I tell you someone is coming to fix it soon. I know it won't be fixed until Monday, because the manager doesn't want to pay the repairman's weekend rate.

> 🔒 **TOP SECRET!** Always request clean linens when you check in. We wash the sheets every day, but blankets often only get washed once a week. And the bedspreads? If there's no visible stain, it's maybe once a month.

9. In this economy, everything is negotiable. If your hotel offers a hot breakfast buffet as well as a free continental breakfast, ask if you can get the hot breakfast with your room. Very rarely will we tell you no.

10. Never use the long distance. Unless you want to pay $10 for a five-minute call, it's best to specifically ask for it to be turned off. We've had situations in which housekeepers have made calls from a guest's phone.

11. If you travel to the same place frequently, use the same hotel each time. Get to know the staff. Regulars are recognized and treated as VIPs. You could get free upgrades, discounts, and more.

12. My official job description: errand runner, toilet plunger, bow-tie tier, towel deliverer, and chef (that free continental breakfast doesn't appear from above). I've also sprinkled rooms with rose petals and dealt with dead bodies. All for about $10 an hour.

13. It Seems to have gone out of fashion to tip your housekeeper. Most are paid minimum wage with the expectation of tips. Take care of them, and they'll take care of you.

SOURCES: Current and former desk clerks at hotels in Mississippi, Kansas, Colorado, Maryland, Vermont, and Washington.

Great Advice

8 TIPS FOR AFFORDABLE VACATIONS—NO PENNY PINCHING NEEDED

Here's how to shop online and get the best prices with the fewest clicks.

1. Become an expert well in advance. Sign up for e-mail alerts and online newsletters, recommends George Hobica of airfarewatchdog.com. It's the best way to familiarize yourself with destinations and prices. In other words, for now, keep your mind open and your wallet closed. And don't forget to ask friends on Twitter and Facebook for their tips.

2. Decide on a few destinations. Now that you have a better sense of what's out there, you want to work backward. Barbara Messing of travel-ticker.com explains, "Don't fixate on one place. Let the deal be your inspiration."

3. Reassure yourself. Before committing, play detective. For videos of hotels, restaurants, activities, and attractions, go to tripfilms.com and insiderperks.com. Tripfilms depends on travelers for their observations, while the videos on InsiderPerks are created by the site's staff. Watch both to get a good overview of your destination. Browse through other families' vacation photos on flickr.com (it's OK—really), and read candid reviews by travelers on tripadvisor.com.

4. Search for the lowest airfare. Experts consider kayak.com the best first step in searching for low-cost airline deals (it doesn't include Southwest, so you'll have to check that airline separately). You'll almost always get a better deal if you're flexible—you can fly out on one carrier and return on another, for example, or fly to an offbeat airport like Bob Hope Airport in Burbank, California (15 miles outside L.A.), or Midway in Chicago. Lock in your rate, but don't pull the trigger yet. (Depending on the airline, you may have 10 minutes to 24 hours to commit, so do the next steps—fees and hotels—quickly.)

5. Find the hidden fees. If you want to know the real price of the ticket, check "Airline Fees: The Ultimate Guide" at smartertravel.com. Will you have to pay for that blanket, the soda, and the pretzels? Some airlines charge up to $100 extra for a seat with more legroom. To find out what your airline charges, go to its website or check the Guide. Then compare bag fees with Fe-dEx, UPS, and U.S. Postal Service rates. "Depending on the route and method," says Hobica, "the cost savings from shipping versus schlepping can range from little or nothing to dramatic."

6. Get a room, then book your flight. Hotels.com features more than 70,000 properties—from small bed-and-breakfasts to all-inclusive luxury resorts—and flags special deals. For unbiased shots of lobbies, rooms, and neighborhoods, go to tvtrip.com. At oyster.com, you get photos, plus the pros and cons. Once you've booked your room, book your flight.

7. Rent a car before you leave. If you don't care which car-rental company you use, head to hotwire.com for deep discounts on rentals, says Anne Banas of smartertravel.com. Check rates for both airport and off-site pickup. (But if there's no free shuttle service, factor in the cost of a cab. Off-site hours may be limited.)

8. Once you've landed, "check in" with Foursquare, a free app for iPhones, BlackBerrys, Palms, and Android phones. Tell your friends where you are, and get their recommendations on the hot spots in town. If they're in the area, they just might join you.

WHAT VETERAN GLOBE TROTTERS WON'T TELL YOU

Great deals happen in the off-season—you just have to know how to find them. We got frequent travelers to reveal when and where those money-savers really are.

1. Off-season doesn't mean the wrong season, when no one wants to go or when you won't be able to experience the best of that area. Some of my favorite travel experiences have been during the off-season.

2. It does mean deals and discounts. Huge tourist destinations are the best bet for sharp discounts in the off-season because these economies are completely dependent on tourist income as opposed to business-travel income.

3. You'll save more on hotels than airfare if hotels can fill an otherwise empty room for 25 or 50 percent of what they normally get. That money is just straight to their profit. Airlines just won't fly as many trips. By far the nicest hotels I've stayed in for very small amounts of money have been off-season deals on major chain hotels, like Marriott, which I get on priceline.com.

4. Getting on the phone often gets you deals. I find a specific deal online or something through the hotel's own social-media marketing efforts or through a discount club like jetsetter.com. Then I call the hotel and try to book it directly, and you in under this Caricom rate."

5. Use community-generated review sites like tripadvisor.com to get the real scoop on hotels and locations. You'll See pictures of rooms and facilities posted by guests, instead of the hotel's marketing time. Plus, you'll get the real deal about the staff, the location, and the overall experience of staying in the hotel.

6. Not that children aren't delightful, but I've been in places where there are huge groups of schoolkids running around making it a much less pleasant experience than it would otherwise have been.

TOP SECRET! Sign up for the city you are traveling to with sites like Groupon and Scout Mob. These discount-finders will send you amazing local deals on spas, restaurants, and entertainment that usually only the locals know about.

7. Cities and major business centers are not as likely to have off-season deals, because there's no off-season for business travelers. It's hard to imagine a season in New York City that's the off-season.

8. You'd be surprised at what you can negotiate. I called a place in Barbados. It was the off-season, and I said, "Is that your cheapest room? What if I stayed a few extra days?" She said, "Well, I can offer you the rate for Caribbean citizens." Caricom is the term for the Caribbean community, and there's a rate for native Caribbeans. It was really easy for her, and it would never have come up online. Only by my calling the hotel did she think of saying, "Oh, we can slip you in under this Caricom rate."

9. If you want to get a taste of the real local culture, ask a waiter, the girl giving out pool towels, or the bartender where to hang out. You're sure to find some great spots that aren't overpriced for tourists.

10. Public transportation is the way to go. If you can figure out the bus system, take it. You can literally save hundreds of dollars taking buses instead of flagging down cabs every time you want to go somewhere.

11. In any season, beware of extra fees. If you can't avoid them or talk them down, at least be aware of additional fees such as extra legroom charges, hidden hotel fees, and rental car extras you don't really need.

12. There are great currency-converter apps that you can download to your phone. Use one if you're traveling somewhere that has a much different monetary system than you're used to, and you won't end up paying $12 American for a can of mystery soda.

13. Refundable tickets can really pay off, especially if you're booking a trip months in advance. Spending an extra forty or fifty dollars up front is a lot better than paying hundreds of dollars in change fees, which all major airlines consider mandatory.

SOURCES: Loren Bendele, CEO, savings.com; Seth Kugel, Frugal Traveler blogger, *New York Times*; Nina Willdorf, former editor in chief, *Budget Travel*.

 Become an Instant Expert
The 5 Easiest Way to Prevent Travel Stress?

1. **Invest in a lightweight, microfiber, rolling carry-on.** You'll be less inclined to overpack and less likely to go over the airline's allowed carry-on dimensions.
2. **Pack one pair of shoes.** Make the ones you wear onboard slip-ons. The Transportation Security Administration (TSA) and your fellow passengers will thank you when it comes time to remove them.
3. **Decant your shampoo.** No need to pack whole bottles into your checked luggage. Buy inexpensive 3-ounce plastic bottles at your drugstore, and decant at home.
4. **Pack one lightweight sweater suitable for day or night.** Unless you're visiting the Arctic, there is no reason to travel with your entire winter wardrobe. Choose carefully, and pack lightweight clothes that can be layered.
5. **Stick with one color scheme.** Our experts uniformly agree that packing clothes that are black or white is the wisest way to travel. Everything will always match, black can be very dressy (or not), white always looks crisp, and you can brighten up outfits with a simple, lightweight scarf.

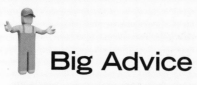

Big Advice

THE SMARTEST WAYS TO TAKE A SPUR-OF-THE-MOMENT VACATION

Sometimes you just need to get out of town, and you really can take a last-minute trip without paying premium prices. But if you just need a break from the office and don't want the hassle of travel, there's always another way to go: home! Use these tips for saving big on a last-minute booking or creating a fabulous "staycation."

How to Book a Last-Minute Vacation

Even if you're a procrastinator, a spontaneous getaway doesn't have to drain your wallet. Here's how to get a great deal when you want to travel quickly.

Troll the travel websites. Sites such as Expedia.com, Priceline.com, and Travelocity.com are treasure troves for last-minute travelers. A few clicks will provide you with the latest transportation and accommodation availability, as well as deals on bundled packages (flight, hotel, car rental) and all-inclusive vacations. Save a few steps by going straight to Kayak.com, which allows you to compare rates, dates, and availability from all of the major travel websites at once.

Register for last-minute travel e-mail blasts. Those same travel websites, and most airlines, offer weekly e-mail newsletters that include up-to-the-minute deals on flights, cruises, hotels, and more. If you're flexible about where and when you travel, finding a great deal to an exciting destination can be as easy as checking your inbox.

Remember the 14-day rule. If they're not fully booked, airlines, hotels, and cruise ships often offer significant discounts two weeks in advance of travel. The key is to get both your transportation and accommodations to line up, so the more flexible you can be about arrival and departure dates, the better.

Go off-peak. Airlines and hotels are less crowded on weekdays, particularly Tuesdays and Wednesdays. If you can book your arrival and departure during the week, you'll have more flights and rooms to choose from. Tuesdays and Wednesdays are also the best days for booking last-minute travel, as prices tend to climb as the weekend approaches. (Remember: When booking your hotel, keep in mind that the best deals on many round-trip flights require a Saturday night stay.)

Try for a last-minute house rental. Despite what real estate brokers might have you believe, vacation rentals can still be found post-Memorial Day. And the good news is, the later the date, the more eager owners are to find renters and the more likely they'll be to offer discounts or accommodate requests, such as flexible arrival or check-out times. Be sure to visit vacation rental sites like vrbo.com as well as contact realtors, and consider slightly off-the-beaten-path locations and properties that are farther from town or the beach.

Have the Ultimate Staycation

The perfect staycation isn't just another day off. It's a way to set your body and mind into total relaxation mode. It means there is no stress about doing extra housework or tackling those home improvement projects allowed—that's too much work! Staycationing *is* vacationing. Here's how to do it:

Unplug your alarm. Turn off your alarm and let yourself sleep as late as you like. Like vacationing, staycationing doesn't require you to clock-in. Go to bed when you want to and wake up whenever—remember a good vacation has no set routine.

Play tourist. Whether you live in a big city or a small town, surely you haven't done everything there is to do. Check out the latest gallery opening, grab tickets to a matinee, hop on a tour bus, or take a trip to your local historical centers. You'll See the place you live from a whole new perspective.

Turn off your phone. Pretend that you're half a world away with little access to your phone. Leave a voicemail that says that you're on vacation and will only be checking messages when you get the chance. Forgetting about your phone will keep you focused on your main goal—relaxation.

Don't check e-mails. Set an out of office reply or a vacation message on your work and personal e-mail accounts and don't peek until you "return" from your vacation.

Don't tackle your to-dos. It's easy to think that your time spent at home can be used to reorganize, clean, and do a few home improvements, but a vacation is no time to do extra work. If you were on an actual vacation would you be upset that your floors at home weren't being scrubbed? No way. Let things around the house stay as they are. Or, for a real treat, hire a cleaning service to come spruce the place up while you're out on the town.

Order in. Hate to cook? Then don't do it. It's rare that you would be cooking your own food if you were out of town, so enjoy the benefits of ordering in or grabbing your favorite take-out. Added bonus: less dishes to clean up.

Go out to dinner. With all of the money you've saved by not going out of town, you can afford to dress up and go out to a fancy dinner. Splurge on the chef's special or the market-priced lobster. Explore some fine dining that you've never tried before, and truly enjoy your night out.

Have a TV/movie marathon. If you've been too busy to catch up on the latest television series or movies, grab some DVDs or go through your DVR list. Missing a few classics on your movie bucket list? Take the opportunity to See some of the greatest movies of all time, all from the comfort of your own home.

INDEX

A

B

C

Caffeine, 61, 65, 124, 305, 306, 310

Calm, visualizing, 312

Camp
affordable options, 172
what counselors won't tell you, 170–171

Cars. *See also* Tires
battery tips and tricks, 198
brake fluid levels, 195
buying tips, 190–191
cleaning and detailing, 199–202
cracked light precaution, 200
driving tips, 192, 193–194
extending life of, 192
gas- and fuel-saving tips, 192, 193–194, 255
insurance, 280
keeping log for, 195
key chain and ignition switch, 195
maintaining, 195–198
paint importance and care, 200
premium gas for, 255
renting, 332
service warranties, 255
waxing, 199, 201, 202
what dealers won't tell you, 190–191
what detailers won't tell you, 200–202
what gas stations don't want you to know, 193–194
what mechanics won't tell you, 196–197
windshield repair, 200

Car seats, 50

Cast-iron pans, 260

Cats
pilling, 181
what they're not telling you, 179–180

Cauliflower vs. broccoli, 143

Cell phones
accessories for, 267
doctor visits and, 96
etiquette for using, 221, 268, 299
exceeding minute/text limits, 267
family plans, 255, 267
free directory assistance, 266
getting out of contracts, 267
moisture precaution, 266
money-saving tips, 255, 266–267
new technology, 268
polarized glasses and, 113
recycling, 47
scam alert, 252
unlimited minute plans, 255
vacation from, 338
what phone sales reps won't tell you, 266–267

Checking and savings accounts, 277–278

Chewing gum
benefits of, 110, 306
removing from hair, 33

Children. *See* Kids

Chimney sweep swindle, 56–57

Cleaning
biggest secret weapon, 22
car, 199–202
clothes, 209–211, 317
computer equipment, 214
dry cleaning, 209–210, 317
home and appliances, 22
jewelry, 82, 233
products, 22, 33–34, 82, 199
recycling hazardous cleaners, 47
with dryer sheets, 199
with vinegar, 22, 199, 211, 214
with WD-40, 33–34

Closets, organizing, 51–53

Clothing
buying tip, 225
cleaning, 209–211, 317
money-saving tips, 271–272
organizing, 51–53
for travel, 335
unused, returning, 52
what dry cleaners won't tell you, 209–210

Wine
buying, 258
stains, removing, 211
Work. *See also* Computers; Job search; Résumés
asking for raise, 304
collection agencies calling at, 274
company stock and, 283–284
e-mails, 268
health- and happiness-inducing activities,
309–311
interacting with coworkers, 296, 299–300.
See also E-mail
knowing what you want to do, 183
level of satisfaction, 184
paranoia alert, 294
productivity enhancers, 305–307, 308.
See also Stress management
protocol importance, 303
running meetings at, 301
salary issues, 302, 303, 304

scary but true antics, 295
sexual harassment charges, 303
top job security factor, 294
unlimited sick day irony, 303
what company nurses want you to know,
309–311
what coworkers won't tell you, 299–300
what HR people won't tell you, 293–294
what IT departments won't tell you, 296–297
what productivity experts want you to know,
305–307
what your company won't tell you, 302–303
Wrinkle Releaser spray, 317

X

X-rays, 110

Y

Yard sale tips, 48–49

Keep discovering new secrets all year long with . . .

America's Favorite Magazine!

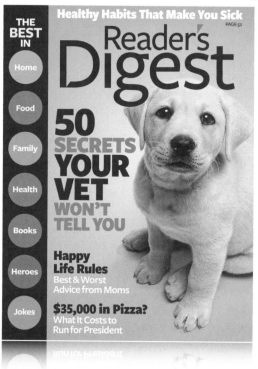

Now you can subscribe
every way you like to read!

Get the BEST DEAL Now!
RD.com/subscribe